Forever Alien

Forever Alien

A Korean Memoir, 1930–1951

by
SUNNY CHE

McFarland & Company, Inc., Publishers
Jefferson, North Carolina, and London

Library of Congress Cataloguing-in-Publication Data

Che, Sunny, 1929–
    Forever alien : a Korean memoir, 1930–1951 / by Sunny Che.
      p.   cm.
    Includes index.
    ISBN 0-7864-0685-2 (library binding : 50# alkaline paper) ∞
    1. Che, Sunny, 1929 — Childhood and youth.   2. Korean
Americans — Biography. 3. Koreans — Japan — Social conditions.
I. Title.
E184.K6C463   2000
973'.204957 — dc21   99-54799
                                                  CIP

British Library Cataloguing-in-Publication data are available

Manufactured in the United States of America

*McFarland & Company, Inc., Publishers
  Box 611, Jefferson, North Carolina 28640
  www.mcfarlandpub.com*

To my mother

Table of Contents

Part II:
Growing Up in Korea, 1944–1951

PART I

A Korean Childhood in Japan, 1930–1944

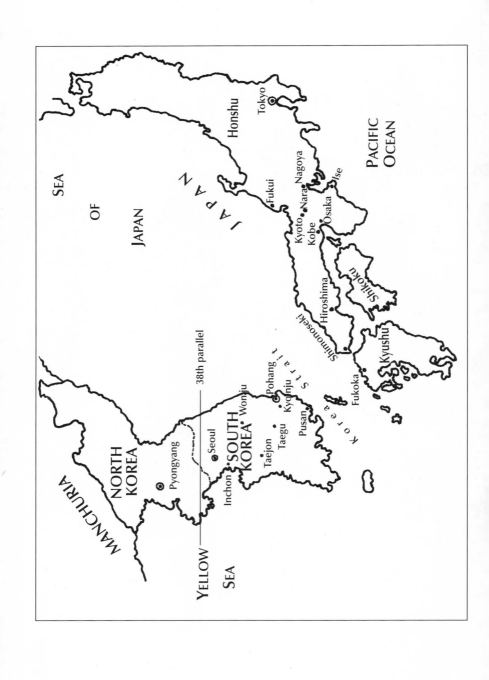

CHAPTER 1

Korean Roots

E ven though I spent most of my childhood in Japan as a child of Korean immigrants, I never felt welcomed to that country or its people. Everything seemed to have conspired to let me not forget that I was a Cho-sen jin (Korean)— our Japanese neighbors, my classmates, my own family, and especially when my Japanese playmates got angry with me for one thing or another. My family stood out, unmistakably Korean anywhere, in our appearance and in the way we behaved. We towered over the smallish Japanese people. My mother insisted wearing her Korean full skirt and chest-high, long-sleeved blouse. And we always spoke Korean among ourselves, at home or out. I never felt part of the land of the Rising Sun, but forever an outsider, looking in. Still I remember my years of growing up in Nihon (Japan) with an aching nostalgia, because of my mother.

As Wall Street was crashing in October 1929, I, Pongsun Che, was born in a farmhouse built by my father and his half-brothers in a little farming village, about two hours' walking distance from Pohang, South Korea, a fishing town on the Sea of Japan.

The farmhouse was typically Korean for the time and place, with dirt floor and thatched roof. The rooms had straw mats laid over a layer of mud-covered rock slabs. For the cold winter weather, these rocks were heated by the oven heat escaping from the adjacent kitchen through tunnels running along the full length of the room.

The farmhouse formed a small, walled-in compound. The main structure was where my parents and the children lived and a separate room-and-kitchen wing was provided for my itinerant grandfather, who was absent for long periods of time. A small mill shed was shared by my family and my uncle's family, who lived on the other side of the dividing wall. The mill was foot-powered with a pounding contraption for husking grain, or pounding it into flour. There was a well near the kitchen, an animal stall for oxen and chickens, and an outdoor privy for a self-contained life.

My father tried to make a living as a farmer but living became harder with a growing number of children on a small plot of land. I was the fourth child, and the third daughter. After two "disappointing" girls, Kiyon and Duli, my parents did everything possible to assure themselves of an heir. When my mother became big with her third pregnancy, my parents climbed an arduous mountain trail to a sacred rock at the summit, to pray for a son. So my big brother, Taiam, was born.

My father, Ungjo Che, was an old man of twenty-five when he married my mother, eighteen-year-old Tongkum Yun. In those days, a girl in her late teens was customarily arranged to marry a boy who was a few years younger than herself. The custom was the tacit acknowledgment that the woman's physical maturity was essential for childbirth and the man's easier part in procreation. Also, the mothers-in-law welcomed fully-grown daughters-in-law to help out with the heavy housework. Against the prevailing notions of matrimony, my parents' marriage was anything but conventional. But then, there was nothing ordinary about my father.

My father was born in the last decade of the nineteenth century, into a landed gentry in Kyonsan, near Taegu, South Korea, the present provincial capital of Kyongsan puk-do. This province was once the seat of the Silla Dynasty, with its capital in Kyonju, during the golden age of Korean history from A.D. 1 to A.D. 918. After a classical Chinese education with a resident scholar, he was to have the genteel life of managing the family estate like his predecessors of the past twenty-five generations. Life turned out to be not that simple for him, by no fault of his own.

My grandfather, so the story goes, was plunged into deep sorrow over my grandmother's death shortly after the birth of their first child, my father. He tried to drown himself in reckless debauchery, drinking, and gambling. As expected by the family tradition, my father began his Chinese classics learning at age seven but had to give it up at thirteen. The dire family circumstances became painfully obvious with the family assets diminished by my grandfather's profligacy. My father had to help his grandmother manage whatever was left of the family land during his father's long, frequent absences.

My mother was one of eight daughters born to a general, distantly related to the Queen of Yi Dynasty (A.D. 1392–1910). In 1910, Japan, victorious from the Russo-Japanese war of 1905, annexed Korea. The Yuns were large and handsome people. Their ninth, the last child, turned out to be the long-awaited son who was as tall and robust as his sisters.

I remember one anecdote of General Yun, a giant of a man. One day he came upon some villagers struggling with a boulder in bridge building across a stream. Rolling up his sleeves, he single-handedly moved the rock into place to the astonishment of everyone, and became a hero that day and a local legend in his own time.

CHAPTER 2

Wandering Koreans

The arrival of Commodore Matthew Perry in 1853 signalled the beginning of the end to the Japanese isolationist policy. Under Emperor Meiji (1867–1911), the Japanese industrialization commenced in earnest. The Japanese wanted to catch up with the industrialized West in a hurry and adopted wholesale the best of the Western civilization. Japan copied the English parliamentary system — the upper and lower Diets — the French educational system, the German (Prussian) military, and the American technology. The nineteenth century German medicine was emulated by the Japanese medicine.

Also, Japan realized that the only way she could survive as an island nation with no appreciable natural resources was by trade, as England had done with her colonial empire during the past several hundred years. Following the English model, the Japanese military expansionist policy was formulated and executed in the late nineteenth century.

In order to keep the industrial production at maximum capacity, Japan had to find readily accessible natural resources and markets. Manchuria and China became the obvious answers to her quest. But Korea, an independent kingdom, was in the way. First Japan had to fight off China in 1895 and then Russia in 1905 before she could have a free hand in Korea. With Teddy Roosevelt's approval at the Russo-Japanese war mediation, Japan formalized the conquest of Korea by annexation in 1910. Now Japan had unobstructed access to the rich deposits of iron and coal in Manchuria and the untapped market in China. They built a wide track railroad through the Korean peninsula to match the Manchurian rail for fast transport of raw materials and finished products.

By contrast, Korea, the "Hermit Kingdom," was caught unprepared to face the overtures from the West for trade and diplomatic relations in the latter half of the nineteenth century. In the end, she was forced to submit to the ultimate victor emerging from the regional wars swarming around her at the turn of the century. So the Korean independence of five thousand years was supplanted by the Japanese colonial rule.

As one of the first colonial acts, Japan took the five-year-old crown prince of Korea to Japan to be reared in the Japanese imperial household and eventually married to a Japanese princess. She banned the Korean language and national symbols — flag, flower, and anthem — and instituted the Japanese laws and Japanese as the official language. The government bureaucracy, commerce, and schools were conducted all in Japanese. The Japanization of Korea was not meant to be the assimilation of the Korean people into the Japanese society, however. Therefore, the Koreans were always viewed as subject aliens with no rights of citizenship.

With various colonial measures dislocating the Korean society and economy, the Koreans found the life in Korea difficult. Some of them cast their eyes beyond the surrounding seas to emigrate to whatever looked promising: the Americas, Hawaii, China, even the Japanese islands. There were rumors of all the land available in Brazil for anyone willing to work for it. The United States of America had a special appeal with democratic openness to all comers. The exotic Hawaiian plantation had its own allure. But the dispossessed Koreans, who chose to emigrate to the Japanese islands, had to face the double jeopardy of the usual immigrants' hardship and a wall of Japanese prejudice and discrimination.

The ultimate Japanese policy toward the non–Japanese was non-assimilation to preserve the Japanese racial purity and superiority. The policies were not always publicly spelled out in the official edicts, but were understood clearly by the governing and governed. Instead of any visible, identifying markings on the Koreans, such as tattoos or patches on clothing, they were marked, nevertheless, by their

birth certificates bearing the original Korean addresses as their permanent domicile. They might have been born in Japan and be second or third generation immigrants, but they remained forever
Korean. The identifying documents kept bright Korean children
from entering the prestigious high schools and beyond. Without
school connections, they were effectively barred from attaining any
position of authority, public or private, condemned to live under
the iron ceiling.

CHAPTER 3

Fukui

Despite the gnawing realization of how fast he was sinking from the landed gentry to a mere farmer eking out a hand-to-mouth existence, my father was pinned down by his family responsibility. As he was increasingly unhappy about himself and worried about what would become of his children, he began to look beyond the sea for a new life.

Like thousands of itinerant Koreans, driven by abject poverty in Korea and lured by opportunities overseas, my father took his meager savings and ventured to search for a place to land in the Japanese archipelago. He started from Kyushu island with a large coal mining industry, through Honshu, to the southern half of Sakahlin island. Sakahlin island had been part of Czarist Russia but the southern half was ceded to Japan, along with the Kuril islands, as the spoils of the Russo-Japanese war in 1905. On Sakahlin island, my father saw the bitter Russian defeat in the miles of burned-out forests torched black by the retreating Russian settlers before the Japanese takeover.

While my father was getting acquainted with the layout of the country, people, and culture, he stopped here and there for a few months, working at coal mines, construction sites, or at any jobs available. All the while, he was learning Japanese. Luckily, the Japanese used the Chinese characters in their writing with the original meanings intact, but with different pronunciations. He found that his old Chinese classics gave him a leg up. The Japanese alphabets, katakana and hirokana, were simple phonetics, easy to master in contrast to the Chinese ideograph, kanji, which numbered in the thousands. One had to master at least five thousand kanjis to read the newspaper.

It is not clear why my father chose Fukui for his family in 1930. As the provincial capital of Fukui Prefecture, Fukui lay on the coast of the Sea of Japan, sharing the frigid sea with Korea on the west and Russia in the north. The Siberian wind, sodden with the mist off the sea, would dump heavy snow in the winter.

Fukui was slow in shedding the nineteenth century feudal traditions and culture when we arrived. The city hall was still ensconced in the old castle, surrounded by a water-lily covered moat, protecting the huge boulder piling and the ancient timbered buildings on it. A wooden bridge arched over the moat into the castle ground with gnarled old pine trees.

When the Che family came to live in a residential enclave at the outer edge of the city in 1930, the town was in gradual transition from rural to urban against its will. Our rented back half of a house — our landlord lived in the front half facing the street across a little stone bridge spanning a stream — had one large tatamied room for sitting, working, studying, eating and sleeping. There was a small entrance where you took off your shoes, a kitchen in the back of the living room with a latrine in one corner, and a small tatamied appendix cornered by the entrance and the living room. It had an unfinished attic with rough boards for a floor for overflow guests.

Our house was in a typical Japanese neighborhood with residential houses intermixed with the stores. A fancy grocery with exotic canned goods and a mini-bar had shaved ice in the summer and working men gathered around the square hibachi for hot sake, even in the summer after a scalding bath. A candy store sold local peaches and persimmons in season. It even had a blacksmith who pounded new horseshoes, or fixed wagon spokes, until one day he disappeared with the horse-drawn wagons, gone out of existence. There was a family-run tie-dye factory which colored our neighborhood stream smelly red, green or blue for days at a time.

In the past, the area had been a country of farmhouses with large kitchen gardens, ancient wells, and fruit trees. Some of them had been impressive estates with rock pilings for foundations for the spacious grounds and the old timbered houses. It also acted as the buffer between the town and rice paddies. I saw a farmhouse being leveled for new rowhouses, to make way for urban living. A Shinto priest blessed the site to drive evil spirits from the new house and from the living. For the foundation of the house, the cornerstones were pounded into the ground by a heavy timber pulled up and down by a dozen men and women using block and tackle. They wore colorful kimonos and headbands with sleeves tied back neatly by sashes, and sang folk songs in rhythmic step with their pulling.

In those days, only newly built homes had indoor running water. Those of us who lived in older houses depended on hand-pumped water in the house, or an outdoor well left behind after the farmhouse was dismembered by the invading city life. Our landlord had his own pump in the kitchen, but we had to draw water from an ancient well. The well was paved with gigantic boulders worn smooth and roofed for the elements of weather. The well was so deep and weather-proofed that in the summer we cooled our watermelons in the icy water and in the winter we saw steam rising from it.

CHAPTER 4

Life in Fukui

When I was about two years old, my father had to return to Korea for his tuberculosis and was gone for five years. My earliest memory of our life in Fukui was a fatherless home where my mother and baby brother, Taikun, were the core center of my little universe. Taikun was born shortly after my father's departure, and he and my mother were inseparable, day and night. He went everywhere on my mother's back, strapped with a wide cloth sash, an obi, and kept warm with a haori, a padded kimono coat, in the winter. He seemed always at her breasts whenever she was taking a break from chores, and he slept on one side of my mother and I, on the other.

My oldest sister, Kiyon, and second sister, Duli, were ten and seven when we came to Fukui and the Japanese law required that they be enrolled in school. They were duly registered and attending the classes right away before they knew one word of Japanese. Right out of a Korean village, my sisters were thrust into an alien world of Japanese urban life with city buses and automobiles. My sisters' long braided hair reaching their small backs was greeted by stares and laughter from the girls with short, bobbed hair and the boys with shaved heads. Their exotic Korean dresses — white, long-sleeved blouses and black, full skirts — and Korean rubber shoes drew more jeers. They stood out like strange creatures among the Japanese schoolchildren in their navy-blue school uniforms. Not knowing Japanese, my sisters had no clue what was being said, or was going on in the class or school yard. They were adrift in a wild sea.

Even teachers began to show impatience with my sisters' inability to respond to the simplest directions. One male teacher in particular tried to get their attention by whacking their heads or desks with a stick he carried for pointing. Intimidation and ridicule turned their first school experience into a living hell. One day, my sisters simply refused to go to school, ending their schooling then and there.

When my father left for Korea, his family had very little money to live on except uncollected money owed by some customers of his Chinese herbal pharmacy. Before my father's illness, his Chinese herb business gave us a living while he was studying to be an acupuncturist. So my sisters went to work at the textile mills which dotted the outlying countryside of Fukui at that time. These mills were small cottage industries, owned and operated by the Japanese families, one of the driving engines for the Japanese economy in the 1920s. My sisters were still children, barely into their teens.

Every morning, they got up while it was still pitch dark outside and breakfasted on a substantial meal of steamed rice, soup, and kimchi, just like the Korean farmers did. Then, rain or shine, they set out on foot to work with rectangular aluminum lunch boxes packed with rice, broiled salted salmon, and kimchi. We didn't see them until it was dark. They worked seven days a week, had no vacation or paid sick benefits, and had to walk a couple of miles each way, even in blizzards. In the winter, they were half-frozen with their frost-bitten hands and feet, red as beets and itchy when warmed. My mother was busy, scurrying around to thaw them out before their supper and getting their clothes dry for the next morning. Warmed through by a hot supper, my sisters would tumble into the cozy bed before starting another grueling day.

On New Year's Day, all the factory workers were treated to a traditional Japanese New Year's feast at the factory owner's home. My brothers and I would wait for the New Year gift box of sushi and mochi that my sisters would bring home from the host. That was the only holiday they had all year. When my sisters started to work in the textile factory, they donned the Japanese kimono with obi (sash) to hold it together, toe-separated socks, and wooden-platform geta (shoes). I never saw them in Korean clothes again for the rest of our stay in Japan.

My oldest sister, Kiyon, was rather pretty, fair skinned and comely-featured like my grandmother, and began to attract attention from the Japanese men. There weren't any young Korean men around. While my father was still in Korea, Kiyon was seduced by the young son of the factory owner where she worked. Faced with strong objections from both families, she and the young man ran away. After some months of no news and my mother's torment, she came home pregnant. Alone, my mother had to deal with the family dishonor and ruin of Kiyon's marriage prospect so that my father would be spared from our problem.

My second sister, Duli, escaped such unwanted attention, being plainer and darker than the rest of us. She was even considered a little slow by the family, especially by our father. My father, in spite of his preference for a boy, adored his first-born Kiyon, but treated Duli as nothing but a nuisance. And Duli obliged by being accident-prone ever since she could walk. As a toddler, she fell into the family well, almost drowning, and the outdoor privy on the farm. My mother had to take time out to celebrate each rescue with rice cake to ensure the longevity of her hapless child.

My big brother, Taiam, three years older than I, was a natural tyrant. Being the first son of the family gave him the inalienable right to an immunity from discipline. I never saw my parents take a thin willow branch to the backs of his lower legs as they did to the rest of us for any misdeed. My parents believed in physical punishment for child rearing, but slapping and spanking were not part of it because of possible injury to the child. There was a family story of my mother's visit to her sister's farm with Taiam, a toddler then. Unable to restrain her little son wandering into her sister's vegetable garden, my mother ended up joining him in rolling in dirt and dust, ruining the garden. He was allowed even his frequent temper tantrums whenever he faced "no" and hitting his little sister, me, for his frustration. I was his scapegoat for as long as I remember.

When Taiam was seven, he was enrolled in Haru Yama Elementary School where my sisters had a disastrous experience. After a few weeks, he decided he didn't like school either. As a firm believer in education, especially for her son, my mother was beside herself. She coaxed, cajoled, and bribed him to go to school, giving him a

Taiam Che and Ungjo Che in Seoul, late 1950s.

penny a day for a while. I could not understand why Taiam would make such a fuss. I was so envious of him going to school while I was left behind without any playmates until they all came home from school.

Unlike my sisters, Taiam in his regulation school uniform was indistinguishable from the Japanese kids in his appearance and speech, except for the telltale Korean name. The Japanese pronunciation of his name was Taikan Sai. Taikan was quickly degenerated into daikon, the Japanese radish which was pickled in rice bran and salt. Because of pervasive xenophobia, he didn't have any friends in school but found his interest and talent in drawing and watercoloring.

As we were so poor, we didn't have store toys. But my brother was full of ideas to amuse himself and often let me into his creative enterprises. When the winter blizzard from Siberia piled heavy snows to the second story of the houses, Taiam would make a pair of skis out of strings and a bamboo trunk. He would bend the pointed ends of halved bamboo trunk over a charcoal heat and convincing skis were born. After a while, he would convert the skis into an improvised sled by nailing a basket on them and take me for a ride. In the winter, our next door neighbor's fallow vegetable garden became the neighborhood ski slope for the kids. We played hours in the snow until half-frozen and red all over from wet and cold.

The summer time was the best time for my brother and me. After the mandatory morning exercise in the school yard and his daily summer-lesson booklet done, he was free for the rest of the long summer vacation day. He took me along to go fishing in the nearby streams or rivers with a homemade fish net and bucket. In spite of loathsome snakes and leeches on our legs, we thought only of the delight in our mother's eyes, seeing the day's catch, small or large. She would prepare even the smallest minnows in soy sauce, garlic, green onion, and hot pepper for the table. One summer, when Japan suffered a severe drought, the whole neighborhood went out to the nearby dried-up river for a rich harvest of carp, eel, and catfish trapped in the riverbed puddles and ponds. For days, we ate nothing but fish.

Sometimes my brother and I would sneak into some neighborhood farmer's ample grounds with its large kitchen garden and fruit trees. In season, we were looking for persimmons, apricots, loquats, pears, peaches, plums, and chestnuts lying ripe on the ground, rich molding vegetation in humid summer heat after the thundershower. Pomegranate with its sweet-sour meat always reminds me of Sakamuni, the founder of Buddhism, who told a cannibal to eat pomegranate instead, as it tasted like human flesh.

Taiam also introduced me to the fascinating world of movies. In Fukui, there were two movie houses, one for foreign movies with subtitles, mostly Hollywood, and the other for Japanese movies of old samurai stories and modern romances. Somehow he found a way to sneak into the movie houses, as a nickel for a movie was hard to come by in those days. One day, he took me into a movie through the back exit door when the door was opened at the end of a showing. This was how I saw dimpled Shirley Temple and Deanna Durbin singing; Laurel and Hardy's antics, and jerky Charlie Chaplin with a white face.

Sometimes my brother would let us see the movie he just saw. In Korean — so our mother could understand — Taiam would describe the whole movie, character by character, blow by blow, and episode by episode. He regaled us with all the misadventures of "fat one" (Hardy) and "skinny one" (Laurel), while my mother was knitting or sewing away. My sisters and I were transported into the fantasy world, all huddled together around the hibachi after supper, in the snowy night. Decades later, I happened to see one of the Laurel-Hardy movies on PBS for the first time, but I felt as though I was watching a rerun, anticipating every move.

Taiam was particularly taken by the samurai movies, and the legendary story of forty-seven samurais avenging their master's death was his all-time favorite. He made his own sword out of a stick and took fencing lessons, kenjitzu, with split bamboo and face mask, at school. I was recruited to fight him with sword but I was too timid to make a good fight.

The first movies were silent. They were always accompanied by a narrator and piano music played in the front pit until talkies replaced them. The old samurai movies were made in the countryside for the battle scenes, but the spell of pretense was broken by a tiny bicycle passing in the distance or an electrical line clearly visible in the background. Years later, when I heard "The Pines of Rome" by Respighi for the first time, I recognized it as the martial music always accompanying the dignified marches of the soldiers and warlords on the horses, going into battle or the visiting noblemen with retinues. They played the same music for all the processions.

Our next door neighbor was a widow living with her bachelor son, a postman. She still had blackened teeth marking her marital status, a lingering feudal custom which made the married women pluck out their eyebrows and blacken their teeth, to separate them from the rest of womanhood. We kids were afraid of her for her red eyes, but the widow let us turn her front vegetable garden into a ski slope in the winter. In the summer, she would plant her vegetables from seeds and fertilize them with raw human excrement like the rest of food growers in Japan. The stench marked the beginning of the growing season and the whole area stank for days until it dissipated, or we got used to it. And she roped around her handiwork with stakes to keep us kids away, but inevitably, our balls rolled into it and she was sure to dash out, shooing us away.

The Japanese wedding was a neighborhood event to liven up life in the 1930s. It was a whole day affair. Before the bride was formally brought into the bridegroom's house, the wedding party had a religious ceremony at the Shinto temple. Then, the bride was taken to the neighbors' houses, one by one, by her mother-in-law in her formal kimono and introduced ceremoniously at the front door. Even in the summer heat, the bride was dressed in a sweeping, layered white silk wedding kimono and wore a bejewelled wig with a white band. Her face was whitewashed against the black wig, penciled black eyebrows and a crimson-red mouth. Her kimono neckline was draped in the back to reveal the nape of her neck painted white, beautiful to the Japanese eyes.

Finally she was brought to her husband's house. Before she could cross the threshold, she was given a ceremonial sake in a flat dish from which she sipped three times and which she deliberately dropped on the ground. The success of her marriage depended on whether the dish was broken into pieces or not. The shattered dish symbolized the finality of her marriage vow, the Japanese version of "till death do us part." In the evening dusk, the bride joined the new family for the wedding feast, while the whole neighborhood, adults and children, gathered in front of the house for the wedding treat. They came to catch the red and white sweet buns with redbean filling, flung from the second floor window. As a little child, I never could get one, but my mother, sisters, and Taiam more than made up for my failure. They would come home with an apron full of sweet buns to feast the wedding. Sometimes, my sisters went back to the place early the next morning, looking for more, overlooked in the dark.

All summer, walk-in entertainments were provided for us kids and the neighborhood as part of living in Fukui of the '30s. As soon as the medicine peddler with his monkey and accordion music gathered enough of an audience in a vacant lot, he would make his pitch for the marvelous, new ointment to remove any unsightly mole on the skin. One time we were so taken by the monkey act, my friends and I followed the man and show to the ensuing stops until we got lost in a strange neighborhood.

Rain or shine, a roving penitent went from door to door, playing a mournful tune on a two-foot-long bamboo flute, with a tubular reed-woven basket covering his head with peep holes in front. Out of curiosity, we children tried to peek underneath the basket to see the face, but the shadow within was too deep to reveal anything. People always gave him some coins for his trouble and wondered what sins he was repenting.

As a forerunner of televised soaps, we had a weekly "paper theater" of melodramas to titillate the neighborhood. A husky-voiced, middle-aged woman in Western clothes made a round of neighborhoods with the summer theater on the back of her bicycle. This portable theater was simply a two-foot by three-foot wooden picture frame with one side open for inserting or taking out the cardboard panels painted with the scenes of the stories. The tales were either old samurai adventures of honor, or the wicked stepmother melodrama of modern times.

Like clockwork, the show lady would appear at an appointed time in the afternoon on a particular weekday and park her bicycle at the same vacant lot, week after week all summer. She announced her arrival by knocking together two hardwood logs throughout the neighborhood. As soon as there were enough customers assembled, she would sell white taffy or seasoned dry seaweed for a penny before she showed us the weekly series. The snack was our ticket. We were anxious to see what happened to the last week's cliff-hangers, and, at the end of the day's episode, we were no better off, hanging in suspense once again. The "paper theater" became a summer ritual for vacationing kids and their harried mothers.

Those long summer evenings brought out old men, lobster-red from scalding hot baths, completely naked except for G-strings. In the summer dusk, with swarming fireflies and twinkling stars in the darkening sky, we kids would gather around someone's grand-father. We pleaded for him to once again tell us about the vengeful ghost, the fox story, or the lore of the black cat with mythical power to change itself into a human form, to right the wrong done to its master. By the time the stories were exhausted, the evening had turned pitch dark. But the spell wasn't broken until a mother was heard calling her child for bed. Still, we were too scared to move. Finally, the bravest would work up enough nerve to run home; only then would the rest follow, screaming as though a deathly hand was about to grab their hair.

Also the summertime brought night-farm markets to the neigh-boring streets with acetylene gas lights and their pungent smell. The night markets became impromptu festivals drawing people out of their stifling houses for summer gaiety. The farmers brought their vegetables, watermelons — red and yellow — and smooth-skinned, bright yellow cantaloupes. Some peddled household wares and oth-ers, toys and ice cream cones. A farmer would auction each water-melon like a valuable art object, starting at a ridiculously high price. But the price gradually came down until a customer would agree to take it. My mother was an experienced haggler. She would wait patiently for a particular melon she picked to come on the block and would not pay one sen more than willing.

My mother would chill the watermelon in the freshly drawn, cold well water until my sisters came home from work. Then we sat on newspapers to catch the drips, and bit into slices of cold, succulent, easily-split watermelon. It was about this time that we had our first "ice cream watermelon." This new variety had a pale, delicate yellow meat, the shade of vanilla ice cream; hence the name. I always thought that the "ice cream watermelon" had a more delicate texture and was no less sweet than the red variety. My mother wasted nothing. When finished, she would gather up the watermelon rinds for the next morning's soup, after first removing the hard skins.

Long before the convenience store became known to the world, Fukui had its own version. All the conceivable peddlers would come by our neighborhood with their wares on their shoulders, bicycles, or handcarts, practically every day. On misty, cool summer mornings, the farmers' wives would bring carts piled high with freshly picked produce: cucumbers, zucchinis, tomatoes, eggplants, beets, all covered with wet burlap. Hearing the hawker's cries, the housewives emerged from their houses for the day's vegetables or basketfuls of squeaky, glistening eggplants, and cucumbers to be pickled with salt and rice bran.

The tofu man would bring fresh tofus — raw or fried. The fishmongers would deliver the freshest sea products, winter or summer; in the summer, the fish was preserved in a bed of ice chunks. In good weather, a pancake man would grill pancakes right in front of the customer. In the summer, the ice cream man cooled off the hot afternoon with cones or popsicles. One summer, pineapple popsicle was a rage for its fragrant, exotic flavor.

Then, there was the rice popper who, for a fee, would pop your rice in a black cast iron, rice-popping contraption, which looked like a miniature cannon. With a loud bang and a puff of smoke, the popped rice was caught by a burlap bag at the open end of the cannon. The whole neighborhood smelled of popped rice all afternoon.

As a Korean child, I was often reminded of being an outsider. But, in a society where children were treasured, my life was still filled with the joys of just being a child. There were traditional festivals for Japanese boys and girls each year. On May 5, Boy's Day "Setku," every Japanese family with sons put out cloth carps — one carp for each son — on a bamboo pole in front of the house for longevity and strength, just like the brave kois swimming upstream.

On March 3, Girl's Day "Hina Matsuri," the family displayed the splendidly clothed dolls of the imperial court. Dressed in the traditional layered court costumes and hairdos, the emperor and empress were placed on the top platform with a miniature golden hand screen behind them as a backdrop and the court officials and courtiers were arranged on the descending platforms according to their ranks. The display even included lowly standard bearers.

I envied my Japanese girlfriends in their beautiful red and gold kimonos with obis tied into butterflies on their backs and their high platform getas for their white tabied feet. I felt the sting of being non–Japanese.

A beautiful kimono always reminded me of a historical anecdote my father often told with great relish at the dinner table. The Japanese kimono came originally from the mourning clothes the Koreans wore for a funeral in ancient times. When the Japanese emissary came to the royal court of Silla dynasty (A.D. 1–A.D. 918) to learn the best and the latest the Chinese-Korean civilization could offer, the mischievous Koreans gave the coarsely woven, hemp clothes with long-hanging sleeves as the finest. Over time, with their own aesthetic taste and ingenuity the Japanese refined it into a fine art form in exuberant colors, intricate designs and improved weaving, eventually surpassing anything the Koreans could produce. The joke was on the Koreans.

CHAPTER 5

Mother

When my father returned to Korea, my mother was left behind with five children in a foreign country, barely accustomed to the alien Japanese ways or their tongue. There was no welfare by the government. Even if there had been one, she would have been incapable of applying for the benefits, being illiterate. But my mother was determined to keep her family together by any means.

Mr. Okubo, a retired government official and the neighborhood honcho, took a personal interest in our plight and tried to intervene on our behalf whenever official documents were involved. It was due to his invisible helping hands that my brother, Taiam, was enrolled at school on time and that I followed him later. One time, Mr. Okubo took my mother, with my baby brother on her back, and me to the city hall for free rice cake, handed out to all charity cases for the New Year. This was the only time I went into the hushed and heavy timbered structure, darkened by centuries of soot and sweat, of a former castle in the heart of the town.

My mother never took to the dainty, restrictive Japanese kimono; her big, unfettered stride made it impossible to wear it with any conviction. She always parted her long, full, dark hair in the middle and wound it tight into a bun at her nape, secured firmly with a large tortoise shell pin, the mandated hairdo for married Korean women. She seemed oblivious of her startlingly exotic appearance, towering over astonished Japanese people around her. Unashamedly, she was thoroughly Korean.

Despite her exotic appearance in full-skirted Korean garb and rubber shoes, the Japanese people found her tall dignified carriage and benign countenance irresistible. Charmed by her gentleness, they treated her differently from the contemptible treatment usually meted out to the Korean immigrants, Cho-sen jins, spit out in name-calling.

The Japanese people, being proudly clannish, excluded all foreigners, particularly the vanquished Cho-sen jins, from their own life and society. But as soon as our plight became known in the neighborhood, our Japanese neighbors brought us their children's old clothes, leftovers from their tables, vegetables from their gardens, and rice cakes during the New Year holiday.

Even a rice merchant fell under my mother's spell in spite of his no-credit policy toward the Koreans. One day, before my sisters' payday, my mother ran out of rice and had to beg the merchant for rice on credit to feed the family. When my sisters got paid, she rushed to the rice store with the pay envelope unopened and asked the rice man to take out whatever she owed. He was deeply touched by her blind trust in him, and her honesty, rare in people, Korean or Japanese. From that day forward, until we left Fukui, he would cheerfully home-deliver, on his bicycle cart, many bushels of rice at a time, even after my mother's death.

My mother earned extra money by taking in tie-dye piece work from the nearby textile factories. She would sew by hand the dotted lines and tied them after pulling the thread tight. Then, the factory dyed tied cloth into flowery designs in various colors. I used to take the tied cloth back to the factory and return with a batch of wet, dye-smelling cloth in a bundle on my back, tied around my neck. Sometimes I had to rest at the side of the road and couldn't get up by myself, weighed down as I was by the load. I had to wait for some passerby to help me up.

Somehow my mother found time to learn knitting. She discovered that knitted wool sweaters, underwear, gloves, and scarves were essential to survive the Fukui winter. She knitted school lunch box covers for Taiam and me to keep our rice warm in the winter cold. My baby brother had a knitted cap with a white ball at the crown, bobbing up and down on my mother's back, under the padded haori on the snowy street.

My mother made homemade yeast with wheat bran for milky white Korean rice wine. She used some of it for herself but sold the rest to Korean families who made their own batches. She made our own soy sauce with fermented soybeans, some of which she sold to other Korean families who preferred the less sweet Korean sauce to the darker and sweeter Japanese Kikoman.

When the warm bright spring sun was pushing up young dandelions and wild watercress, my mother would be out with my baby brother on her back and me in tow, scouring the untilled fields, rice dikes and country roads. This excursion into the countryside was her long-awaited rite of spring. The wild greens we picked were the first honest-to-god greens we had tasted since the last harvest time in autumn. She would blanch and season the greens with crushed garlic, parboiled and crushed sesame seeds, soy sauce, and hot bean paste. It was an eagerly awaited treat after eating nothing but pickled cabbages, daikons, and dried turnip tops for vegetables all winter.

As the growing season marched toward summer, the watercress in the clear, swiftly running streams would be replaced by freshwater snails, nature's gift for protein and gourmet eating for Koreans. Koreans ate the boiled and shelled snails in vinegary, hot sauce. For some reason, the Japanese shunned them.

Too poor for meat, nevertheless my mother would buy a bucketful of beef innards cheap from the Korean peddler, about ten sens. She would clean the insides of intestines, throw them in a large, black iron kettle with heart, liver, stomach, and sauté them with handfuls of garlic, green onions, red peppers, and soy sauce. A few hours of slow simmering produced a delicious, rich soup without one fiber of muscle meat. Before cooking, she would slice up some pieces of raw liver, sprinkle salt and serve it up as an appetizer. Koreans considered raw liver good for health but shied away from raw fish like sashimi, a cultural eccentricity.

In spite of our poverty, my mother would be overcome by her pity for the poor fisherwoman peddling from door to door in the winter. In deep snow and cold, the peddler trudged along red-faced, weighed down by a bamboo pole slung across her back, with baskets of oily, rich-flavored, large sardines, hanging at both ends of the pole. Out of the bucketful of fish my mother bought for a good price, she salted away a good part and we had broiled sardines for days.

When it came to feeding what my mother considered a healthy diet for her brood, she would forget her natural reserve or pride, and go begging. She frequently stopped by the kamaboko (fish cake) maker for discards — heads, tails, bones still connected in whole pieces. After a gentle simmering, an aroma of rich fish chowder would permeate the whole house in the snowy winter. After a while, she became a familiar face around the shop, and sometimes a kind worker would slip in a whole fish or two among the discards. She was shameless in asking for discarded tops of daikons or half-rotten grapefruit from the greengrocer.

In the fall, when the persimmons were harvested, the neighborhood candy shop would sweeten the hard unripe persimmons by soaking them in huge vats of warm water. The process took tartness out of the fruit for sweet, tasty eating. For us, the store would set aside overripe persimmons so that Taiam or I could pick them up for our ready desserts.

My mother never felt comfortable in using any of her daughters' earnings for her own personal pleasure. One luxury she allowed herself was smoking a pipe, a long-stemmed Korean pipe. When the winter was safely over and the weather was good, she would take out our wicker baby carriage for scrap iron or firewood collecting with my baby brother and me while Taiam was in school. She was sure to find a good deal of metal scraps in the open-air pit in the back of Fukui Technical School buildings, a couple of blocks from our house, across the river. She took the scrap metals to a nearby dealer for some tobacco money.

The Technical School was nationally well known enough to merit an imperial visit some time in the 1930s. One fine day, the schoolchildren with Rising Sun flags, together with the throng of ordinary people, lined both sides of the major street from the railroad station, passing through our neighborhood, to the school. People came from near and far to pay their once-in-a-lifetime personal homage, in deep bows, to Emperor Hirohito and the Empress, who passed by in a large, black car. In public appearances, the Emperor wore a Western suit while the Empress wore long flowing white Western clothes with white hat and parasol in the summer. All of the officials were white-gloved, even the policemen. The ordinary Japanese on the street, however, never really saw the imperial personages, as they were too busy bowing to have even a peek at them. A gaze on their godly persons was unthinkable, considered an impudence.

The harvest times in the country meant a bonanza of free food for a poor family like ours. The potato fields, after harvesting, yielded not only small potatoes ignored by the farmer but also a few overlooked, good-sized ones. The discarded daikon tops, outer leaves of Chinese cabbage, and green onion tops were gathered up to be dried in the braided straw ropes for winter vegetables. It was during one of these gleaning times one summer that we almost lost my baby brother. As usual, he was placed in the wicker baby carriage on the country roadside, next to a muddy drainage ditch, while my mother was gathering discarded vegetables in the nearby field. I was to keep an eye on my brother, who was then about two years old, restless and rocking the buggy. How long I was distracted from my charge, I don't know.

When I looked up, I saw my mother running toward us and, in a flash, pulling my brother's head out of the ditch. Racing to the nearest stream, she frantically tried to clear his mouth and nose of muck with her fingers. She feverishly washed his mouth with stream water until the baby was able to cry. Then, she cleaned up my brother in the stream and sat down, all spent, on the grassy bank for breast feeding, a final clearing of his throat and a comfort. My mother never scolded me about the accident but I knew it was my fault.

Kimchi is what makes a Korean Korean. It is a time-honored social institution as well as a defining national food. In Korea, every family makes its own kimchi in the fall after the harvest. The whole family participates in this annual national ritual, taking many days. Kimchi unites us Koreans like nothing else does, not politics or religion. Korea is a nation of kimchi addicts.

It is the filling which makes kimchi so unique. It is made by combining crushed red hot pepper, mashed garlic, sliced ginger, julienned green onions, oysters, tiny shrimp, anchovy, even chunks of herrings, and salt. The varieties of kimchi were created by varied combinations and differing proportions of filling ingredients. Kimchi makes strong contrast in taste and smell to other pickles.

First, the Chinese cabbages and daikons are "killed" by salt until they become limp. Then the cabbage is filled, leaf by leaf, with the spicy filling. Cubed or whole white radishes were mixed with the same filling, or any variation thereof for a variety. Before modern refrigeration, kimchi was preserved in a huge glazed stoneware crock, about three or four feet high and two feet in diameter. Varieties of kimchi were put in separate crocks for distinct tastes, and for the winter, the crocks were buried in the ground near the kitchen, with straw roofs to keep out the snow and protect it from freezing.

Since, in Fukui, we did not have the usual courtyard nor the proper crocks for kimchi making, my mother did the best she could. She would make kimchi in the largest crocks available and keep them in the drafty kitchen corner. But it didn't keep too well, or too long. When the spring approached, we had to eat the moldy kimchi any way we could, by washing off the white mold and cooking it in a soup. My mother wasted nothing.

Garlic in kimchi was a dead giveaway for the Koreans in Japan. Kimchi eaten at every meal saturated the whole body with garlic whose fumes escaped through every pore on the skin. Cho-sen jins were virtual walking garlic plants, especially to the Japanese who did not use garlic in their cooking at all.

CHAPTER 6

Going to School

One of my memorable childhood events was going to school in April 1936, April being the start of the Japanese school year. That year I was "nominally" seven years old, as Asians get one year older on New Year's Day. I had a shaky start for my schooling on registration day.

Since my mother was illiterate, speaking very little Japanese, Duli, my fourteen-year-old sister, was sent along with me to Haru Yama (Spring Mountain) Elementary School for registration. Taiam was starting his third grade that year. As my sister was hardly literate herself, in no time she was thoroughly baffled by the paperwork and fled home without telling me. Not finding my sister anywhere in the milling crowd of parents and children in the auditorium, I too came home, not knowing whether I was in or not. On the first day of school, I simply showed up.

It could have been Mr. Okubo who came to my rescue, once again. Having served in Korea as a colonial administrator, he showed uncommon interest in the Koreans. He was also a devout Buddhist and family man with a university-educated son. Often I saw Mr. Okubo standing under the dim glow of a naked light bulb hanging from the ceiling of our main room, trying to read some documents. Not many Japanese neighbors came to our house unless they were bringing things for us, but Mr. Okubo never hesitated to come to our place and stay for a chat. The image of an old gentleman in elegant silk kimono trying to communicate with my mother, a poor, illiterate Cho-sen jin, keeps alive my faith in man's basic goodness.

I was registered as Hozen Sai, the Japanese pronunciation of my Korean name, Pongsun Che. Thereby, I turned into a balloon from a gentle phoenix, the meaning of my given name. Hozen sounded very much like hosen tama, a balloon in Japanese. Che turned into a fierce animal as a Sai was a rhinoceros in Japanese. So I became, willy nilly, a balloon in my little world.

The first day of my school, I put on a new navy-blue serge sailor suit with white tie and square collar with two white stripes, and white knee-high cotton stockings. I put on my first pair of sneakers. My school supply — pencils, an eraser, and crayons — were carried in a leather bag on my back. The boys had their school caps and navy-blue uniforms with shiny brass buttons in front and Nehru collar. They looked like little "student princes" out of Sigmund Romberg's operetta.

Haru Yama Elementary School was a neighborhood school, as everywhere else in the country. Everyone walked to school, teachers, students, and janitors who rang the bell hanging from the eave, near the teacher's office, for classes and recesses. There were two classes for each grade. The first and second grades were taught by women teachers who stayed with the same class for two years. From the third through the sixth grade, the male teachers took over and sexes were separated. Each teacher taught all the subjects with the textbooks issued by the national government. Education was a national responsibility and everything was decided by Tokyo, including the training of teachers in Normal Schools throughout the country.

I loved Mrs. Sigeko Matsui, my first teacher, who was tall for a Japanese woman. Realizing that I was a disadvantaged Korean child, she arranged to give me a free hot lunch at school in the winter and encouraged me with approving nods and smiles at all my efforts. I was an eager student. At the end of the day, I could hardly wait to go home and show off my school papers bearing perfect scores. My mother couldn't read the numbers, but saw the circles on my papers, very few crosses. Swept up by my shameless gushing, she would join in my triumph of the day.

Even though we had two male janitors, they did not do any cleaning except keeping a huge kitchen spotless. The kitchen was a traditional Japanese kitchen with big cast-iron pots sitting on a cement-cased oven and there was always tea being brewed for teachers. It also had a tatamied area, elevated above the concrete floor, with sunken hibachi in the middle for charcoal heat for the winter and the tea kettle. I saw now and then the other first-second grade teacher nursing her baby there. The teacher was always so huge with a baby and looked tired all the time.

We students did all the cleaning of the school after classes: classrooms, hallways, privies, and the auditorium, which was in constant use on the rainy and wintry days from morning till the end of the day. We did the windows, too. And waxing, on our hands and knees with soft cotton rags, turned the wooden floors and hallways into shiny mirrors, tempting us to slide on our stocking feet. In the morning, we parked our shoes in designated pigeonholes of shoe racks in the entrance room, except when we were out in the school yard.

On the Emperor's birthday, all of us came to school in formal attire. Women teachers came in long-sleeved kimonos and deeply pleated long serge skirts over the kimonos, and men teachers were in "swallow" tails. Even the janitors came in suits, instead of the usual sweaters. My mother bought me a yellow, loosely-woven wool blouse with gold-striped square sailor's collar and a pink satin bow. This, along with a good serge skirt, became my formals for some years. For economy, my mother always bought my clothes at least two sizes too big so that they would fit me at least for a few years. The first year always needed shortened sleeves and a couple of tucks around the waist.

We assembled before the imperial portraits on the dais in the auditorium. With white-gloved hands, the principal reverentially removed the Imperial Decree on Education, written on a scroll, out of a tasseled lacquered box and read it in his formal samurai voice. Somehow his stylized reading sounded like my father's rhythmic reading of letters brought by our Korean neighbors. At the end of the reading, we all responded with deep bows, singing the national anthem for everlasting nationhood, as long-lasting as it took for "a pebble to become a moss-covered ancient boulder." To mark the occasion, each student received two rice buns with sweet red bean filling, red and white for joyous holiday.

In 1937, Japan invaded the Chinese mainland to punish the Chinese government for its boycott of all the Japanese goods in retaliation for Japanese control over Manchuria. In 1931, to consolidate its hold on Manchuria with its rich natural resources, the Japanese set up a Manchukuo government with a puppet emperor, Henry Pu-yi.

Shortly after the Shanghai landing, our teacher told us about our brave Japanese soldiers fighting in China for the Japanese glory. She urged us to do our bit of patriotic duty by writing to our heroic men and set aside a class time to do our letter writing. We never received any reply, though.

The Japanese government underestimated the Chinese resolve and resources, domestic and overseas, to resist the Japanese aggression. The relatively quick and easy victories the Japanese military won over China, Russia and Korea around the turn of the century must have lured her into thinking that the internally divided China was no match for the determined Japanese war machine.

On the other hand, the Chinese considered themselves to be the center of the world, as the name of the country implies, and looked upon the Japanese as an upstart offspring of Chinese culture. To my father, the Japanese aggression was like a grandson striking back at the grandfather, Korea being the father who had introduced Chinese characters and high culture to Japan throughout the centuries. The Japanese invasion violated the Confucian principle of filial duty, among other things.

Faced with the foreign invasion, Nationalist Chang Kai-Shek and Communist Chang Hsueh-Liang united to repel the invaders. The formidable Japanese forces, however, had quickly seized the Chinese coast and the immediately adjacent interiors. After the fall of Nanking, Chang Kai-Shek moved its capital to Chung King, a remote interior city on the Yangtze River, close to Burma. The choice of Chung King was dictated by the necessity for arms supply through the backroad from abroad. The Burma road, finished by the American engineers and Chinese coolies in 1938, brought the sorely needed war materiels with "Flying Tigers" as the air escorts. The American-educated Madame Chang Kai-Shek played no small part, selling the Chinese cause to President Franklin Roosevelt and the American people.

The year 1937 was a momentous year for our family life. My father returned, cured of tuberculosis. He had also become a Christian.

For five years, among the scenic splendors of majestic waterfalls in the Diamond Mountain resort of North Korea, my father underwent the acupuncture and Chinese herb treatment for his illness. Since the resort was a favorite vacation spot for Westerners living in China and Korea, he unavoidably encountered the vacationing missionaries. So, one day he found himself converted by a Canadian Presbyterian missionary to Christianity. He was a changed man. No more drinking, gambling, womanizing, smoking, and no dancing or lipstick for his daughters.

Our leisurely, no-school Sundays were gone forever. Early Sunday morning, we all dressed up and walked to the Korean Presbyterian church, across the town, beyond the main railroad station on the east side, for Sunday service. We even attended the Wednesday vespers. We rarely took the city bus or the local train running along the city perimeter, the fare being too much for the whole family.

Our young minister conducted the church services entirely in Korean with his wife playing the portable organ. The upstairs of the rented house was our church and the downstairs was home for them and their three daughters. As my father was a learned man, he was made an elder right away for the small congregation of about two dozen Korean families.

Each year, the whole congregation looked forward to Harvest Day and Christmas Day festivities for the communal feasting on cakes, candies and fruits brought by everyone. And there were always enough leftovers to be divvied up among the families to take home. My parents usually brought a big tray of Japanese mochi in pink, white, and mokusa green. I never could quite understand, though, the connection between the infant Jesus and Santa Claus, with our disguised minister passing out the presents.

At one Christmas pageant, I inadvertently gave a comic performance of a Christmas story in Korean. I couldn't read the script in the Korean alphabet, however, and the minister's wife painstakingly coached me in the approximate sounds to copy. The way I

mouthed the story, it came out like the mangled words of a drunk-
ard, far from what I had intended. The solemn celebration of Jesus's
birth turned out to be not so solemn after all. The laughter ruined
everything.

Once again my father resumed the responsibility of a bread-
winner and set up the Chinese herb pharmacy with imported herbs
from China and Korea. In our living room, he had an apothecary
chest with one hundred small drawers, ten drawers across and ten
drawers stacked up, with each drawer divided into two compart-
ments with identifying herb names. A Chinese herb manual prescribed the amount and what herbs to be taken, how often, and how
long. A small hand scale was used to measure precisely the small
quantities of herbs. A scary-looking slicer, with a bottom blade sta-
tionary on a wooden board and a top blade acting like a guillotine,
reduced the bulk herbs to manageable bits. One evening, Taiam,
trying to help our father, almost sliced off a good chunk of his
thumb.

My father also restarted his postponed medical training to be
an acupuncturist, under a Japanese practitioner. His teacher, a war
veteran with a limp, conducted classes at his home where he also
practiced his medicine. In the 1930s, the general medical practi-
tioners usually practiced their trade out of their own home, and
home visits were routinely carried out. Now I saw my father at home
all the time, studying or dispensing the Chinese herbs.

The return of my father was a rather trying adjustment for my
mother. His constant presence at home put an additional burden on
my mother, who still had her hands full with housework and care
for her working daughters, school kids, and a pre-schooler. New
demands from my father took away the little personal freedom and
space she had enjoyed in his absence. Now and then, I spied my
mother sneaking in a few hasty puffs of her pipe behind my father's
back.

Upon my father's return, my mother was simply told that she
and her children were Christians. It was quite a shock. She had been
a Buddhist all her life, but she went to church obediently and tried
to understand the new god who didn't look like us Asians and for
some reason died a horrible death on a cross. Singing foreign songs

Ungjo Che in Fukui, Japan, 1937 or 1938.

(hymns) accompanied by an organ was all so new. Sometimes, I saw her nodding with eyes closed, lulled by droning sermons.

Her old habit died hard. She still prayed to Buddha on each birthday morning, with the offerings of birthday breakfast, before we sat down to our breakfast with a Christian prayer. She wanted to cover all the religious bases, just in case.

Finally, my mother had to tell my father about Kiyon's indiscretion and her own pregnancy by another man. I do not know who the man was, but knowing my mother, who befriended all the strangers coming to our house for help, or just overnight stays, I would not be surprised if she was a victim of her own generosity. After hearing all about the family troubles for the first time, my father flew into a rage and threw a wooden rice bucket at my mother. This was the only fight I had ever seen between my parents. Afterward, I watched my mother trying to put together the broken rice bucket without a word. From the blurred image of my mother getting an acupuncture treatment from my father, I surmise that she had an abortion. Soon after, my mother was pregnant by my father.

As our family was readjusting to our father, he had a near-fatal accident while crossing a rope-constructed suspension bridge over a river in the countryside one dark night. Practicing unlicensed medicine at the time, he was called to an emergency case by a Korean man. Ever since his return from Korea, we noticed that he had developed impaired night vision and was wearing horn-rimmed glasses for reading. That night in pitch dark, remote country terrain, he fell off a flimsy bridge onto the dry rocky river bottom, breaking a couple of vertebrae in the midsection of the spine, but luckily not the cord. He was brought home on a jerry-rigged stretcher by some men on foot.

The next morning, my father directed my mother to assemble certain Chinese herbs in prescribed proportions and brew the concoction for him to drink three times a day. And then, he taught her how to insert the acupuncture needle into certain spots on his back, hands and legs. Where he could reach, he did it himself. His Chinese influenced idea of mending broken bones was that the fractures must be healed without immobilizing the healthy parts of the body. He was, therefore, dead against the body cast which was the accepted remedy at that time. By his reckoning, good blood circulation was essential to all healing.

It took a couple of months before he could gingerly walk around, a little bent, and his height was thereafter shortened by a couple of inches. It was a good thing that my sisters were still working in the factory to keep the family going.

My teacher, Mrs. Matsui, must have found out about my father's injury. Toward the end of one school day — I was a second grader then — she asked me to come to her desk near the front blackboard. Without any explanation, she simply handed me a brand new school uniform and gently told me to take it home.

CHAPTER 7

Death of Mother

I never suspected that one moonlit winter night was the last night I would spend with my mother all to myself, going to the public bath. It was shortly after the 1938 New Year. She was already limping painfully with a boil on her thigh.

Within days, she was laid up with the swollen, infected thigh. The smell of death seemed to penetrate into our little home. Kiyon was home from work in her advanced pregnancy by her persistent boyfriend, and Duli was keeping house.

In the beginning, my father treated her boil with acupuncture and mokusa — dried herb burned over the acupuncture hole. Only it got worse. My father's reluctance to bring in the Japanese doctor was based on his deep-seated contempt for modern medicine which too frequently produced wrong diagnoses and resulted in unnecessary surgeries half the time. My father charged the modern doctors for opening up the patients to find out what's the matter with them. Perhaps his personal bias might have cost him dearly in family tragedy and personal grief. In his last-ditch effort, he consulted a Japanese M.D. but it was too late. Her huge thigh was draining, filling the whole house with sweet, pus smell.

While my mother was dying from gangrene, my father's half-brother came from Korea, looking for work. On the very arrival night, my uncle had to see my father committing an infanticide: Kiyon gave birth to a boy in her little tatami room. Killing his first grandson must have taken something out of my father, but his hatred against the Japanese man overcame everything in the end. My father, accompanied by his half-brother, left with a bundle into the night, to the downtown river which cut through the center of Fukui.

Shortly, my mother too gave birth to a boy but he lived only a week. Duli tried to save the baby, but he was already weakened by my mother's blood poisoning. My mother was delirious with fever and had no milk for the baby. Racked by fever and thirst, she asked for watermelon in the middle of winter. My father, knowing that she was beyond hope, found an imported watermelon at the downtown fancy grocer and didn't even bother to haggle over the price. One bite was all she could swallow.

On February 28, 1938, my mother died, surrounded by her husband and children. Just before she died, she made sure that she saw my baby brother and me, who were kept away from her in the little room. Her wordless search for our faces changed my father's mind and we were brought in just in time. My father, sisters, and brothers were inconsolable, but strangely I could not cry.

The Christian funeral for my mother was an event for the whole neighborhood to see. This was the first non–Buddhist rite they had ever seen. While dying, my mother made my father promise to lay her in a Korean coffin (rectangular). Barrels were used by Japanese for coffins in those days, and the corpse was placed in the barrel in sitting position with legs crossed, palms together in the Buddhist's prayer, and its neck was deliberately broken to make sure that the lid would not pop open. My mother thought that the Japanese coffin was barbaric. By law, all the corpses were cremated since the land was scarce, even for the living.

My mother was laid in the only good Korean dress she owned in the custom-made coffin on a makeshift pedestal in our living room for three days — the mandated wake in case the doctor made a mistake. We heard tales of the dead rising out of the coffin after a few days of unconsciousness. On the third day, we held a Christian funeral service in our living room, officiated by our minister, and we all saw my mother's infection was dripping through the coffin onto the tatami underneath. The Japanese neighbors came to offer their Buddhist prayers and Mr. Okubo cried. We had no idea that she had so many friends among the Japanese.

After the service, we took my mother to the crematorium in a black curtained funeral car. The crematorium was equipped to take only barrels and we had to place one end of her long coffin into the hole with the rest slanting out of it. Just before Taiam lit the fire under the coffin, for the last time we were allowed to see my mother's face. She was serenely asleep with rosy cheek bones. Since our church did not have a graveyard and we did not belong to any Buddhist sect, we kept her ashes in an urn on a shelf for the time being.

Taiam and I had one week of no school for mourning. Suddenly, the house was so quiet and the happiest time of my childhood was gone forever. My five-year-old Taikun seemed so lost and bewildered with all the party-like commotions and the sudden disappearance of our mother. Overnight, he was changed from a carefree, laughing little boy into a subdued, quiet one.

After the funeral, my father gathered us together to discuss what we must do to carry on without our mother. My sisters were to keep house until they got married. The younger ones would take over the domestic responsibilities as time went on. Kiyon was eighteen and my baby brother, five.

Within a year after my mother's death, my father passed the Prefecture's licensing examination for acupuncture. For his practice, we moved to a better address with prominent public exposure. He rented the largest house of a recently built, two-storied, three-unit row of houses in our neighborhood, just a stone's throw away from our old place.

The downstairs front room became my father's examination office, furnished entirely with the European furniture. An examination bed with straw stuffing and brocade covering, a leather swivel chair for himself, a swivel stool on wheels for the patient, and a glass-front cabinet on a table, were all placed directly on the tatami floor. He set up his Chinese herb dispensary in the upstairs front room which doubled as a bedroom at night for some of us children.

Above the front door, he advertised his specialty with a billboard, a sheet of metal painted white, announcing arthritis, ulcer, tuberculosis and so on, both in Japanese and Korean. For an emphasis, a vertical wooden sign, "Acupuncture Clinic," in elegant Chinese calligraphy was placed near the front door, perpendicular to the house so that the street traffic would not miss it.

After some initial hesitation, his practice took off with the bold-faced advertising and pre-license reputation. My father's growing reputation was not altogether due to the efficacy of acupuncture as much as his common sense approach to the human body. To his thinking, the body was nothing but a finely tuned and chemically balanced machine with a soul. Therefore, it was daily meticulous maintenance which had a direct bearing on good health. How often I overheard my father admonishing his patients about smoking (throat and lungs were not smokestacks), drinking (disastrous to the personal health and family finance), good nutrition, and adequate sleep. He told patients to refrain from sex during the treatment. His brand of medicine, under the Japanese license, was mostly influenced by the holistic Chinese philosophy of the human body, proven by centuries of experience.

Despite his critical views of Western medicine's undue dependence on surgery as a cure-all, he loved Western technology. Soon he was making house calls on his beloved German bicycle, sleek and gleaming with chrome, a swan among the ugly ducklings of Japanese bicycles. My family, seeing more money than ever, was bitterly reminded of a Korean fortune teller's prediction of long ago that, if and when my mother lived past her thirty-ninth birthday, she would be in clover thereafter. She was thirty-nine years old when she died.

My sisters stayed home and tried to keep house. But it was an unmitigated disaster. They had no inkling of how the Korean household was run, with annual kimchi making, homemade soy sauce, or the fine art of boiling rice without burning. They had no feel for seasoning. Their factory job left them poor homemakers. We all missed our mother's magic with scraps of food.

Kiyon, out of boredom or love, resumed seeing her Japanese boyfriend, surreptitiously. She would see him while the whole family was away for church services. Once again, she tried to run away with her boyfriend, but for our next-door widow, who discovered my sister's bundle of clothes stashed in her tool shed. Confronted by the discovery, Kiyon grabbed the bundle and ran, with our father and us children chasing after her.

Between our neighborhood and the main commercial strip,

there was a long block of Buddhist temples of various sects, lining up both sides of the street. Kiyon disappeared into one of these temples and hid behind the rows of gravestones within the wall. After being spotted by my sharp eyes, she was brought back home, humiliated and angry. Shortly thereafter, she succeeded in running away, but it didn't take too long before she came home pregnant, again.

Desperately, my father sought out our minister to find a husband for Kiyon. He was willing to endow her with a generous dowry to any Christian Korean who would be willing to take her off his hands. So a husband was found for her, a rather gentle and educated coal miner from Fukuoka, Kyushu island. Months after the white church wedding, Kiyon gave birth to a Japanese-Korean boy, and her husband accepted and loved him as much as his own subsequent children. Even my father seemed to adore his "first" grandson on their home visits.

Her life as the wife of a coal miner was not an easy one. She did not know how to live within her husband's wages. On home visits, they arrived in shabby clothes and, after staying for weeks, they left in new clothes and loaded down with new household goods for their home. Kiyon unwittingly confirmed a Korean adage that "Daughters are all thieves."

CHAPTER 8

The Third Grade

I started the third grade with a male teacher. From now on, the boys and girls followed the segregated educational paths with separate classrooms but equal basic academic subjects.

However, there were some variations to the basic theme to acknowledge the different social roles they were destined to play in Japanese society. The boys began a more athletic regimen such as kendo (sword fighting), a vestigial samurai culture, and judo (self-defense maneuver). The girls took sewing lessons from a woman teacher, learning how to sew a button or hem a skirt.

As the Sino-Japanese war was raging in China in 1939, our school day began with more vigorous morning calisthenics to the accompaniment of John Philip Sousa's marches. We marched with "Stars and Stripes Forever" booming from the outdoor loudspeaker, without knowing anything about the music itself at the time.

Our school had another record, which a teacher played on a hand-cranked portable record player. Whenever a sad emotion must be evoked in the students viewing the heart-wrenching scenes of school movies, on cue Camille Saint Saëns's "The Swan" from his "Carnival of the Animals" was played. I still remember a movie about a national hero who rose from a humble, rural background into national prominence by his hard work and his family's sacrifice.

While "The Swan" was playing, the hero, a youngster, trudged through deep snow to his home in the country, running away from the harsh regimen of work in town. When he reached home, cold and hungry in the evening twilight, he saw his mother drawing water from the well, instead of a servant. It turned out that his family had made the financial sacrifice for his future in town. Finding that her son quit his apprenticeship, on the spot his mother ordered him to turn right back with no pause for food or thaw. "No pain, no gain" was driven into the young Japanese minds in our school lessons.

CHAPTER 9

Stepmother

After Kiyon's marriage, Duli tried to keep house but failed miserably. It was becoming obvious to my father that he needed a new wife to look after the family and household so that he could concentrate on his thriving medical practice. Once again, my father enlisted our minister's help. Thus, my stepmother came to us from Korea as a "picture bride" for my father.

My stepmother was a widow with an eleven-year-old daughter who had been reared since birth by her paternal grandparents in the country. My stepmother had worked as a Bible woman, a church worker dealing exclusively with the female congregation in sex-segregated Korean society, after graduating from the Presbyterian Mission school in Taegu, South Korea. She was everything my mother wasn't. She was a picture of Korean femininity, daintily featured and fair complexioned with petite feet. My mother always wore men's rubber shoes as the woman's biggest size wasn't big enough for her enormous feet.

When my father told us that we were about to have a new mother, I was glad. For one thing, I was thoroughly sick of bad cooking. To my thinking, my new mother should be better in some ways than my mother, being educated and a professional Christian. It didn't take too long after the wedding feast held at our house and attended by the whole church that we began to feel the great gap between our expectations and reality.

My stepmother was no mother. She was an iceberg by nature, not capable of any warmth even to her own daughter. Her icy chill was felt by us children right away. Her indifferent cooking from the lack of interest and talent did nothing to soften our apprehension. We quickly gave her a nickname, "the Siberian Wind," behind her back. My father, too busy with his expanding practice and so relieved to have a full-time housekeeper, was oblivious to the subtle but profound change in his home.

From my stepmother's perspective, perhaps she was too disappointed by the drudgery of domestic responsibilities for a family of five children. The life of a single career woman, by comparison, was a lark. She might have been misled into thinking that marrying a physician was the road to easy street, bringing up her daughter in the lap of luxury in the Depression. She didn't know, or somebody failed to tell her, that there were no servants. As soon as my stepmother got settled in, Duli went back to her factory job, gladly giving up the housekeeping.

My stepsister, Jinju (Pearl), was a rather soft, moon-faced, and plump girl, just like her name. The first time we saw her, she looked like a scared white rabbit, blinking at the harsh light of sun after hibernation. She too had to discard, reluctantly, her long pigtail and Korean dress for the Western clothes to go to school. I don't know whether it was the lower Korean educational standards, or the poor grades from her rural school that she was put one grade below me, even though she was a year older. She turned out to be a middling student with very little intellectual curiosity.

Jinju was a stark contrast to me. She lived up to her name, soft and nice, while I was a tomboy, sunburned, freckled, and quick in limbs, mouthing everything on my mind without a pause. In no time, my sharp tongue got me into trouble with my stepmother and arguments with Jinju. Showing off my good marks from school did nothing to endear myself to them either. I really wanted Jinju for a friend, after growing up with brothers as companions for so long, but it became obvious that she and I were not compatible.

I took pleasure from my studies and my father noticed. To my embarrassment, he would openly praise my good grades in front of my Japanese playmates. Privately, he urged me to become a medical doctor, and never broached the subject of marriage and family even in casual conversations. He was a feminist decades ahead, in the wrong time and the wrong place.

My big brother, Taiam, took our mother's death very hard, but even harder when our stepmother appeared. He seemed to have found a target in our stepmother for all the bitterness and frustration he felt. Her cold, indifferent attitude toward us only fueled our natural resentment. He started to rebel openly by complaining about school.

One day, Taiam got himself a job delivering newspapers for his own spending money. He would get up at 3:00 A.M., pick up his papers at the collection point, and deliver them before breakfast. In no time, his grades plummeted to the very bottom, as he either cut classes too many times or slept through them. It was his way of showing how desperately unhappy he was about life's injustice. My father was beside himself, but seemed powerless to do anything about his rebellion.

My younger brother, Taikun, started school without a hitch after our father returned. All the light seemed to go out of him though, when our mother died. She was the sun and moon for us kids. Taikun became a withdrawn, indifferent student and always looked lost. He was so quiet that the family forgot that he was even there. The rebellious Taiam and I, ever so quarrelsome, seemed to get more attention from our parents than we wanted, but Taikunnie was left all alone to shift for himself. Soon he was stealing money from our father's wallet to buy candy or things he wanted. (To fight tooth decay, my father wouldn't have any candy in our house while we were growing up.)

One scorching summer afternoon, he was caught sneaking into a nearby farmer's kitchen garden and the farmer's wife tied him to a fruit tree for punishment, under broiling sun. I don't know how long he was left in the hot sun before someone came to our house about his predicament. When I saw his pitiful, bedraggled look, drenched in muddy sweat and burnished red with sunburn, my heart cried out to him. The little boy was abandoned by his mother, so he thought, and then by the whole family in benign neglect, truly an orphan in his own home.

On the surface, my family seemed to be whole again with my

father's remarriage. With a great sigh of relief, he went back to his medicine with gusto. For the first time in his life, his practice was bringing a good, steady income. He could see that, under my stepmother's charge, we had an orderly life with regular meal times, a clean house, and the laundry done in timely fashion.

My parents even had silk sheets on their futon bedding, my stepmother's idea. One day coming home from school, I saw my stepmother pleased as punch with her new black lacquered Singer sewing machine with golden curlicue designs and a foot pedal for power. From then on, I often found her sewing away, oblivious to the world around her. She was most happy when making dresses for herself.

My first inkling that all was not well with our family life was when I happened to catch my stepmother's hate-filled glare. I was showing my father that I needed a new summer dress. My dress was a few summers old and finally had a big rip in the back from sticky sweat. Earlier, we were in a dress shop, picking out Jinju's new wardrobe of Western clothes, but nobody noticed my several-seasons-old, faded dress. My stepmother's killing look sent a chill down my spine.

Taiam, who had already made up his mind that he didn't like our stepmother, and I began to vocalize our grievances about slights, imagined or real, and her favoritism toward her own daughter. She would put more chunks of beef in her daughter's soup bowl and packed more rice into Jinju's lunch box than mine. In the beginning, my father tended to write off his children's complaints as part of adjustment. After all, she was a Christian and, for a time, had been a Bible woman.

As the tension between his new wife and us children escalated, my father was forced to take off his rose-colored glasses and see things from his children's point of view. My bickerings with Jinju did not matter much. But Taiam's open rebellion in taking up the newspaper delivery and Taikun's stealing began to alarm him. About the same time, my father had his own misgivings when he heard, during a tender moment, my stepmother confess that she loved him more than God. That was sheer blasphemy to him.

What sealed the chasm between our stepmother and us children was that she threw our mother's ashes into the nearby river without telling anyone in the family. There were only two things to remind us of our mother, her ashes and a group picture of our church picnic, taken the last summer our mother was with us. Now, her ashes were lost in the Sea of Japan, but my stepmother's cruel act only crystallized our love for our mother and beatified her in our memory forever.

From then on, we treasured the photograph of our church picnic. My mother was standing in the back row with my baby brother (about four years old) and me in front of her. My father, Taiam, and Duli were standing elsewhere in the back, behind the children. The picture clearly showed that I was holding back Taikun by his left arm while he was about to run up close to the camera, mounted on a tripod with a black cloth over it. Taikun stood slack-jawed in wonderment, his right shoulder and foot pointed toward the camera. My mother was pictured exactly the way she always was and will be remembered: tall, erect, and gently smiling in her white blouse and gray wool skirt.

We were badly prepared for our stepmother. Neither the wicked stepmother of the summer "Paper Theater" nor my Japanese playmate's stepmother warned me about the cold fish of a mother I was to have.

My playmate was about my age and we visited each other's house to play with our dolls, especially on rainy days. Her father owned and operated the fabric dyeing factory, right next to their residence, a few houses from my house on the other side of our street.

Upon the death of my friend's mother, her father purchased a geisha for his new wife. After the life of song and dance in fine kimono and dead-white makeup on her face to entertain men with samisen and koto, her stepmother took on the ordinary housewife's life. The family saw one day how hard the stepmother took the sudden death of my friend's younger brother after a short illness. She was utterly inconsolable at his Buddhist funeral service, conducted by the priest at their home. An abandoned, open crying in public was a rarity for Japanese.

CHAPTER 10

Moving to Nagoya

In 1939-40, with the Sino-Japanese war sliding into a stalemate in China, "China Night," out of a Chinese war movie, was a rage among the Japanese people. Through war movies, they became aware of the exotic land of China and its people with a sing-song tongue.

But ominous clouds were gathering over Europe. The Munich appeasement of 1938 whetted Hitler's aggressive appetite and emboldened him, with encouragement from his Axis partners, Italy and Japan, to swallow up Sudetenland and Czechoslovakia. Eventually, Hitler invaded Poland in September 1939, despite the non-aggression pact he signed with Stalin only a few weeks earlier.

The Polish invasion was the last straw for Great Britain and France, both of which declared war on Germany on September 5, 1939. But the following six months saw very little military engagement except in the Baltic countries which were overrun by Russia with the notable exception of Finland. Finland put up a fierce resistance in a brief Russo-Finnish war, but in the end she had to accept a deal from Russia, granting Finland a token autonomy.

Sometime early in 1940, my father decided to move his family to Nagoya on the Pacific coast, known for its salubrious climate. Here we would be away from the terrible winter and the painful memories of our mother. Also he had heard about a sizable Korean community in Nagoya for his trade.

Leaving Fukui was an anguish for me and my siblings. We were leaving our childhood behind, perhaps forever, with all the reminders of our cozy nest under our mother's wings. For years thereafter, I often dreamed that I returned to our Fukui neighborhood, frantically trying to see everything I missed so much, before waking up. We never returned, even for a visit.

Just before moving, my grandfather came from Korea to live with us. He was everything I had heard and more: an autocrat with a steel rod for his spine. He was a sight. In a nation of small-statured people, he stood out like a giant, but elegant, white stork — bearded, with a black horse-hair pipe hat with wide brim and strings tied under his chin. He always wore white cotton in the summer and silk in the winter — a Korean outfit consisting of a jacket with ample sleeves and generous pockets, baggy trousers tied at the ankles, a flowing outer robe, and white cotton socks, all hand-sewn.

He always carried a long-stemmed tobacco pipe which he sometimes used for something other than smoking. A couple of times, some naughty Japanese kids made a mistake, jeering and coming too close on the street, and, without a word, my grandfather whacked their heads with the pipe without breaking his stride and remaining stony faced.

My grandfather never accepted Christianity or anything foreign. A life without pleasures — alcohol, tobacco, a woman — was unthinkable. He commanded due respect from us all, including his grown son, my father. He felt humiliated, eating with us at the same table, three generations together. Old Korean protocol dictated that the proper distance be maintained by having, among other things, separate trays of meals served to each generation.

One day, my grandfather asked my father to get him some lumber. For days, my grandfather, with a jackknife, painstakingly whittled, shaped, and sanded the wood smooth before lacquering it black, into an octagonal tray table with four Queen Anne legs. Before this time, the family never suspected he was a wood carver.

I don't remember too much about the train ride from Fukui to Nagoya, only the embarrassment I felt in front of the Japanese passengers, of my grandfather ceremoniously eating a banana unpeeled. He never had such a fruit before. Half-eaten, he gave it back to my stepmother, complaining that it was too tart for him. It was embarrassing to me who knew how my grandfather and my father took themselves to be far superior to the Japanese, calling them "Wenum" (foreigner) in their own homeland. They never forgave Japan for taking Korea.

Nagoya was quite a change from Fukui. The Siberian winter of Fukui was replaced by balmy Pacific climate with hardly any snow, kept away by the warm Pacific currents. Nagoya was the center of commerce, the third largest city after Tokyo and Osaka, in pre–World War II Japan. It was a bustling metropolitan city with trolley cars fanning out to the edges of the urban sprawl, almost touching the rice paddies.

The city had one of a few Japanese feudal castles that were well preserved as national treasures. The government buildings and an army base clustered around the castle and its vast parade ground, used for the military maneuvers and training. After the attack on Pearl Harbor, anti-aircraft guns were installed to protect the seat of government.

The Nagoya castle, about three hundred years old, was the tallest building in the city, dwarfing all other buildings. On a clear day, from our street, the castle looked like a mythical bird soaring into the sky on the wings of sweeping tiered roofs. Solid gold, flipping fish decorated the four corners of the top tier roof and could be seen from a distance, like shiny quarter moons.

CHAPTER 11

New Home in Nagoya

Our rented, two-story house was several blocks from the east end of a trolley car line, and the rice paddies were just a few blocks farther away from our neighborhood. There were still a few farmhouses left in the area, intact with bamboo groves and threshing courtyards.

Our house faced a side street across from a firehouse with a fire lookout tower for spotting smoke with binoculars. In the back of the fire station, which fronted a wide, major street intersecting our side street, were an old Buddhist temple and a Shinto temple. The two stood side by side, spanning the whole block between our side street and the next, facing away from us. In a way, the new neighborhood was reminiscent of the Fukui place we left behind, having the remnant of rural Japan around us, except the government sanctioned and supervised a "red light" district a few blocks west of our neighborhood.

I doubt that my father was aware of the whorehouses so close by when he rented our house. At that time, prostitution was legal and considered a necessary service by the Japanese society. There were about half a dozen streets, each a couple of blocks long, with red-lighted whorehouses facing each other. There were eating and drinking places on the periphery, a health clinic to contain venereal diseases, and a public bathhouse.

The prostitutes had their own, self-contained world. They pretty much stuck to their own place and rarely mingled with "ordinary" people in the area. Still I saw them at our public bathhouses now and then. They stood apart, as they were better groomed and clothed. Some were rather young and some were older, but never truly old. The rumor was that when a young girl was sold by her father, the proprietor of the house had the privilege of deflowering her before offering her to the public. Abortions were routinely performed to keep the income flowing from the human investment.

My family was settled in the six-room house with a token garden, within the wooden privacy fence in front. My father set up his practice in two rooms and the family lived in the remaining space. He had his Chinese herb pharmacy set up in the downstairs front room which doubled for the patients' waiting room. The apothecary chest was lined up against the only wall of the room and the bulk herbs in brown bags were hung from the ceiling in rows. Soon the room took on the herbal smell of an Italian kitchen and it wasn't at all unpleasant. The upstairs back room became the treatment office, leaving the sunny south front room for my parents' bed/sitting room.

The downstairs back room became the children's bedroom at night and study/dining room during the day. There was a small room off the upstairs landing, which was used for the out-of-town patient, with his family member in attendance. This new house had running water from a faucet sticking out of the concrete base outside the kitchen, al fresco— no fear of freezing in this climate. What a luxury to have our own water source.

After an initial slow start and a little coaxing from the handbills distributed by his children from neighborhood to neighborhood, my father's practice took hold and expanded, in time beyond the Nagoya metropolitan area into other cities, spread by word of mouth.

Shortly after we came to Nagoya, my first cousin Youngii came to visit us from Korea, on his summer vacation from Normal School. Ever since my family came to Japan in 1930, we corresponded extensively with his family and knew him well from school pictures his mother enclosed in the letters. His mother was the only younger sister out of seven my mother had and they were particularly close. Youngii's father, a small farmer, died suddenly while my cousin was still in grade school and his three younger siblings were very small.

My mother took the tragic news from her sister very hard and cried. That was one of the very few times I saw my mother cry.

My cousin, Youngii Kim, was a brilliant student and my aunt was determined that her son was not going to be a farmer. She encouraged him to go on to Normal School for teachers in Taegu, the provincial capital, after passing a grueling entrance examination. She assured him that she would somehow manage to run the modest farm by herself. It turned out that a rich farmer in the village promised to underwrite Youngii's education and my aunt became his mistress.

Youngii was my love at first sight. I fell in love with the serious-faced schoolboy staring intensely out of his grade school picture. As he graduated from the elementary school with honors and went on to Normal School, I kept my forbidden love all to myself. As life went on, my platonic love for my cousin became my secret refuge of pleasant reveries to escape unhappy moments. When he visited us for the first time in Nagoya, Youngii was more handsome than I ever imagined from his pictures. That summer he was a proud and self-assured young man.

We children were all enrolled in a brand new school, Lower Iida Elementary School, except for Taiam who went to nearby East Middle School. I was put in Mr. Kurota's fifth grade girls' class. Mr. Kurota was a no-nonsense type of strict traditionalist who took bushido literally, the "Way of Samurai."

The bushido was the code of conduct based on the principles of the feudal warrior (samurai) caste, and the military elite in power then adopted it as their own. It exacted an absolute obedience to the Emperor, loyalty to the nation, and an honorable death over the disgrace of surrender.

Mr. Kurota was an ultra-nationalist who had absolute faith in the superiority of the Japanese race and the divine destiny of the Rising Sun to rule all Asia and beyond. He took it upon himself to prepare the future generation for the national task of molding the physical and spiritual characters of his charges by the Spartan discipline of bushido. Despite his chauvinistic attitude toward women, at times he seemed to be carried away by his own zeal and forgot that we were girls.

Mr. Kurota was a small man, the son of a farmer who became a teacher after training at Normal School. He bicycled to school across the city from his farmhouse on the other side of the city, rain or shine. He was red-faced on arrival and stayed red the whole day until it was time to go home. A scowl was a permanent feature on his face and, when he tried to smile, it turned into a grimace. His flat-top crewcut made his coarse black hair stand up like a brush and his swaggering gait was menacing. His disciplinary slapping and hitting with a stick were not reserved just for us girls in the fifth grade, but for anyone anywhere, unfortunate enough to be caught violating any school rule. Whenever a student saw Mr. Kurota coming straight at him, he was completely petrified with terror.

To toughen us, he would wait until we could barely hold our pencils before allowing any stove heat in the classroom. He also forbade us to wear warm socks on the cold wooden floor until all our toes were swollen red with incipient frostbite. At times, I wondered if he was angry that he was not picked to teach boys and took revenge on us girls. I half suspected that the thoughtful principal and other teachers winced at some of Mr. Kurota's excesses and misguided zeal, but they could do nothing except present a united front to the students, as a professional courtesy.

I don't remember too much about the subjects he taught but I certainly was not impressed by his scholarship. Besides, he took an intense dislike toward me for being Cho-sen jin and a Christian to boot. I never could get any better than C on any subject, a disappointment after high marks I received in Fukui. I was picked on for frequent slappings in the face until my ears rang, all for trivial or mere suspicions. I began to hate school.

CHAPTER 12
Life in Nagoya

The summer of 1940 was a disastrous time for Europe, as Hitler blitzkrieged through Denmark and Norway in April, Belgium and Holland in May and, at the end of June, took France. This was a heady and joyous time for the Japanese government and people with victorious news of the Axis partner, Germany. Then, the London raids by the German Luftwaffe commenced.

While the ominous war rumbles were heard on the other side of the globe, the summer of 1940 was a carefree and adventurous one for me. I learned to swim. My new Japanese playmates in the neighborhood took my siblings and me to an old feudal estate, converted to a public park with a children's pool. The pool was a large round concrete wading pool with shallow water around the rim and the middle reaching about four feet deep. With my friends' coaxing, I was able to float with my face down and breath held as long as I could. After that, everything came easy. All summer we tried to come to the pool as often as possible except when I came down with infected ears and eyes. The water was so polluted with urine that we even called it the "pee pool."

During this summer, I was introduced to world literature. Denying us children the radio and phonograph player — they were becoming part of the Japanese domestic scene, but my father considered them to be frivolous time wasters — he had to give us something to occupy our summer time.

He bought us the Japanese translations of *Crime and Punishment* by Dostoevsky, *Les Misérables* by Hugo, Abraham Lincoln's biography, and short stories by Western writers. *A Midsummer Night's Dream* by Shakespeare was taken as a fairy tale and Hamlet was viewed as a romantic, not a tragic character, by us naive readers. Among the young, Chopin, the pianist, was the ultimate romantic, dying young of tuberculosis, deeply in love and surrounded by the beauty of his music.

To balance the literary exposure, my father brought us the Chinese historical novel *Three Kingdoms* by a well-known Japanese author. Soon my big brother branched out into the Western philosophies of Nietzsche and Kant, but I stayed with the light literature.

I recall that Nietzsche was a very popular philosopher among the young budding intellectuals in Japan in those days. My recollection is that his writings were exploited by the Nazis and Japanese militarists for their political agenda. It was not a coincidence that the 1930's "documentary" movie of Hitler's rise to power, by Leni Reifenstahl, was called *Will to Power*, which happened to be the title of one of Nietzsche's books. The irony was that Friedrich Nietzsche's writings in the nineteenth century did not endorse dictatorship nor anti–Semitism. In fact, Nietzsche even broke friendship with Richard Wagner, the composer, over these points, according to some. Yet, in those days, Hitler and Nietzsche were ideologically linked in the Japanese minds.

My father also felt that we were old enough to understand the troublesome international events swirling around us. He started to explain the meanings behind the Japanese newspaper headlines and his own interpretations of the world happenings. This was the beginning of my love for all things political, domestic or international. As the only time my father could be with us was the dinner time, our dinner table became a round table discussion on the latest news from Europe and Asia, and his own analysis of those events. He urged us to keep up with daily newspaper reading.

As soon as we settled in Nagoya, my sister, Duli, found a factory job in a textile mill run by a Korean family, near the Nagoya castle. There was no direct public transportation from our house to the factory, so she was forced to walk at least five miles each way to work every day. It was not an economic necessity for her decision. Was she seeking her independence, or an escape from our stepmother?

There she met a young Korean man, a mechanic, who kept the machines in working condition at that factory. She fell for him, head over heels, her first love. I could tell something was happening to her. She was shopping for new kimonos and grooming herself with careful makeup on her neglected face. One day she confided in me that her boyfriend was walking her home after work.

She did not tell our father about her boyfriend out of fear that he would not approve of him, being a non–Christian. Nor did she want to risk our father ordering her to stop seeing him. She kept her romance away from our father as long as she could, until he started arranging her marriage to the son of our church elder. All her life, she had never asserted herself for anything. The family took her for granted. Now, for the first time in her life, she wanted something just for herself with all her being. She was prepared to defy even our father. Just days before the engagement meeting, she decided to elope with her man to Osaka where his brother lived.

It was a Sunday in the summer. She was off work and uncharacteristically moody that morning, instead of being busy with family doings with her younger siblings. Shortly after lunch, she asked me to go for a walk and had a bundle in her hand. About several blocks from our house, she told me that she was going away to live with her boyfriend and that I must turn back home. My worst suspicion became true, and I started to cry, insisting I go with her. And I kept following her. At the end, she got angry and shooed me, ignoring the stares of passersby.

That evening when I finally told my father about Duli, he swore her dead and forbade us to have any contact with her ever. He was acting as a knee-jerk patriarch, caring more about his lost face in the eyes of the church people than any concern about the welfare of his daughter. How I wished my mother had been alive then. She knew exactly how to calm my father's temper and would not let him indulge himself too long in his self-righteous rage. Somehow she would have gently diverted his attention to what he could do for his daughter under the circumstances.

I don't know if my sister wrote any letters home from Osaka, but knowing my father, all would have been destroyed, unread. One evening, about a year later, Duli, her husband and brother-in-law showed up at our house unannounced. When informed about their presence downstairs, my father simply went berserk. Racing down the stairs, he told them to get out of his house, throwing after them the gifts they brought for the children. He would not let them set foot in the house or stay overnight after a long train ride.

Taiam remained very much an indifferent student in his two years of middle school, but had the good fortune of having a wise, understanding teacher. Under his teacher's guidance, Taiam ventured out into various sports and found swimming to be to his liking. His fast growing height was an advantage in his swimming competition and he became one of the best in school.

Just before finishing his last year of middle school, when all the graduating students had to decide what to do with their lives — going to one of the trade schools, pursuing higher educational goals, or going to work — my brother, accompanied by our father, was called in for a conference with his teacher.

Taiam's teacher was the oldest teacher in the school, teaching beyond his retirement with the wartime shortage of manpower. In his quiet, gentle way, he touched a responsive chord in my brother's rebellious nature and got him to apply for the specialized field of medicine, acupuncture. I suspected the teacher of collaborating with our father on the choice of career. The teacher, in his matter-of-fact way, simply laid out, for my brother to see, the road map showing which way led to a lifetime of ditch-digging, or alternatives to a more satisfying life.

Taiam was readily accepted by Nagoya Acupuncture Institute and commuted by trolley car to the far end of the line through the downtown, six days a week except on Sunday. He had a new school uniform, the university uniforms of the day — navy blue serge with special school brass buttons, Nehru collar, a tri-cornered cap, and a long, full-length cape to match. The cape made my tall brother look like Count Dracula in the American movie. He was particularly amused by the awe he inspired in his fellow trolley passengers who unconsciously stepped aside for him in standing-room-only crowds.

Miraculously the new uniform and school transformed him into a serious student with a new purpose. Do clothes really make a man?

His love for drawing became a great asset for him when he had to draw the anatomy of a man: the skeletal system, the blood circulatory system, and the body organs. New outlets for his artistic talent boosted his self-confidence as nothing else did before.

His required German language class served only to pique further his newly-found joy of learning. Probably the mandated German for medical training was a holdover from nineteenth century Japan's infatuation with anything German in science and medicine.

For the summer amusement, Taiam drew, from photographs, a picture of Thomas Edison with a white thatch of hair and near-sighted squint, and one of Ludwig van Beethoven with piercing eyes, a quill pen paused in midair, and a notebook in his hand. My father had them framed and hung on the waiting room wall for all to see.

Jinju seemed to have found her sea legs, too, to navigate the waters of the big city. Her placid nature took in the turmoils of the move and new school without a complaint. At times, she looked like a duck serenely floating in a pond, oblivious of goings-on around her. Nothing ruffled her feathers.

Taikun seemed to be just tagging along, in his subdued way, objecting to nothing and demanding nothing. He was doing schoolwork well enough, but put no heart into it. He simply made the required motions in his distracted way. Sometimes I would catch his faraway look, lost in his thoughts. Remembering our mother and Fukui?

My father did not believe in a weekly allowance for his children, as long as they were well fed and adequately clothed. He did not buy into a new notion that found acceptance in many Japanese families, namely that discretionary money gave the children a sense of personal freedom, as necessary as the air they breathed. So Taikun, like the rest of us, except timid Jinju, resorted to devious ways of getting spending money: helping ourselves to our father's wallet, or asking for money for feigned school supplies and expenses. It was one of these uncovered wrongdoings which led to a broken leg for Taikun.

One evening, Taikun was once again being scolded for taking money from our father's wallet. Afterward, Taiam took Taikun outside in the dark starless night for a brotherly talk, away from the self-righteous sneers of our stepmother and Jinju. On the way back to the house after the talk, in the dark Taikun missed the little wooden planks bridging the tiny drainage ditch between our concrete front walk and the street. Not seeing that Taikun's foot was stuck in the ditch, Taiam impatiently pushed him from the back and broke his right shin bone against the concrete edge of the front walk.

That night my father put a homemade splint on his leg after first setting it straight. We all felt terrible for Taikun. Taiam must have felt worse, but strangely he never showed any remorse. Probably this was the first time Taikun had received undivided attention and solicitous care from the whole family since our mother's death. He certainly relished the unexpected dividends from weeks of no school and the pampered status of an invalid. Even though Taikun did not express openly his anger against Taiam for his injury, I have a sneaky suspicion that he never forgave Taiam for it.

In the summer, Taikun, too, had swimming lessons and became an accomplished swimmer like Taiam. But I learned to swim "free style" by watching other kids.

With my father's practice prospering, my stepmother purchased a Western wardrobe which fit snugly into the Buddhist altar alcove in her room. The fruitwood wardrobe had a place for hanging suits and overcoats, with hand-carved heavy double doors, a vertical skinny mirror next to them, a couple of small drawers underneath the mirror, and a few drawers wide enough to secure the wardrobe bottom.

My stepmother also made contact with her sister living in Osaka. Soon we had social visits from my stepaunt and her small children, but we, the Che children, never felt any kinship to our new relatives. Evidently the feeling was mutual. We noticed that our stepmother began to visit her sister quite often.

CHAPTER 13

The Coming War with America

In September 1940, the relations between Japan and America turned openly sour. Officially, the United States stopped sending steel and iron scraps to Japan. Japan, in turn, retaliated by making *official* the Axis alliance for economic, political, and military cooperation with Germany and Italy. In reality, they had been partners for some time. Buoyed by the spectacular victories of their Axis partners in Europe, the Balkans and in the eastern Mediterranean, the Japanese were convinced that they were on the winning side. The war with the West was inevitable, so they calculated, to fulfill the Japanese hegemony in Asia under the banner of "Coprosperity Sphere in Asia." The people and the government were quickly united in the Japanese manifesto "Asia for Asians," a front for her desperate need for natural resources in southeast Asia.

Alarmed by the possibility of German submarines reaching American shores, Franklin D. Roosevelt, in 1940, urgently prepared for war in both the Atlantic and the Pacific. He asked for and received appropriations from Congress for war materiel, a national draft, and to have the Monroe Doctrine reaffirmed. Under his "Lend Lease" agreement, the United States supplied beleaguered England with surplus warships and arms. The isolationist "America First Committee" was no match for the rising tide of the American people's sympathy for their English cousins and the persuasive power of charismatic Franklin Roosevelt.

63

Until Hitler made the fatal decision to attack Russia on June 22, 1941, despite the covert American support we were prepared to hear any day about the fall of Great Britain. Hitler's invasion of Russia put the Japanese government in a quandary once again. Just two years earlier, the August 1939 non-aggression pact signed by Russia and the Nazis forced the Japanese government to accept its long-time foe as a newly minted friend, forgetting the 1905 Russo-Japanese war and the bitter relinquishment of the southern half of Sakhalin island by the Russians. The confusion was evident among the ordinary Japanese people who took every word of the government's pronouncements without question. One was reminded of the Americans' confusion toward the flip-flopping positions of Russia toward Hitler during the same period.

Faced with the necessity of helping its new ally, Communist Russia, in solidifying the Anglo-American bond, and clarifying the war aims, the "Atlantic Charter" was announced by Roosevelt and Churchill in August 1941.

Meanwhile, Japan, with the permission of the Vichy French government, occupied French Indo-China on July 23, 1941, threatening all the strategic positions and natural resources of the Allies in the South Pacific and the Philippine islands. From the experience in the ongoing Sino-Japanese war, the military-dominated Japanese government came to the conclusion that without an uninterrupted flow of raw materials for the war industries, no victory was possible.

Now perched on Indo-China with a massed Japanese army from China, Japan was hungrily eyeing oil, rubber, tin, and other strategic materials in Malay and the East Indies. The occupation of Indo-China also assured ample rice from two annual harvests for feeding both the Japanese people at home and the soldiers. The Japanese takeover, however, brought instant retaliation from the Americans, British and Dutch, by freezing all of the Japanese assets in their respective countries. The war storm was fast gathering momentum.

In early 1941, as a new war was looming on the horizon, my grandfather decided to return to Korea. His decision, entirely personal, had nothing to do with the coming war. He had had enough of "foreign" living and the reduced status he suffered in his son's house. He had to share a room with his grandchildren. His commands were not absolute. The atrocious manners of his grandchildren were beyond the pale. We children kept forgetting *not* to address our grandfather from the standing position. The old protocol dictated that we spoke to him only from the seated position of a supplicant, no matter that we were on the run. He wanted to die in his homeland, with his dignity intact.

I don't know how he managed to travel on the Japanese train to Shimonoseki and take a ferry to Pusan, Korea, without knowing one single Japanese word. He was also too proud to ask for help from anybody.

In 1941, war propaganda was pumped up and the signs of new war preparations were everywhere. The Tokyo government decided that all the school children should know how to swim. Somebody, deep in the bowels of the central government bureaucracy, saw the vastness of the Pacific Ocean on the map and it dawned on him that most of the Japanese soldiers could not swim. In a crash program, all the public schools had swimming pools installed in the playgrounds and swimming became an urgent national priority. For the first time in the Japanese public education system, sports became as important as academics. Six days of school except on Sunday, we started the day with the morning assembly: singing the national anthem, the principal's exhortation for the day, vigorous calisthenics, and marching to Sousa.

When I started the sixth grade in April 1941, I was praying that we would get a new teacher. I was not the only one. My classmates groaned audibly when Mr. Kurota strolled in for another year. He was getting more fanatical about the Japanese sacred mission for the world, Asia in particular. He could not invoke the name of Emperor Hirohito without choking on his tears. The academic subjects were getting a short shrift as his tirades against the injustice suffered by Japan at the hands of the racist West became more frequent. After a while, we were bored with the same litany, day after day.

Then unexpectedly, I had an escape, for a little while anyway. The Education Ministry announced a month-long seashore camping trip for the weaklings among school populations. In May, all the sickly students in Nagoya schools were rounded up. There were two girls from my school. I volunteered to be one of them. In my case, it was a pure ruse to escape from Mr. Kurota and my stepmother, even for a short time.

Such a delicious sense of freedom, free from it all, to see the sparkling blue Pacific bathed in early summer sun, and feel the soft sea breeze on my cheeks. Barefoot, collecting sea shells in gently lapping waters made me forget all about my trouble at home and with Mr. Kurota. I tried my "free style" swimming in buoyant ocean waves, pungent with seaweed.

The camp was made up of several dormitory rooms with about twenty girls each and two teachers assigned to each room. The teachers were easygoing about the rules and the token school lessons in the morning were meant to merely ease our guilty conscience, knowing that the other school kids in the city had their noses in the regular school works.

Students thrived in the seaweed-scented breeze and on the pampered schedules of naps and nutritious meals. For the first time, I tasted fresh strawberries with milk and sugar. I wished I could stay between sea and sand forever. This was the beginning of my love for the sea.

When we returned to the city, my campmate from our school was met by her smiling mother at the train station. Nobody came out for me. I took a trolley car to the East End and walked home the rest of the way, dragging my suitcase.

CHAPTER 14

Pacific War

The Pearl Harbor attack on December 7, 1941, was like a bolt of lightning out of the summer sky, even though for some time the Japanese people were anticipating an impending break with the West. We had no clue as to what form, when, or how this inevitable break was to come. When it finally came, we could hear a collective sigh of relief, as though the national boil was finally lanced. The next day, Prime Minister Hideki Tojo, an army general, declared "The Great Pacific War" on the United States and Great Britain.

The government-controlled and -censored radio and newspapers went into high gear to crank out the Japanese rationalization for the surprise attack and the war to liberate Asia from Western colonialism. "Coprosperity Sphere in Asia" became the Japanese equivalent of the American Monroe Doctrine, Asia for Asians, only under Japanese domination. The government painstakingly enumerated every slight, every wrong, every injustice and every indignity Japan had suffered at the hands of the Western colonial powers in the past and present. Racism became a two-edged sword, against the white man's power and for the Japanese domination.

After all, Japan was anointed 2,600 years ago by the divine hands of Amaterasu Omikami (Goddess) whose direct descendant was the present Emperor Hirohito. She had inalienable moral and racial superiority to rule over all of Asia. The "Coprosperity Sphere in Asia" was used as the propaganda slogan to mobilize not only the Japanese, but also the Asians to be subjugated.

My father was delighted with this latest Japanese adventure for his own, perverse reason. Knowing the enormous power of the American technology and the inexhaustible raw materials the United States commanded, he saw the beginning of the end of the Japanese empire.

When I arrived at school that morning, the whole school was abuzz with the news of the Pearl Harbor attack, and everyone seemed to be caught up in a euphoria of pride and fever-pitch patriotism. The daring military exploits were minutely described and repeated with relish. How silently the massive naval task force had moved close enough to the targets on the Hawaiian islands for the planes from the aircraft carriers to strike. And how heroically mini-submarines were launched into Pearl Harbor for suicidal attacks on the American Pacific fleet from under the sea on that Sunday morning.

Mr. Kurota was in ecstasy, predicting great victories over evil America and its allies. We could not do any school lessons that day. Every class had a map of the Pacific spread over the blackboard and the students set to memorize the exotically strange names of the islands and the natural raw materials they possessed. Every day thereafter we followed the advances of the Japanese flag sweeping down the Pacific toward the South Pacific. It looked as though the Japanese forces were unstoppable.

In lightning succession, Hong Kong fell on Christmas Day. Early 1942 saw Manila fall and, shortly, "invincible" Singapore, the British gateway to East Asia and the Pacific, capitulated with the surrender of its forces. These were heady times for the Japanese. The daily newspapers headlined the latest conquest and the newsreels paraded the captured British and Dutch soldiers to feed the war frenzy. Within a half year, the Japanese took the Philippines, all the British and Dutch possessions in the East Indies, and Burma.

In April 1942, I started to attend East Middle School. On April 18, the Japanese sense of invincibility was shattered by the daring Doolittle raid launched from the American carrier *Hornet* six hundred miles away on Tokyo and three other cities, deep in the main island of Japan. The rapid-fire victories after Pearl Harbor had lulled the Japanese people into thinking that this was duck soup.

I do remember one cloudless afternoon when, hearing an airplane approaching toward my elementary school yard, I looked up and saw a huge plane, bigger than any I had ever seen before. It was flying low, barely clearing the treetops and school buildings, and a pilot was clearly visible. Because of the insignia of a white star on the side of the plane, I suddenly realized that it was not a Japanese plane.

I raced home and saw from my street that the plane was already well along toward the Nagoya castle and the civic center of government buildings and an army base. I could see the frantic puffs of anti-aircraft shells bursting all around the lone plane, cruising unhurriedly. It did not drop any bomb.

My father was ecstatic with the news of the raid. His faith in the military power of the United States was vindicated and it was only a matter of time to prove that he was right all along about the final outcome of the war. He was most impressed by the relatively noiseless performance of that marvelous flying machine. All of the Japanese aircrafts, by comparison, were small, ear-piercing tin cans.

The Doolittle raid was a potent psychological jolt to the Japanese who realized that they could not hide from a determined foe. The thoughtful people in Japan saw that she was now in a life-and-death struggle for her very survival.

CHAPTER 15

Graduation

When the war came, my sixth grade class was right in the middle of preparing for the all-important entrance exams more fortunate students were to take for admission to the high schools in early 1942. These high schools, segregated by gender, were ranked on the basis of high standards and the prestigiousness of schools. Those students who did not make it had two years of middle school to fall back on and delay for a time, so as to decide what to do with their lives.

Under the war emergency, Mr. Kurota set aside the usual academic subjects and focused on the progress of the war. What islands, what cities or strategic places were captured on what dates were memorized and drilled every day. The classroom was a war room.

Even though Mr. Kurota tried to discourage me from applying for a high school by keeping my grade fixed on C, nevertheless I defiantly tried for a prestigious school, knowing full well that it was a futile gesture. I simply wanted to have the experience of facing the solemn-faced inquisitors of whom I had heard so much. These examiners looked at everything essential to judge the intellectual abilities of the applicants: family background, father's occupation and social status, and the manners and clothes of the student. Moreover, I was so tongue-tied with fright that I couldn't answer the simplest questions like my name and address without stuttering.

Just before our graduation, Mr. Kurota invited the whole class to his farmhouse for a traditional Japanese dinner one Sunday. We girls took the streetcar to the end of the trolley line and walked a mile or so to reach his house. One of my classmates, a grocer's daughter, took a box of oranges, a rare treat, as the class gift.

After we were ushered into the main room of the heavy-timbered, darkly weathered old farmhouse, we sat on our legs to hear Mr. Kurota's rambling monologue on the Japanese values, until we couldn't feel our legs below the knees.

For the dinner, we were seated in a square, facing each other. Each student was served individually on a small lacquered tray — reminiscent of old Korean custom — rice, vegetables, a soup in individual lacquered dishes. A couple of class leaders (teacher's favorites) sat in the middle of the square, extra rice in rice buckets ready for seconds.

While my Japanese classmates were politely picking at their food, it took only two bites for me to empty my bowl of rice, and unhesitatingly I asked for seconds. The serving girl looked startled at my speed but gave me, rather reluctantly, more rice. Shortly I asked for a third helping, but this time she, appalled at my audacity, pretended that she did not hear me. So after all the traveling, I came home hungry. But I had a glimpse of how the Japanese people kept themselves daintily small.

It was a national policy that every elementary school graduate made a pilgrimage to the national shrines and visit the historical monuments. When the graduation trip came up, my father, being a good Christian who did not acknowledge any other god but his, protested to Mr. Kurota about the religious dilemma I would be put into. Predictably, Mr. Kurota pounced on this protest as a confirmation of his long-held suspicion that Cho-sen jins were anti–Japanese and could not be trusted. In front of the whole class, he berated me for refusing the time-honored national homage to the Japanese heritage, after being so willing to go on the seashore camping trip. My love for adventures moved me to side with Mr. Kurota, overcoming my own father. So I went.

We visited three historical cities: Ise, Nara, and Kyoto. First, we went to Ise Gin Gu to see Ise Shrine, the most sacred national shrine, to pay our homage to Amaterasu Omikami, literally the Great God of the Heavenly Shrine. But actually it is a goddess with an interesting story.

About 2,600 years ago, so the legend goes, her brother played a mean trick by throwing a freshly killed animal on her. Angered by the mischief, she hid herself in a cave with a boulder closing the entrance. Suddenly the whole world plunged into a complete darkness and people couldn't do anything — nothing grew in the fields, fishermen could not fish, hunters could not hunt, and hens could not lay eggs. So people decided to coax her out of the cave, but nothing worked.

Finally, somebody came up with an idea to lure the goddess with merry-making noises of dancing and singing. Sure enough, her curiosity got the better of her and she decided to peek through the crack. Then, she saw a beautiful lady looking at her. She did not know that it was her own reflection on a mirror hanging from a tree branch across from the cave entrance. Gradually, she was lured out of the cave and all was well with the world again. Not only did she start the long unbroken imperial line, but she was also the founder of the Japanese nationhood.

I always had questions about Amaterasu Omikami but never had the nerve to ask them in my class. For instance, in a patriarchal society like Japan, how on earth did a woman become the fountainhead of this male-dominated nation? Why not her brother? Why was her father passed over for this honor? Was the matriarch, the goddess, of the Japanese tribe the beginning of the Japanese nation? Was the Chinese influence with Confucius' philosophy and ethics responsible for the transformation of Japan into a patriarchal society?

Shintoism is a state religion established expressly to help consolidate the political powers, held by the warlords (samurais) throughout the Japanese archipelago, into the hands of Emperor Meiji (1868–1911). The mythical tale of Amaterasu Omikami, the Sun Goddess, gave the divine origin to the imperial line and endowed the imperial authority with the Japanese version of a divine right. The divine claim was designed to overcome the resistance from regionalized feudal powers and face the growing foreign (Western) threats since the appearance of Commodore Perry in 1853. Shintoism reached a fevered pitch during the Pacific war when the government propaganda touted the unbroken 2,600 years of the imperial line, even though Japan's oldest written history went back only to the eighth century. The beginning of Japan's nationhood has always been shrouded in mystery and myth, but recent archaeological findings in royal burial mounds of a seventh century Korean mural and the sixth century Chinese artifacts raise uncomfortable questions about her accepted faith.

Ise Gin Gu (Ise Shrine) had three sacred treasures — the mirror, used to lure the Goddess out of the cave, a sword, and a necklace. I have forgotten the legendary stories connected with the other two sacred objects. After a hot, dusty walk — we walked everywhere after the train rides between cities — how cool and hushed we pilgrims felt in the immaculately kept grounds of the shrine, densely surrounded by an ancient forest. We purified our body and spirit by washing hands and rinsing mouth in cool, clear spring water from the moss-covered stone basin with bamboo dippers. Whitely clad, the priest officiated at the worship, and I was, despite myself, deeply moved by the solemn rituals. I could almost sense the presence of god.

Nara, the second town we visited, was the original seat of Buddhism in Japan since that religion had been introduced by Korea around A.D. 500. The largest bronze statue of a sitting Buddha, tarnished black by centuries of the open sky, was a testimony to the Japanese people's devotion to Buddhism. An old temple of enormous timber blackened by burning incense, human sweat and dust; a gigantic iron temple bell rung with a hanging beam at the side, still giving out deep-throated gongs; and an ancient and weathered stone pagoda — all were footprints left by the foreign imports of long ago.

Kyoto was the last city we visited. It was, for many centuries, the seat of the imperial power before it was moved east to Tokyo. We saw the centuries-old imperial palace, low-lying, one-story, wooden structures with definite imprints of the Chinese architecture. The buildings were well preserved, surrounded by exquisite grounds with a garden, and a pond with gigantic, glittery kois (carp). A graceful red bridge arched from the shore to the teahouse in the middle of the pond. You can almost see how, in ancient times, the courtesans entertained themselves with music and poetry in the teahouse, awash in moonlight.

The Japanese gardener, profoundly influenced by the Zen philosophy, tried to recreate nature in the garden without betraying any trace of a human handprint. Every blade of grass, every patch of moss on a rock, every flowering bush and tree, every pebble or boulder, was carefully considered and placed in seamless harmony to replicate nature itself. Even the meandering stepping stones on the ground were designed to compel man to cast a downward look in proper humility and deference to nature. Man's ultimate place in the universe is in the union of man and nature. By contrast, the Western garden celebrates man's conquest of nature and man's power to improve on his surroundings. Man is the master of the Western universe.

It was not, however, the architecture nor the garden which intrigued me most on that day. It was the squeaks in the floorboards. Barefoot, we the tourists were walking through an old wooden corridor of the palace, and came across the "Nightingale Floor." It was nothing but deliberately and strategically placed floor squeaks in the winding corridor passing by many rooms. This was the security system of yore. Any assassin sneaking in at night would be detected by the squeaks and his target would be alerted instantly. After all these years, the floor still sang like a nightingale.

Starting on March 10, 1945, until the end of the war (August 15, 1945), sixty-three Japanese cities were firebombed every night by American Air Force planes under the command of Major General Curtis LeMay. But the three cities I visited as a school child were spared from the fiery fate due to the American war planners who had a respect for cultural heritage.

Kyoto was particularly spared from the atomic bomb, as Secretary of War Henry Stimson adamantly demanded that it be taken off the target list submitted by General Leslie Groves in charge of the Manhattan project. Mr. Stimson had spent his second honeymoon in Kyoto some years earlier.

CHAPTER 16

Middle School

After two years of Mr. Kurota, I felt so liberated in middle school, as though a heavy black cloud was lifted off me. Under the fair-minded women teachers, I began to do well again academically. The middle school was coeduational; boys' and girls' classes were segregated in separate buildings, taught by male and female teachers respectively. The only times we were thrown together were during the recess and the morning assembly when the whole school, students and faculty, went through the daily rituals of singing the national anthem, bowing to the east to our Emperor, and receiving our principal's patriotic words of wisdom. The assembly ended with vigorous calisthenics in our undershirts, even in winter.

In addition to the basic academic courses required for all the students, the girls had "girls only" courses to prepare for home-making roles to be played in the society. We had advanced sewing lessons with sewing machines, making our own dresses after cutting rayon fabrics on dress patterns. The cooking lessons were carried out in a specially outfitted kitchen classroom with the gas burners in the middle of long tables. We learned to steam rice, sauté vegetables, and make miso soup, a must for the Japanese breakfast.

We even had the Western etiquette lessons on how to eat with forks and knives, the English version of not switching hands for a dinner fork, and how to let the waiter know if you were finished. For mystifying reasons, we were also taught how to sit and get up properly from the European straight chair, and even tested on it.

The students were given group swimming lessons and certificates were awarded for meeting the nationally set standards of accomplishments: the distance of underwater swimming under one breath and endurance swimming, any style.

On a national hike day, all the teachers and students set out to march along miles of country roads with our lunches in our backpacks. The countryside was studded with huge vats of rotting human excrement collected from the townfolk and the pungent smell perfumed our entire route. The country aroma might have assaulted the city noses but it only reminded me of the countryside gleanings I had with my mother and baby brother in Fukui a long time ago.

The annual May Field Day took on a special meaning in war time. The boys were urged to test their strength, stamina, and skill to the utmost in marathon, jumping, discus throwing, and running. The Korean boys, being bigger and taller from robust kimchi diet, monopolized the top honors in every sporting event, not a fair contest for the Japanese kids. The tall, lanky Korean boys loped along, like ostriches, a half lap ahead of the rest of the runners, who were all bunched together far behind. Thereafter, they were called "ostriches."

Speaking of "ostrich," I believe it was a Korean athlete who won an Olympic medal for marathon running under the Japanese flag in the 1936 Berlin Olympics. My father was proud and sad at the same time as the Korean athlete had to compete under the "foreign" flag.

There was a war-veteran teacher who had an army uniform on without insignia and leather cavalry boots to his knees, twirling a riding crop. He acted as though he was still in the army and we students speculated as to why he wasn't: age or war injury. He presented a fearsome figure, tallish, muscular for a Japanese, a stark contrast to the rest of the faculty. He presided over our morning assembly with orders barked military style and a take-charge attitude. He was determined, it seemed, to turn the snot-nosed kids into fighting soldiers.

One morning during the assembly, the ex-army officer spotted one of the "ostrich" boys failing to come to attention as he ordered. He never gave a second chance. He jumped off the dais, grabbed the boy, and punched his face hard. Just in time, the boy's teacher (Taiam's former teacher) came to rescue him from further injury than a broken nose. Being tall, the student was at the far end of his class line and did not hear the order. Sometimes the Korean boys' natural advantages worked against them.

CHAPTER 17

War Time

The Pearl Harbor surprise attack was a colossal blunder of the Japanese military strategists who misunderstood the implications of the isolationist sentiment in "America First" and the Republican party of American politics. They took the vocal, political dissent as the lack of will to fight in war.

They also misjudged the American character. They thought it, softened by self-indulgent life, could not stomach the sacrifice and deprivations demanded by war. Just as Hitler misunderstood the English people by the off-the-cuff remark of Nietzsche, "Man does not strive for pleasure: only the Englishman does."

Once the will of the American people and the mighty power of American industry were united, the outcome of the war was a foregone conclusion. It became a question of when and how. It was a sleeping tiger they aroused, not the "paper tiger" they counted on. After the initial rapid victories, the Japanese people did not hear much spectacular war news for a few months until they read about the epic naval battles in the Coral Sea and off Midway island (May–June 1942), costly to both sides. These naval engagements turned out to be a decisive turn of the war for the American forces.

Right after Pearl Harbor, the Japanese secret police swiftly rounded up suspected or possible saboteurs. Its primary target was the resident Koreans with some education, the leaders of the largest ethnic group in Japan. Our Presbyterian minister, Reverend Pak, was the first one to be interrogated and imprisoned for a year. Then the church elders began to take their turns in time.

Hearing that my father was the next suspect, one day he quietly slipped away from home without telling his own children where he was going. He went into hiding at Kiyon's home in Fukuoka, Kyushu, until the heat was off. My stepmother knew where he was and why, but did not share the information with us in fear that our loose lips might jeopardize his safety. A dark cloud descended over our family while he was gone.

When the paranoia began to subside, my father returned, but soon was called in by the police for questioning. He was asked about any knowledge of Syngman Rhee and Il Sung Kim, two well-known underground activists for the Korean independence movement from abroad since 1910. Syngman Rhee was associated with the Western democracy and Il Sung Kim was a Soviet trained Communist. My father lied and pleaded ignorance, thus escaping probable imprisonment.

Even though my father was not actively involved, he knew about the underground agitations. Eventually, timely intervention by Japanese Christian ministers on behalf of the Korean churches had a tempering effect on the witch hunt by dispelling suspicions of the seditious thought and acts of Korean Christians.

By this time, all the nationals of the hostile Western countries were repatriated to their homes, and now and then I saw a Westerner, tall and fair-headed, on the street — the Axis nationals or Catholic priests from Italy.

The closest I came to suspecting anyone of spying was the father of my Korean playmate, our westside neighbor. He would mysteriously disappear to far-flung places like Manchuria and, after months of absence, he would pop up just long enough to collect mail and clean laundry. Even though they were Koreans, they looked and acted Japanese. They spoke flawless Japanese and wore Japanese kimonos by preference. My playmate and her younger brother lived with their mother in comfortable circumstances even though there was no visible means of income or no discernible job held by her roving father, a burly, big man with coarse manners. We gossiped that he might be connected with some labor movement or Il Sung Kim the Communist. In those days, the labor activist and the Communist were interchangeable.

The only possible treason my father could have been charged with during the war was that he was an ardent admirer of President Franklin D. Roosevelt and his wife, Eleanor. Setting aside the privileged life of the American aristocrat and the discomfort of his polio, Roosevelt pursued selfless public service for his people and country during the Great Depression and World War II. My father believed that if it had not been for Roosevelt being at the right place and time in the history of mankind, the world would have been quite a different place under the dictatorship of the Axis. He was a diehard Roosevelt Democrat from afar.

Initially, all young Japanese men of certain age categories were automatically conscripted to serve in the military. But the Korean young men, either in the Japanese islands or in Korea itself, were exempted from conscription. For good reason, the Japanese government could not trust their loyalty to Japan or the Japanese new order in Asia.

But as the advancing Japanese military forces spread themselves thin all over the vast Pacific and Southeast Asia, the manpower shortage became acute. The government began to call up the older, married Japanese men without children to man the supply lines and construction crews. Even Korean men were lured with the promise of spectacular wages, unheard of earlier.

As the tide of war began turning against Japan, "volunteers" were recruited from the cream of the Korean community: young men with a high school or university education in Japan and Korea. These recruits were used as the ground maintenance crews, under close supervision, at the air or naval bases in the Japanese home islands, away from the sensitive front lines.

Once I was sent to the city hall by my father to collect his medical fee owed by a Korean lady whose husband was serving in the Pacific. When I presented the bill to the city bureaucrat, he found out that the man's account had accumulated an enormous sum of money, unbeknown to his wife, far more than the amount due. He saw a chance to pocket the difference. He asked me to sign a blank receipt without any monetary amount written in. Obediently, I complied by affixing my father's seal, which I carried with me, under my father's name on the receipt. In Japan and Korea, the personal seal, made when one became of age, stood for one's signature on documents.

My father often heard from his patients about the lonely hardships they endured, not hearing from their loved ones for months, not receiving their wages, or not knowing whether they were dead or alive. Their poor command of the Japanese language and ignorance of how to deal with the Japanese government red tape exposed them to fraud and exploitation.

A couple of years into the war, our eastside neighbor was conscripted to serve in the Pacific. His young wife was left alone in their two-room rental house, a part of an old farm compound which housed two other families also living in rental quarters. The farmer-landlord occupied the old farmhouse with thatched roof. Shortly after her husband's departure, the young housewife got together with a pregnant prostitute from the nearby red-light district and decided to adopt the baby when it was born. Usually the masters of the whorehouses did not allow the pregnancy to be carried to full term and abortions were the usual procedure to ensure a timely return on their investments.

But love intervened under the most unlikely circumstance. A customer and his prostitute fell in love. Before the man was called overseas for military service, he spent all his time with this woman and she became pregnant. Out of a patriotic sense of duty or a romantic gesture, the proprietor of the brothel allowed the woman to bear the child on the condition that the baby be put up for adoption.

For months, the obviously pregnant prostitute was seen coming to this lonely housewife's place with packages for the baby bed, clothes and toys. These two young women, linked together by accident or fate, planned together joyously, like sisters, for the coming birth of the baby. When a baby boy was born, he had two doting mothers waiting on him.

His biological mother visited every day to breast feed the baby. The infant breathed a new life into their empty lives after their men were gone to war and gave them hope in their fearful moments. Like any new infant, the baby thrived on the unsolicited cooing from all of us women and children in the neighborhood.

As the war went on, the government stepped up its propaganda with censored newspapers, war posters, and patriotic movies. There was a Roosevelt poster, with his smiling face touched up to look like a foreign devil with a cigarette holder sticking out of his clenched teeth, and a Churchill poster with the British prime minister looking like a stuffed pig, pink and bald. We were horrified at an American soldier pointing a rifle at human bones, highlighting the atrocities committed by the Allied soldiers. The Japanese government took hard the loss of Guadalcanal (August 1942) in the Solomon Islands to the American marines, and started the war slogan "Forget *Not* Guadalcanal."

These propaganda messages were effective, by and large, in frightening the people into redoubling their war efforts and in mobilizing them for national survival. But my father read between the lines of the war coverage in newspapers, saw shadow numbers behind the battle kills, and sensed the implications of moving battle fronts. He was a vintage political pundit without a portfolio.

Shortly after Pearl Harbor, a movie was made to glorify the intrepid Zero pilots and one-man minisubmarines attacking the American war targets in the Hawaiian islands, from the air and undersea. The supreme sacrifice of the suicidal attackers in the experimental minisubmarines was memorialized, and the pictures of the submariners, young men in navy officers' uniforms, were plastered all over the front pages of newspapers and prominently in the public places for many days.

Propaganda movies were exhorting all citizens to accept willingly, as patriotic duty, the rations of food and consumer goods, and to conserve gas and wood for cooking. We were also warned of danger lurking among us: the Fifth Column. The strident war movies were sometimes softened with a romance woven into them, and in one movie, we saw the heroine waving goodbye to her love, flying into the blue yonder.

The movies were usually preceded by newsreels of the latest battle scenes in the sky, the sea, and on the ground. The newsreels had the same introductory picture of the invincible Japanese naval fleet slicing through the open Pacific on the way to somewhere, always accompanied by stirring "Anchors Aweigh" by Charles Zimmerman, or something like it.

As a belated attempt to draw Koreans into the war efforts, the Japanese government decreed that all Korean residents in Japan must Japanize their Korean names. In the past the Japanese preferred that Koreans be readily identifiable by their Korean names, and the proud Koreans like my father wanted to hang onto their names as the last vestige of their Korean identity. The critical manpower shortage in ever widening war in the Pacific, however, overcame the past policy toward Cho-sen jins.

After hard soul-searching, my father came up with a token compliance to satisfy the edict, and, at the same time, his Korean loyalty. He took the town name of our ancestral family seat, Kyonsan, pronounced it in Japanese, and our Korean surname *Sai* (Japanese pronunciation of *Che*) became *Nagayama*. He did not bother to change given names except Jinju's and mine. My *Hozen* was changed to *Matsuko* (child of pine). The common Japanese girls' names end with "ko," meaning child. Now I was Matsuko Nagayama, an apparent Japanese but hardly one within. It was my father's tireless drilling throughout my childhood that I never forgot who I was and was proud of being Korean. In a way, he overdid it by insisting that I was even better than the Japanese. Jinju became Umeko (child of plum). Still, the school and the neighbors knew we were Koreans.

All over the country, the schools were urged to pitch in with endeavors for the war any way they could. Academic subjects were sandwiched between working in the sweet potato fields, sporting events, and air raid drills. We went to the countryside to help the farmers harvest their grain crops as their men folks were gone to war. We planted and harvested acres of sweet potatoes in the sun to make alcohol for the war machines.

We also fanned out to the hillsides to collect pine resin for pitch and tar, to make fuel for tanks and trucks, so we were told. It was a hot and sticky job, chopping off the pine branches and stumps with hatchets. Our hands, arms, and clothes were smeared black with sun-baked, gooey pine sap, and we all smelled like tar. Even though I liked my academic work, particularly my new English class, working in the fields and hillsides with my classmates and teachers under the blue sky was an enjoyable diversion. It even took on the air of a picnic outing although without picnic basket.

The war rationing was hardly unexpected. All the staples like rice, soy sauce, oil, and sugar were promptly rationed with coupons, and vegetables, meat, and eggs soon followed. The Japanese people used a lot more sugar in their cooking than the Koreans who ended up bartering surplus sugar for other necessities. My family gave away our extra sugar to the fire station for their meals.

Despite rationing, we had enough to eat and wear in wartime Japan before the air raids began. We always managed to find extra rice or clothes or shoes on the black market. Routinely, Korean peddlers came around with contraband, and my father hoarded bolts of men's suit and overcoat materials, all worsted wool. My stepmother bought up hard-to-find silk brocades or dress fabrics whenever offered.

The government ordered that we stop wearing any floppy clothes like kimonos and skirts. All the women and girls had to put on baggy pants over blouses or kimonos, narrowing at the ankles, like the farmers' wives in the fields. Men had to tie their pants legs with strings at the ankles, too, as though they were riding bicycles. No more the sartorial splendor in white for my father's summer attire, from the Panama hat to the white linen suit to the white shoes. They were banished for the duration of the war.

All the households were required to have a wooden barrel always filled with water for air raids. In the summer, little mosquito larvae were wriggling in green, slimy water and, sometimes in the winter, a thin layer of ice formed at the top of the barrel in a rare cold snap. It is amazing that we did not all come down with malaria in the summer. Nobody but me seemed to be worried about how a barrel of water could put out a house fire.

We covered our windows with black cloths to hide our city from the enemy airplanes at night. We had bamboo spears, "one hundred million bullets of fire," issued to every household to face the invading enemy soldiers for the last fight before mass suicides. The government propaganda led us to think that suicide was the only honorable way out when the sacred homeland was violated. The people were beginning to think what had been unthinkable. An honorable death was much preferable to the disgrace of surrender. It was fight to the last man.

All the while, the whole nation was praying for Kamikaze II. The people prayed before their family altars and the local Shinto shrines for the second coming of the Kamikaze (Divine Wind), which some called a seasonal typhoon, that sank the invading Mongols' armada centuries before.

Around 1942 or 1943, my normal school cousin's younger sister came to live with us from Korea. She came for her congenital heart condition, to be treated by my father. Even though she knew that she was dying and would never see her mother again, she was determined to see the world outside her little village. Her heart was so weakened by the disease that she could barely walk.

Once in a while, I would carry her outside on my back so that she could get some fresh air and see our Japanese neighborhood. Everything must have seemed strange and exotic to her, but she said very little. As her end came closer, she could not lie down any more and had to sleep sitting up. She struggled for every breath. She was only eleven years old when she died in her sleep. Her second brother came from Korea to take her ashes back home.

My father's half-brother stopped by on his way home to Korea, to get some acupuncture treatment on his incipient black-lung. He had been working in the coal mines and became too sick to continue.

Admiral Chester W. Nimitz, commander-in-chief of the Pacific fleet, decided early on that control of the air was crucial to winning the Pacific war. Thus, he concentrated on building bigger and better aircraft carriers and airplanes. Knocking out four Japanese aircraft carriers off Midway island in June 1942 turned out to be the pivotal point of the war in the Pacific.

In 1943, the Japanese forces tried to get through New Guinea to Australia, the last bastion of Western colonialism in the Pacific, but the American forces, strengthened by the control of the air, repulsed them.

Then, the Americans commenced the strangulation strategy of "leap frogging" north, taking the most strategic islands for American bases of operations and leaving the Japanese forces in between, stranded. Even the heavily censored newspapers could not quite conceal altogether the ever tightening noose that was approaching the Japanese home islands.

While General MacArthur was in Australia, preparing to fulfill his promise to return to the Philippines, the Marshal Islands were secured. Guam and Saipan in the Marianas were the next targets to be taken in July 1944.

CHAPTER 18

Going Home

As the Pacific battlefronts came closer to the Japanese home territory, the Japanese government took more drastic measures of self-defense. Nagoya city hall urged the citizens to disperse to the countryside to minimize the concentrated casualties of inevitable air bombing. The citizens were asked to go back to their hometowns in rural areas, to live with country relatives or friends. It offered them an incentive, city subsidies for moving expenses.

My father, increasingly nervous about the imminent American threat, decided to move the family back to Korea. He gladly took the serendipitous offer of money from the city hall. We were one of the first families to take advantage of this unprecedented government largess.

Later we learned that, once the nightly air raids commenced on March 10, 1945, everyone wanted to get out of the cities. Thereafter, the city governments had trouble keeping enough people in town to put out fires.

In March 1944, my father hired three professional packers who arrived early at our house to begin packing the household goods, the cumbersome Western furniture for his medical practice, all the books, and even his treasured German bicycle. It took one whole week of packing everything meticulously in wooden crates, protected by straw.

Each day, the packers were offered hot tea for their packed lunches and at the end of each working day, they were treated to warm sake and the Japanese hors d'oeuvres of broiled dry squid.

On the last packing day, my father paid them handsomely with an unexpected large bonus and was surprised by their unfeigned gratitude in repeated deep bows.

Considering the distance and many transfers on different modes of transportation they had to travel, our possessions survived the trip remarkably well, not one dish broken or one bicycle spoke bent. The crates had to be transported first on bicycle carts, as no trucks were available, to the Nagoya train station. There they were put on the train to Shimonoseki, the westernmost seaport of the Japanese main island, and then transferred to a ship crossing Tsushima Strait to Pusan, the southernmost seaport of the Korean peninsula. At Pusan, they were loaded onto the Korean train but did not reach the final leg of their journey to Pohang, South Korea, until after changing trains at Kyonju.

Since Taiam had one more year to go before his graduation from Nagoya Acupuncture Institute, my father made an arrangement with his cousin Pek for Taiam to stay with his family until graduation. Cousin Pek was the son of my father's paternal aunt and had a spring manufacturing company in Nagoya, producing all kinds of springs for the Japanese war machine. Once Cousin Pek and his mother came to dinner at our house. The old lady was the female version of my grandfather, slim and dignified. By working part-time in Pek's defense factory, Taiam escaped the required "volunteering" for military service.

Cousin Pek had done very well financially with his military contracts and lived a sumptuous Western-style life, complete with a feather bed. To me, the feather bed represented the ultimate of the urbane, sophisticated life I had read about in Western novels and seen in the American movies. For some reason, his feather bed impressed me as nothing else did. I didn't know much about him or his family, but always remembered him as the one with the feather bed.

Shortly after Taiam graduated from school in March 1945, Cousin Pek, too, came back to Korea, barely missing the fiery air bombing of Nagoya. He managed to bring all his assets intact after selling his business.

Since my second sister, Duli, was unceremoniously thrown out of the house, along with her husband, we had no word from her. Kiyon with her two young sons and her coal-mining husband remained in Fukuoka, Kyushu island.

Going home? It was a homecoming for my parents and Jinju, but for my brothers and me, it was another story. As a three year old, Taiam had very little recollection of the Korean life. I had no memory of Korea. Taikun was born here in Japan.

Whenever I heard "going home," I always thought of the old Fukui home where my mother kept her brood safe and sound with her fabulous cooking under her protective love. The image of her standing in front of our house, calling us to supper with her embracing love lighting up her face, was seared into my soul and going home to Korea did not feel right. The return to our homeland felt more like going to an unknown, new country, leaving home and all the fond memories of my mother and my childhood behind.

Still I tried to calm my uneasy feelings by telling myself that no longer would I ever be a Cho-sen jin and a perpetual outsider in Korea. Besides, I would be seeing, for the first time, my mother's dearest sister, the mother of Youngii. I would be part of the extended clan family with cousins, uncles, aunts galore on both sides. My cousin Youngii had graduated from the normal school and was teaching at an elementary school in Pohang, our destination. Above all, I would be seeing more of Youngii, even though he had no inkling of my uncousinly feeling for him.

March 21, 1944, was one of the few dates from my childhood in Japan to survive the time's forgetfulness. With my mother gone, I didn't mark my parents' birthdays nor my siblings'. Today, I can't even remember the national holidays we all knew so well in Japan. I had no idea until now how wrenching our departure from Japan must have been to etch that day into my memory forever, along with the day my mother died.

On March 21, 1944, we boarded the train to Shimonoseki after bidding teary goodbyes to my big brother. I was afraid for his safety. Please, God, hold off the air raids until he graduates, I prayed.

I sensed that we were seeing the calm before the storm as the train was chugging along the verdant countryside, rice fields not yet filled with water, thatched farmhouses flitting out of sight. We passed Osaka, belching black clouds out of factory smokestacks; Kobe, a cosmopolitan seaport with a long history of Western exposure; and peacefully innocent Hiroshima which was fated to be on many people's conscience on August 6, 1945. But on the day we passed through, Hiroshima looked like any other mid-sized Japanese city of gray, low-lying tile-roofed houses with narrow streets snaking through them.

We reached Shimonoseki in the evening. We spent the night on the waiting room benches waiting for the ferry which was to cross Tsushima Strait early the next morning. The whole waiting room was crowded with sleeping adults and children, and their possessions.

In the middle of the night, I had to go to the restroom and came back to where my family was all huddled together, fast asleep. When the morning light started to stir people awake, I was shocked to stare into the blinking eyes of a young Japanese couple just awaking. By mistake, I crawled between them under their cover and they didn't notice it. So, unexpectedly, I spent the last night in Japan in the bosom of Japanese strangers.

PART II

Growing Up in Korea, 1944–1951

CHAPTER 19

So This Is Korea

On that cold, gray morning of March 22, 1944, I should have known, at the sight of an old wreck of an unpainted ferryboat, that my fantasized Korea was about to be shattered bit by bit and that I was in for a rude awakening.

The ancient weather-beaten bucket was a poor excuse for a ferryboat, carrying mostly Koreans between Shimonoseki on Honshu and Pusan on the Korean peninsula. It was nothing like the sleek, white luxury liner I had seen in American movies. I watched, with sinking heart, the streams of Korean families burdened with infants and children, struggling with suitcases and bundles containing their earthly possessions. They were crammed into the ship's already overflowing hold and gradually filled every cranny they could find to huddle together, under the stairs and along the passageways.

It was a fearful time to cross Tsushima Strait, separating the Japanese islands and the Korean peninsula, with brazen American submarines lurking below the sea and the seasonal storms taking their part in sinking ships. We faced a double jeopardy, from above and below the sea.

There was no food available on board and soon enough I found out why. Once the boat started to cross the turbulent strait linking the cold Sea of Japan with the warm Pacific Ocean, it was tossed around like a Ping-Pong ball among the heaving, dark blue swells. In no time, the passengers lost whatever they had in their stomachs. Most of them never made it to the ship's lone restroom, and the whole ship began to reek of nothing but vomit. The people were so violently seasick that they forgot all about our imminent dangers from the sea. In the evening twilight, we finally reached Pusan.

Often I had wondered how Korea was named by the West, when the Korean people, Hahn-min, called their own country Hahn-gook or Hahn country. Evidently the West made some contact with the Koryo dynasty, one of three kingdoms — Silla and Paekche being the other two — ruling the Korean peninsula from A.D. 1 to A.D. 918. Korea was known to the West as "Corea" as recently as the 1930s when some English writers were still spelling Korea with "C." Was "Corea" a corruption of "Koryo"?

Throughout the history of Sino-Korean relations, however, the patronizing Chinese emperors called the client outpost Korea Cho-syun, "a land of morning calm." Japan, upon annexing her in 1910, kept it and pronounced the name Cho-sen in Japanese. After the defeat of Japan by the Allied forces on August 15, 1945, the Korean people took back the original name of their country, Hahn-gook, leaving "Korea" to the West.

True to the old Korean proverb "Hahn-gook is a shrimp crushed in the battles of whales." For centuries Korea felt put upon by her aggressive, expansionist neighbors: China, Japan, and Russia. As European world explorers were prying open the southern seaports of sixteenth-century Japan, exposing the country to exotic peoples, cultures and Christianity, the Yi kings tried to seal off Korea in the following centuries, but they failed. Undaunted by the occasional shipwrecks on the rocky shores off the southern tip of the Korean peninsula, the Western explorers managed to breach the coasts now and then, and sometimes to a disastrous end.

In the second half of the nineteenth century, Japan was emerging as a fledgling Asiatic power under the Meiji modernization policy. Korea's self-deluding, closed-door policy left her totally unprepared to face her ambitious next-door neighbor, Japan, who was hungry for raw materials for her burgeoning factories, and markets for her products.

At about the same time, China and Russia began to sense a potential rival in Japan for the dominance of the region of Korea and Manchuria.

Around the turn of the twentieth century, Korea was like a

rabbit sitting on its hind legs with its paws tucked to its breast, frightened to death, while the Russian bear, the Chinese tiger, and the Japanese wolf fought over it. Actually, on the map the Korean peninsula does look like a rabbit, attached to the Asiatic continent by its head and long ears, facing China across the Yellow Sea.

After emerging as a victor from the Sino-Japanese war of 1895 and the Russo-Japanese war of 1905, Japan formally annexed Korea in 1910. Japan then pushed aside the feckless Korean king, who had been a Japanese puppet for some time. Thus, Korea became part of the growing Japanese empire but a fierce Korean pride resisted a complete wipeout.

Groggy from seasickness and wobbly from the rolling ship, my first impression of my homeland was sickening disappointment. I even felt hurt and betrayed. My weary eyes could see only the shabbiness of everything all around.

While my family was led to an inn by a hotel man carrying a kerosene lantern, I tried to see the town as much as the waning daylight would allow. The streets were not lighted, nor were there any signs of streetcars or modern buildings befitting an intercontinental seaport.

The houses we passed were made of mud and straw, unlike the Japanese houses of wood shingle and white plaster. The streets were mud, packed smooth by foot traffic, and the people were ragged and patched. The town looked woebegone from poverty and neglect.

After eating meatless soup with rice for supper, we shared a room with several other families, giving us barely enough space to stretch out full length on the bare floor.

The next morning's light did not improve on my first impression, nor did the town itself. It only deepened my disappointment and confirmed my suspicion that the town or Korea itself was a backward place, left behind fifty years ago by the mainstream life of the fast moving world. Perhaps this was precisely the reason why my father wanted to bring his family into safety, away from the insane, war-crazed world.

We got on a wide-track Korean train, not well-kept and clean like the Japanese trains, and rode to Pohang, about eighty miles north of Pusan, on the Sea of Japan. After the Japanese train ride through the luscious countryside along the Pacific coast in the early spring, the Korean landscape looked bleak and barren. I could see the muddy countryside with poor, stony fields, sparsely forested hills, thatched mud farmhouses, and people clad in soiled gray Korean dresses, all melted into one drab picture.

Ever present oxen carried heavy loads along the roads or pulled the plows in the fields. I saw farmers bent under loads twice as tall as their height, on A-frames. Women carried large mason jars on their heads in rhythmic gaits, ferrying water from the well or human manure to the vegetable patches. Young girls with long, braided hair and their mothers did the family laundry on the river rocks, as they gossiped with neighbors, while frolicking children played nearby.

An eerie feeling came over me that we were stepping out of modern twentieth century civilization into an African village life. At the train station, my family stood out like a sore thumb. We were wearing smart Western clothes, complete with leather shoes, a hat and a walking stick for my father, among the milling other passengers in monotonous white or black native dresses and traditional rubber shoes or homemade straw slippers.

In peace or wartime, machine-milled fabrics were not available in Korea as they were in the Japanese islands. Even in the middle of the war, the black market in Japan proper was thriving for rationed consumer goods, and the Japanese people were able to uphold their traditional aesthetic sense, shibui (tart), in their choice of color and design.

For the Korean people, most of the fabrics were made by farmers who grew cotton, hemp, and silk from silkworms fed on mulberry leaves. Their wives wove fibers into bolts of cloth to be marketed in town. Due to the lack of skills and dyes, the fabrics were either bleached white by the sun, left their natural color, or dyed black. The rich and well-connected elite, however, seemed to find ways to obtain silk brocades in multi-colored floral designs, even during the wartime shortages.

By preference or necessity, Koreans wore mostly white which showed every speck of dirt while the Japanese preferred somber-colored clothes in the fields and for daily chores. The only Japanese people who wore white were the Shinto priests and brides, signifying purity.

Koreans did not have the fanatic love for bathing like the Japanese had. Any self-respecting Japanese house had a hot tub, and the public bathhouses were within easy walking distance in any town. The Koreans did not bathe on a regular basis, but they were a clean people in their own way. The women took great pride in keeping their mud houses and kitchens spotless against great odds. Their family laundry was done without the help of a washing machine, indoor running water, or commercially produced soap. Farm wives made their own soap from ashes.

Despite pervasive poverty, Koreans, by and large, exuded robust health, with ruddy cheeks and sturdy limbs. I attribute it to their penchant for garlicky, mouth-burningly hot, spicy food, eaten in generous portions at every meal. Koreans tended to be taller, bigger-boned, and more muscular than the Japanese who were short and slight, even dainty. In Japan, I saw how Japanese ate small portions of simply seasoned food, artistically arranged, decorously served, and daintily eaten.

Koreans were industrious people who believed in and depended on child labor from early on. As soon as a toddler could navigate around the house and courtyard, he was taken along as an observer by sister on her chores, and later as a mother's helper. Idleness was considered worse than being crippled or even dead. It is no wonder that Protestant missionaries had no trouble in proselytizing them into accepting Protestant work ethics.

Because of my bilingual upbringing, I understood ordinary conversation in Korean around me. But as soon as I opened my mouth to join in the conversation, I noticed Koreans looking at me askance. Unbeknownst to me, I had acquired a distinct Japanese accent in my mother tongue, which my parents insisted had to be spoken at home in Japan. From then on, I was treated as an outsider, despite my protests. After being a gaijin or foreigner in Japan for most of my life, I was hoping that I would be accepted as one of them in Korea. It was a foolish thought.

We got to change trains at Kyonju, the ancient capital of Silla Dynasty (A.D. 1 to A.D. 918). The Silla civilization was noted for its arts, science, and the adoption of a new religion, Buddhism. In the sixth century, it was Silla who exported Buddhism to the primitive island country called Japan, across the sea. Regrettably, we did not stay to see the royal tombs of huge, grass-covered mounds or the Silla artifacts.

The railroad from Pusan was the major artery linking Japan and Manchuria, threading its way through the major Korean cities of Taegu, Seoul, and Pyongyang in the north. Pohang, our destination, was at the end of a side track off the intercontinental railway, going east from Kyonju to the Sea of Japan.

CHAPTER 20

Pohang

By the time we pulled into the Pohang railroad station, I was anxious to see a reassuring, familiar face to ease my mounting apprehension at our homecoming. How glad I was to see my beloved cousin, Youngii, waiting for us. How handsome he looked and he had taken on the air of a man, befitting to teach the third grade boys at Pohang Elementary School.

Pohang is at the rabbit's tail on the Sea of Japan, if my simile is taken seriously. It was a sleepy little fishing port, forgotten by the world. During her rule, the Japanese government used Korea mainly as a bridge to transport raw materials from Manchuria to industries on the Japanese islands, and as a buffer to protect the backside of Japan. Out of mistrust of Korean loyalty, Japan did not have any war installations, industrial or military, in Korea. Therefore, the whole of Korea remained relatively peaceful and surprisingly untouched by the urgencies of an ongoing war in the Pacific. Furthermore, Pohang was pushed aside, ignored by the major rail traffic.

Youngii had already rented a Japanese house for us, with a Japanese tatami wing with a hot tub and a Korean wing with two Korean on-dul rooms heated by an adjacent kitchen. On-dul was an ancient radiant heating system. The heat and smoke from the kitchen traveled through the flues under the stone floors of the adjoining room. The stone floor was covered with mud spread smooth and finished off either by an oiled-paper floor covering, or with straw mats if a family was poor. During cooking, the room was heated at the same time; "waste not, want not" at work, Korean style.

Youngii also saw to it that we recovered all the shipments of our household goods and even helped to trace my father's prized German bicycle. Somebody at Kyonju station had held the bicycle back, thinking that we might forget about it. In those days, thievery was rampant and half-expected in poverty stricken Korea.

Pohang was the county seat with two high schools, one for boys and the other for girls of better-heeled families, after finishing public school, which was provided for all students through the sixth grade. The city had electrical lines for light in public buildings, for streets, and in some affluent homes, but there was no electricity, no coal. War came first. The town was in complete blackout, involuntarily and unnecessarily because the town was not marked on anyone's war map. Kerosene and candles lighted homes at night.

The town's economy was truly local. Surrounding farming villages would bring in farm products and the fishermen would return the favor with the fruits of their own from the sea: fish, including the oily whale meat much loved by Koreans, seaweed of all varieties, and the delicacy of aphrodisiac sea cucumbers, eaten raw with vinegary hot sauce.

There was a stretch of sandy beach near the town but one never saw any woman or girl swimming in daytime, only topless men and boys in their knee-length underwear, fishing or gathering seaweed. They had no idea of swimwear. And it was considered a scandal of grave consequence for a female to appear in public, bare-armed or bare-legged even in the hottest dog days of the summer.

All government business was conducted in Japanese only and administered by the Japanese officials acting in a supervisory capacity. But Korean was still spoken everywhere else, at home, in the markets, and even in the government offices, except when speaking to Japanese superiors. I noticed that the Japanese nationals in Korea never learned to speak Korean, nor socialized with the natives, no matter how long they lived there. Schoolchildren were taught in Japanese with the Japanese textbooks and became bilingual by necessity.

CHAPTER 21

Life in Pohang

Our rented Japanese house was the largest of three houses clustered together around the common well. The other two were of typical Korean construction, smaller and laid our in a mirror image to each other with a wooden fence and the well as the divider. Our compound was on the northerly outskirts of the town, smack in the middle of wheat fields, making the clustered houses float in a sea of wheat rippling in the breeze and later ripening in the hot sun.

One reason that Cousin Youngii rented the big house was to accommodate all of our furniture, even temporarily. My father told my cousin that he had not decided where to settle his family and an ordinary Korean house would not do to house all of the belongings we managed to bring from Japan. Moreover, choices were severely limited as no new houses were built anywhere during the thin days of the war.

Our landlord lived with a smallpox-scarred wife and two children in an impressive old Korean house with heavy tile roof, a few hundred yards away from our compound. He was a public scribe by profession, and for a fee wrote public documents or private letters for the illiterate people. His knowledge of the intricate bureaucratic rules and games to be played made him an invaluable mediator between the government and the people.

One of our immediate neighbors was a young shipyard worker, married, and supporting his teenage sister and widowed mother who were living under the same roof. After we arrived in late March, we did not see much of him. He left for work before dawn every day, including Sundays. Later in the summer, however, we saw him around the house. We learned that he had contracted leprosy.

It was a death sentence for him and a catastrophe for his family. Leprosy in Korea was shrouded in old superstition and medical ignorance. Lepers were abandoned by their own families and eventually became roving beggars with no eyebrows, lopped-off noses, and no fingers or toes, all eaten away by the disease. Some Western missionaries set up a leper's colony on a nearby island to isolate and care for them, but there was no known cure then.

By the time the sick man and his mother, fearful and desperate, consulted my father about the illness, the disease had already advanced beyond the point of no return.

Five years later in the summer of 1949 when I was visiting my cousin Youngii from Wonju, I stopped by to see our old neighbors. The shipyard worker's wife was gone and he was cared for by his mother and sister. His sister, a couple of years older than me, had lost any hope of getting married and having her own family. The Korean society, out of fear, mercilessly ostracized lepers and their families. His aging mother was driven to scratch out a living as a door-to-door peddler.

Shortly after we were settled into our house, the Catholic family of a Korean agricultural official for the county moved into the third house. He had a large family of several children and another one on the way. There was also a servant girl to help out his wife.

The lady of the family was striking: slim, tall, and regal in bearing. She had a creamy, blush complexion, unusual among the paper-white women of the Korean elite. Her face was long with an aquiline nose, a strong chin, and hazel eyes. Her mother was visiting from Taegu one day and she was a typical Korean lady with delicate features. From neighborly conversation, we gathered that her mother once worked in the Catholic parish in Taegu. Many years later when the not-so-celibate private lives of Catholic priests became known around the world, I began to wonder if our neighbor lady wasn't the product of a Western priest and a Korean mother.

Our Catholic lady seemed well educated and cultured, even sophisticated for the time and place where we were thrown together by chance. When she dressed up in silky, flowing Korean dress in muted colors and subtle floral design to attend social occasions, she turned herself into a Madonna in Korean garb, serene and untouchable.

One afternoon she saw a matinee performance of a well-known Korean ballerina, trained by the Bolshoi Ballet Company in Moscow. Breathlessly, she recounted how tales were told, without words, in the finely nuanced gestures and body movements of the dancer. One particular story was about a Buddha coming alive after a deep meditation or death itself. From a motionless, sitting position, a muscle in her face twitched and her eyelids slowly lifted. Her palms parted from a praying position. The wobbly limbs found the legs, and finally the Buddha broke into a fury of motion in resurrected life.

I wonder today if there was some hidden political message for the imminent rebirth of Korea. There was a speculation, even then, about the ballerina Che being a Korean patriot and a Russian-trained Communist spy. During the desolate years of the Japanese colonial rule, Korean people were not picky about the source of resistance. Evening shows were impossible with no electricity, but for the afternoon performance, the movie house was overflowing with excused government workers and entertainment-starved townfolks, spilling out into the street.

With wartime scarcity, there emerged a clear division between haves and have-nots. The haves were on an inside track with the government and commerce. The have-nots were left out in the cold. Our government official was able to feed his growing family very well on his government salary. His family had plenty of rice, even the sweet rice for cake making, soybeans for soy sauce and paste, oil for kerosene lamps, and even rubber shoes. They lacked nothing and lived better on a meager salary than we who had money but no connections.

Having Catholic neighbors was the first close encounter with Catholicism I had. They prayed to the same god as we Presbyterians, but a little differently by crossing themselves. A crucifix on a chain, hanging from the neck, reminded me of the persecution of the Japanese Christians by the feudal lords who forced them to choose between faith and death by stepping on a crucifix on the ground. I was intrigued by their liberal views on drinking, gambling and smoking — yet celibacy was imposed on their priests.

Now and then, I saw the government official come home late, drunk and singing. His wife would hustle him into the house, but the next day he was his old jovial self again, playing with his children. Despite his drinking binges, he was a good family man.

After my family settled in for a transitory stay in Pohang, my father took off in search of a permanent home for us and his medical practice. But first, he visited our family cemetery in Kyonsan near Taegu. Despite his conversion to Christianity, he could not quite shed the Confucian mandate of ancestor worship.

Our family had owned a hill covered with burial mounds for over two dozen generations. My father wanted to pay a special homage to his grandmother who had raised him after his mother's untimely death in his infancy. He had a vivid memory of his grandmother struggling to keep whatever was left of the family farm in his father's absence. Naturally, he had no recollection of his mother.

My father spent the whole summer and part of September 1944 looking over likely places for settlement in Taegu, Taejon, and even as far north as Seoul. He finally came upon Wonju, a county seat in the mountainous inland province of Kangwon-do, about eighty miles southeast from Seoul.

I am not exactly sure how he came to this place. He might have been shocked by the exorbitant real estate prices in Korean cities, or he wanted to take his family as far away as possible from the impending invasion of fearsome American armed forces closing in on the Japanese islands. The war news was not good at all for the Japanese.

In July 1944, Saipan, Guam and Tinian (Marianas Islands) were taken by U.S. forces and used as bases for bombing raids on Formosa and the Japanese home islands. Years later, viewing a PBS documentary on the Pacific war, I was particularly horrified by the film footage of suicide leaps off a sea cliff by the Japanese civilians, old, young, and mothers with small children in their arms, during the Marianas Islands battles. Even though this information was not declassified by the American government until recently, rumors were rampant in Japan then about the heroic suicides of Japanese soldiers and civilians alike during the war. Some of the suicides might have been assisted or coerced by fanatic soldiers.

We found out that the food ration was practically non-existent, even for essential rice. We would have starved if we had depended on it entirely, as there was no rice in the marketplace either. In Japan, rationing was well organized, efficient, and ample enough to have surplus to give away or to be used in bartering, until the American air raids began. But in Korea, we had to use our personal resources to feed ourselves. If it had not been for Youngii, we would have starved. He somehow obtained the precious rice to tide us over while our application for rations was halfheartedly processed by city hall bureaucrats. Nothing came of it.

One evening, Youngii suggested after one of his frequent visits that I go to his rooming house with him that night to bring back rice the next morning. He lived about a couple of miles from our house and it was too late to return with rice that evening. My stepmother quickly objected to the idea on the point of propriety. Without knowing why, my cousin and I blushed as though we had already committed a shameful act. We felt soiled by her obscene implication and uncomfortable by what she was thinking. Did she know how I felt about Youngii?

My stepmother was hoping that my cousin would take an interest in her fifteen-year-old daughter, but was dismayed by the lack of any encouraging sign from him. In the end, Taikun was sent along as my chaperone to Youngii's rooming house that night.

Out of preteen innocence, I was very much in love with the idea of romantic love fanned by the Japanese and Western love stories, but it was the platonic variety. If I had understood the consequences of love, physical and social, I might not have daydreamed so much about the beautiful world of romance.

I often fantasized what it would be like to spend the night with my cousin in an embrace, a spiritual communion, unmarred by anything physical. When the opportunity finally came, it was nothing like what I yearned for.

Several boys were waiting for Youngii for a private tutoring when we arrived at his house that evening. The room was so hot from the heated floor that we had to keep the door wide open all night to let in the cool April air. Around eleven o'clock, we finally stretched out on pallets on the floor with Taikun between my cousin and me, but because of my overstimulated imagination and the stifling heat, I could not sleep until I finally dozed off from exhaustion.

My cousin grew up with a younger brother and two younger sisters, all sleeping together in the same room. The social taboo on incest usually inoculated family members against any dangerous thought. I was perfectly safe with Youngii in spite of my infatuation. He had no trouble falling asleep, a sure sign of a clear conscience.

I must have been quite a sight in the morning, bedraggled and disheveled from tossing, fully clothed, all night. This was not exactly the way I wanted Youngii to see me, but there was no hiding in his small room.

My forbidden love for Youngii remained a secret all these years until now, as I mentioned him in my diary only as X. So I foiled my big brother's snooping later on.

The whole town of Pohang seemed to notice my cousin, the handsome new schoolteacher in town. A university or teacher's degree was a prime achievement in the backwater fishing town of Pohang. As soon as he started to teach third grade boys, the town folks vied with each other to get him to take their spare room for lodging, especially the parents with marriageable daughters. His reason for picking the Pohang teaching position was to be close to his mother who still lived in his home village about ten miles away and, at the same time, to have a better opportunity for his own life in a bigger pond.

All of the attention he received, wanted and unwanted, was not lost on Youngii, but he seemed not to let it go to his twenty-two-year-old head. He seemed wise enough, beyond his young age, to pick and choose the best offer or opportunity for his life's goal. A comfortable life was a good measure of success in those days in poor Korea.

I was pointedly made aware one day of what a stunning effect Youngii's good looks and comely demeanor had even on a casual onlooker. When I accompanied my cousin to the city hall on the matter of ration application, a pretty young clerk happened to see Youngii standing at the counter, and was instantly transfixed, staring hard at him. I was sure my cousin noticed her, but he never let on that he was even aware, nor turned his head in her direction. I could not help feeling that his studied nonchalance was calculated to inflame further the young woman's interest. Helplessly she fell for it.

Surprisingly, an attractive, well-educated woman, liberated enough to work in a government office, did not know the first thing about the subtle but complicated game of courtship. Being so obvious about her romantic attraction was the surest way to lose the interest of a highly sought-after man. In a way, I was shocked by her brazen stare. The prudish social rules of straitlaced Korea gave her no second chance.

Shortly after my overnight stay at my cousin's lodging, he moved to a bigger, more affluent household with a senior high school girl. The girl's parents must have had some ulterior motive for having him as a lodger, but I didn't see any hint that he was keen on the girl. All that summer and into the month of September, Taikun or Jinju and I would drop off his laundry, washed and ironed, and pick up his dirty clothes.

Visiting Youngii on these summer evenings, for any excuse at all, was the first taste of exquisite moments in my life. When Youngii was not tutoring boys for their high school entrance exams, he would bring out his guitar and play European classical pieces. Enchanted by the melodic guitar music in the fading summer twilight, I was hopelessly lost in its spell and struck dumb at the same time. I didn't want to break the magical moment by even asking about the music he was playing, and how I wished that it would go on forever.

Years later on another continent, I saw Andres Segovia enthrall a San Francisco audience with his classical guitar repertoire in solo performance. I was swiftly transported back to that summer of 1944, and my beloved cousin with his guitar and dreamy, faraway look.

CHAPTER 22

My Favorite Aunt

Youngii's mother was my mother's most favorite out of her seven sisters. By frequent correspondence with this sister, my mother had kept in touch with home throughout our thirteen-year stay in Japan.

In Nagoya, my father treated my cousin's younger sister for a heart condition until she died, while we followed, step by step, the progress of Youngii's education. It was this aunt who took my father into her home for his recuperation from tuberculosis treatment in the Diamond Mountains. Now her son was helping us acclimate ourselves to the Korean life after a long absence abroad.

Shortly after our arrival in Pohang, my aunt came to visit us in our rented house. Her resemblance to my mother was remarkable; a younger version in features and familial mannerism and genteel carriage. She cried when she saw Taikun and me, remembering her dead sister.

My cousin must have told her that we needed everything and anything edible. So she brought us rice, homemade soy sauce and paste, both mild and hot, things not readily available in the market which had plenty of seafood but not much else. Whenever we visited her modest farmhouse, she would always insist that we take home a package of food, including grains and fresh vegetables, and never let us leave her home empty-handed. In Korea, we call the generous person "big handed" and certainly she was. Perhaps this label was very apt in the country where nobody cooked with measuring cups and spoons. Everything was measured by pinches, fistfuls, and handfuls in the kitchen.

When I visited my aunt in her village, once in a while a well-dressed man would come to see my aunt, sometimes during the day, other times at night. I was never introduced to him, but I had a distinct impression that he was avoiding me, whispering with my aunt and leaving shortly. I didn't know who he was, but later, from my gossipy stepmother, I learned that he was my aunt's benefactor and lover.

The man was the richest man in the village, with extensive land holdings and some commercial interests in town. He kept my aunt's family together after the sudden death of her farmer husband. Without the financial and farming help from this man, my aunt had no way of keeping her small farm going with four children, the youngest at her breast. On her own, the education of her children was simply out of the question. Youngii's education would have been impossible without the generosity of this man.

Even if I had known at the time the whole truth about their relationship, I would not have loved my aunt any less.

While my father was away that summer, I had a terrible row with my stepmother with unforeseen consequences later on. Taikun and I used to take out the family photo album to look at the family pictures and, particularly, the church picnic picture taken in 1937 with our beaming mother standing in the back row. To pass the time, we reminisced the happy times with our mother in Fukui.

One day, to our horror, we discovered that somebody had neatly scratched out the face of our mother in the photo. My stepmother, when asked, insisted that she did not know anything about it, but offered that perhaps our Catholic neighbor's kids might have done it. I did not believe her. Why or how would they have singled out my mother among complete strangers in the picture? There was no doubt that it was my jealous stepmother who didn't want us to have even the last physical reminder of our mother. Goaded by my pointed questioning, she tore up the photograph into tiny pieces in a rage. In an instant, the only physical image left of my mother was gone forever.

Crying, I walked miles through the dusty, deserted countryside and over the hills to reach my aunt's house late that afternoon. Quietly my aunt listened to my tearful story of the photograph, but she did not say much. I could feel, nevertheless, her heart was aching for her sister's children but she could do very little.

The day after my arrival, my aunt asked me if I would stay with her youngest daughter while she went on an overdue round of visits with her sisters who lived in the villages on the other side of Pohang. Her second son was away on a teacher training program out of town. I was flattered that my aunt would trust me, a fourteen year old, with her house and her school-aged daughter. My pride swelled up within me to meet the challenge of my first housekeeping assignment.

I got up with a chorus of roosters from all over the village, and my day started with a hot breakfast of rice and soup. I washed, cleaned, polished, and swept the on-dul rooms with straw mats and the mud-packed kitchen floor until I thought the little farmhouse shone like a new moon. My girl cousin entertained herself and was not in my way, nor was she a help.

When my aunt came home from her journey, she was amazed that I hardly used the rice she put out for the meals before she left. I was fast becoming a frugal housekeeper. She also found that I had rearranged her dresser chest into neatly folded and organized piles of clothes. However, she discovered to her chagrin that the huge stoneware jars of homemade soy sauce and paste, clustered together on a stone pavement near the kitchen in the courtyard, had cracked and chipped lids. They were the sorry casualties of my overzealous cleaning, too cumbersome and heavy for me to lift and not to drop them back down so hard. Though complimentary about my good works, she was probably glad to see me go home after a week.

Before we left for Wonju in the fall, Taikun and I briefly stopped by to see another aunt, older than my mother, at her farmhouse, not far from my birth village. Though care-worn as a ne'er-do-well farm wife, she looked just the way I remembered my mother: sturdy, tall, and dignified. There was an unmistakable family resemblance among the sisters. Even though I never met the rest of my aunts or my only maternal uncle, who was born just in time to save the Yun family line from extinction, I felt I had met them all.

CHAPTER 23
My Father's Brothers

Uchong-myon, "Bird River–village," was my birthplace. I was born at 743 Sege-dong, or World Lane. Somebody had a rather grandiose idea about the place or himself in that obscure little village, about ten miles south of Pohang. It was listed as my permanent domicile on all legal documents, identifying my ethnic origin for political and other purposes in the Japanese-occupied world in which Koreans found themselves since the 1910 annexation.

The permanent domicile separated the native Japanese from all others, lumped together as gaijins (foreigners). Specifically, Koreans were called Chosen-jin, the people of "Morning Calm." Once a gaijin or Chosen-jin, always an outsider, no matter that one was born and lived all his life in Japan. This policy is very much alive today, I hear.

My father and his younger half-brother had built their farmhouses side by side on World Lane, which wound around a gently sloping hillside, just wide enough to let an ox-pulled cart pass through. When my family emigrated to Japan in 1930, my father's other half-brother took over our farmhouse. They were still there when we visited them in the summer of '44.

After their courtesy calls on us in Pohang, we visited their families on farms several times that summer. I saw firsthand the harsh life of a Korean farmer trying to eke out a meager living from the poor, hilly land with the help of an ox or two. The whole family, wife and children, toiled from dawn to dusk. It was an endless cycle of chores for women and children: tending chickens and hogs, milling and spinning, all in addition to the everlasting housekeeping. Human waste was the only fertilizer, cheap and dependable, and hand-forged and hand-carved farm implements were the only tools to coax the stony fields and terraced rice paddies to yield against their nature.

By the time we came back to Korea, the older half-brother had just died from black lung, contracted in the Japanese coal mines, and his widow and three children were still living in the farmhouse built by him. Strangers would never have guessed that these brothers were related to my father by looking at them. Their different mothers gave them a stark contrast in physical appearance. My father was slim, tall, and delicate. His brothers were born farmers, ruddy-faced and stocky. From the family gossip, I learned that after the death of his first wife — my father's mother — my grandfather, still in his teens, had lost all his bearing in life. He became irresponsible in the family affairs, and married again carelessly. My grandmother Yew was from a more respectable yangban family than my grandfather's, related, however tenuously, to the last Korean royal family. Yangban at the turn of the century was the ruling elite class made up of landowners, government officials, and scholars in the learned Chinese classics.

My widowed aunt, short and thickened all over by heavy work, and her three young children were trying desperately to keep the farm going without a man in the house. The oldest boy was fifteen, working like a grown man with only an elementary education. His two younger sisters had never darkened the school door. Before their father's tragic death, the children were already helping their mother work the farm while their father was away working in the Japanese coal mines in Honshu to supplement their subsistence.

The whole summer, all went about their chores barefooted, to make their homemade straw shoes last longer. Even in sizzling summer days, the mother and her daughters worked in the fields and around the farmhouse, always properly covered with tattered, soiled, long-sleeved Korean blouses with cuffs rolled up, and full ankle-length skirts. They would get up in the morning with the roosters, and take their noon break in the shade in the field when the older girl would bring their hot lunch in a large, wide-mouthed wooden bowl, carried on her head. They did not go to bed until the animals had been looked after, and they had a hearty hot supper, even in the summer heat. Botulism, I suspect, was kept at bay with freshly cooked, hot summer meals in the country where refrigeration was not known.

There was no radio, no newspapers or magazines for information or amusement, let alone books for the mind. Farm work was a hard and grueling, year-round job. But when the traditional festivals came, they let their hair down with a vengeance.

The country folks made a big deal out of the Chinese New Year celebration and the Harvest Day, set by the harvest moon, right after the rice threshing in the fall. Each event lasted at least one week. Joyously, the whole family would pitch in for weeks of furious preparation for the holiday feasts. All businesses, government offices and farm works were completely shut down. The people honored these holidays by gorging themselves on rich food: beef, pork, pheasant, infinite varieties of rice cakes, the holiday dishes of fern shoots, transparent noodles sautéed with julienned vegetables and shitake mushrooms. And the holiday musts: "water kimchi" and "sweet wine" of rice with no alcohol for women and children.

The men would dress up in the traditional Korean outfits of snow white silk or cotton trousers, rather baggy and tied at the ankles with ribbons, and matching long jackets with vests. Women and girls decked themselves out in rainbow colored, empire-waist blouses and sweeping floor-length skirts. To make these festivities lively, the farm folks, except the Protestant Christians, brewed homemade, milky white rice wine.

Wine loosening up inhibitions, men had boisterous parties of singing and dancing to the old folk songs. One of the old favorites was called "Ariran," a song about a woman wishing her errant husband sore feet to keep him from going too far astray. These parties were strictly male-only affairs. Wives and sisters would scurry around, making sure that they had plenty to eat and drink, and that no harm came to them.

In a segregated society like Korea, the only way the sexes met was through arranged marriages. Marriage was a social contract brokered by the unlicensed and volunteer marriage broker for both families. Man and woman never met, except by appointment.

For the timely relief from the hand-to-mouth existence, these hard-working people also counted on occasional weddings, funerals and hangobs, the sixtieth birthday blowout for both men and women. This landmark sixtieth birthday celebration was the first time the woman was treated on an equal basis. After a lifelong, second class status, hangob was a belated coming-out party for her. Like other Asian sisters, the Korean woman was very much under the thumbs of men all her life, dictated by the Confucian codes. As a daughter, she was under her father's domination, as a wife she was ruled by her husband, and as an old mother, she was controlled by her son.

During the war years, my farming relatives had to give the government allotted quotas of their rice, barley, wheat, and cotton for nominal prices. The remainder of the harvest had to stretch out the entire year to meet their own needs. When they needed cash for other essentials like kerosene, candles, matches or sesame seed oil, they would take some of their food supply to the open market in Pohang to barter for whatever they needed.

The market day was a whole day affair for my farm folks. They were too poor to ride the local bus and walked both ways to Pohang with their loads on their heads or carried on A-frames. Still, they considered the market day a farmer's holiday and made the most of their trip by taking in the sights and sounds of the town.

Every time I visited my relatives in the country, I could not help feeling that I was nothing but a nuisance, intruding into their busy farm routines. I was made to feel useless as they would not let me help in any way I could. For them, I was not prepared to work, dirty or not. I was dressed in fancy city clothes and my delicate white hands were strangers to farm chores. So I was often left alone in their farmhouse during the day while the whole family worked in the fields.

One lazy afternoon, I visited the temporary burial mounds of my grandfather and uncle under a stand of pine trees on a hillside, close by our farmhouse. My father hadn't a chance as yet to move my grandfather to our ancestral cemetery in Kyonsan. Lying on famous Korean short grass and listening to droning cicadas and the gentle whistles of the sea breeze rustling the pine needles, I imagined that my mother was visiting with me in spirit. I tried to visualize the life and times of my parents and older siblings before they emigrated to Japan in 1930, the busy farm life with rambunctious children and my grandfather wandering in and out at his whims.

I could not help feeling the outrage of injustice in such a harsh life my country cousins had to endure while my family and I enjoyed a rather easy and idle life. I wasn't the only one who felt this unfair turn of fate as I saw the dark, resentful look in the eyes of the dead uncle's oldest boy, as he was struggling under the enormous pile of harvested barley on his back. Before he reached manhood, by arranged marriage, he had to assume the responsibility of a man. Painfully, he watched his widowed mother working in the field like a hired man. And he stood by helplessly as his younger sisters were indentured by circumstances to the dismal prospect of life on a farm. His family pride was hurt when he realized that they were no better than landless peasants. To him, the yangban title sounded hollow.

My father's other brother seemed to be doing a little better than the widow's family. However, as I always stayed with the widow on my visits, I didn't get to know him and his young family very well, although they lived on the other side of the dividing mud wall. This uncle was not as welcoming and rather standoffish. I suspected he was also struggling to feed his family.

I began to see the unbreachable chasm between the world my blood relations lived in, and mine. Blood might be thicker than water, but the blood tie alone was not enough to close the gaping gulf of knowledge and experience I felt between us.

They seemed to be stuck in the feudal world where electricity and radio had not touched their simple primitive lives. The global geopolitical world wars had not disturbed their preoccupations with the relentless cycles of growing seasons and their ingrained obedience to Buddhism and Confucianism. Totally oblivious to the death struggles being waged in the Pacific and in Europe, they were pretty much left alone to pursue their immediate tasks of birth, death, and how to feed in between.

The fear I felt for my big brother's safety in Nagoya and my married sisters' fates, with the ever threatening American forces closing in on the Japanese home territory, could not be shared with my relatives. They had no conception of what modern armaments could do to the people and buildings.

Furthermore, my family's conversion to Christianity put us beyond their comprehension. The worship of a foreign god from the West was taken as an unpardonable treachery.

My world was expanded beyond the Japanese archipelago and the Pacific Ocean through the American movies, Western literature, and European music. How could I share or even talk about Chopin or Victor Hugo with my country cousins?

Perhaps I could have talked about these esoteric subjects with Youngii, but whenever we were together in the same room at our house, or in his lodging with other people around, my brain froze and my tongue fell silent, overwhelmed by euphoria, so exquisite and so new.

I felt alone and alien in my own birthland of "Morning Calm," and I suspect that, if my relatives had been less polite and more forthright, they would have said that I was a queer wenum (foreigner) to them with a thick Japanese accent.

Nevertheless, I hated to see the summer go and dreaded the return of my father from his search for our new home, to take me away from my beloved cousin.

CHAPTER 24

Wonju

Wonju, Kawon-do, was about eighty miles southeast of Seoul on an inland rail line between Seoul and Kyonju, a mountainous, rural region of the country. It was a county seat with its offices in a centuries-old building on a pedestal of stone piling with broad steps leading into the building. It was roofed over with slate-gray tiles, sporting animal heads at four eave-ends, and painted Chinese-red outside, now faded to a salmon-pink. It was a signature Chinese architecture. The building was protected by a chest-high, tiled-roofed mud wall with a heavy wooden front gate enclosing a spacious courtyard in front of the main structure.

The town of Wonju had one elementary school and one secondary school, a boys-only agricultural school, reflecting the farming economy of the area. There was a broad shallow river winding down the rocky bottom from the surrounding mountains where the whole town came out to do family laundry, even in the snowy winter. For the hottest days of the summer, the women and girls under the cover of darkness dared to come out for skinny-dipping with joyous abandon in the warm river water.

Despite its inland location, isolated from the thriving coastal cities and commerce, the town was chosen by the American Methodist Mission to locate a regional mission for the church. Before the Pacific war, there was a large Methodist congregation with a handsome, red-brick, Western style church building and three two-storied, red-brick missionary houses, atop three knolls on the western hillside, overlooking the entire town and its environs.

One of the hard mud-packed town streets went along the south wall of the county government in the town center, passed in front of my house due west, then climbed a northerly curving hillside to reach the Methodist church. Farther on, it connected the three missionary houses on knolls, like beads on a string, and eventually came down the gentle slope on the north side of the town, merging back into the main road connecting the town with the railroad station a half mile father north.

These missionary houses were abandoned by the American missionaries shortly after the outbreak of the Pacific war in December 1941, and the Japanese military occupied them throughout the war. Meanwhile, the Methodist church was barely surviving, with a decimated membership under the Japanese surveillance, and persecutions of the church leaders by interrogation, torture, and imprisonment without due process.

I wondered why my father chose Wonju, a place of nowhere, for our home, but seeing the prominent church presence with its implied influence over the town, I began to see his reasoning. It was his Christian faith that clinched his final decision above anything else. When he saw the impressive red brick Methodist church with a cross-topped spire on the hillside presiding over the town, surrounding rice paddies and fields, with a river running through it all, he took the idyllic scene as a divine sign.

The town also had a provincial government-run hospital at the south edge and even sported a movie house of sorts among the small stores clustered around two commercial strips, running along the west side of the river.

Originally, our house was to be a one-story inn; a u-shaped structure with one of the long sides facing the street. It was a hybrid of traditional Korean architecture with Japanese elements incorporated into it, including ceiling-to-floor sliding doors papered over the latticed wooden frames. It had just been completed when my father came upon it. As an inn, the house was larger than the average residential house with six on-dul rooms and four kitchens to heat those floors. The street side of the u was extended by the roof-to-ground, double wooden front gates which bridged the house structure and the privy on the other side of the entrance.

It had an inner courtyard inside the u whose open end faced east, and a vegetable garden in the back with a shallow utility well. An unpainted picket fence separated us from the Japanese family of an agriculture schoolteacher living in the back of our house. The house had a tile roof and an electrical line into the house, but no electricity except for one or two hours a month, so that the revenue-starved local government could send out the monthly bills.

By the time my father returned with the news that he had purchased a home in Wonju, the summer was gone and the fall was in full swing with its busy harvest time. When we finally arranged for transportation of our household things and arrived in Wonju by train, the people were just finishing up their kimchi making. They were bedding down their homes for the Siberian winter with piles of firewood and stores of grains, and vegetables were buried in the ground, both fresh and pickled.

Finally unpacked and settled into our new house, we found ourselves pitifully unprepared for the bone-chilling winter in this land-locked town in this mountainous country. Our house was not well designed for prolonged, sub-zero winter temperatures from December through February. The Japanese rice-papered sliding doors couldn't keep out the penetrating Siberian cold as well as the narrower, shorter Korean doors. And when we tried to buy firewood and food for the coming cold, the market was bare. We would not have made any kimchi that fall had it not been for the help of church neighbors.

The first winter was seared forever into my memory for the relentless misery of the bone-aching cold and gnawing hunger. Rice and other scarce food such as beef were supposed to be rationed, but this, like everything else in Korea, was long on official intent and short on delivery. In order to survive in wartime Korea, one had to know the right people for things one needed. One had to know a rice merchant for rice, a butcher for meat, a woodcutter for firewood, or a farmer for chicken and eggs. Without Cousin Youngii in Wonju, we were entirely on our own to starve and freeze.

I don't know how we would have survived our first winter in Wonju without half-rotten sweet potatoes. In the middle of the 1944-45 winter, discovering that the stored sweet potatoes commandeered from farmers for alcohol were rotting in the underground storage on the slope just below the missionary houses, the government released them to the townsfolk. The rotten potatoes were not good enough for war, but were welcome to the starving people.

We had to cut off half of each potato before steaming the mutilated remains to be eaten with soup. Without some kind of soup to wash it down, the steamed potato was too dry to swallow. It had a lingering alcohol smell which made it seem as if we were taking an antiseptic. Even so, we had only two meals of this each day for weeks on end, stretching into a bleak couple of months.

With no reliable fuel available, the five of us — my parents, Jinju, Taikun and I — had to squeeze into the main room for sitting, eating, and sleeping. Often in the morning, we saw a bowl of water frozen solid in the room. It became clear that somebody had to gather firewood in the nearby hills if we were to survive. Taikun, then twelve years old, got himself an A-frame and scoured the countryside for twigs, dry leaves, and brush to burn.

My father and Taiam were incapable of adjusting to new situations, having been thoroughly brainwashed by Confucian codes of conduct, which, among other things, prohibited the yangban men to even enter the kitchen, the woman's domain. They could be dying from hunger or thirst but would not think of helping themselves. They were the prisoners of their own mindsets, and women accepted and enforced this notion as a given.

But Taikun was willing to help with chores, bringing fresh water from the well up the road, in two buckets swinging by ropes at both ends of a pole slung over his young shoulders, chopping firewood, or tilling the kitchen garden we started first thing in the spring. Born and raised in Japan for the first eleven years of his life, his experience in a foreign soil might have had a liberating influence on his ideas about the parochial mandate of the Korean gentleman class.

Strangely, my stepmother and Jinju never seemed to be concerned about how cold and hungry we were. They would rather huddle around the warmest spot in the main room floor with extra clothing on than do something about it.

When Taikun and I were out in the countryside, picking up

broken tree limbs and gathering fallen pine needles into a burlap bag, we felt unexpectedly free and happy. Reminiscing about our mother always revived our spirits, gladdened our love-starved hearts, and warmed up our shivering limbs in the bleak winterland. With all of her things gone, the only thing Taikun and I had left was our memories to share freely in those moments of privacy. Being away from our stepmother with dark scowls was a time to rejoice.

We thought my father's practice would never catch on in the new place that winter. The few patients who wandered into our house for consultations found, to their dismay, that my father had to examine them in our chilly living quarters owing to the lack of heat in his medical office. Without the professional surrounding of confidence-inspiring medical accoutrements, my father's healing power seemed to be questioned.

Whenever he had a farmer for a patient, therefore, he was forced to ask for rice as his fee, but it was not easy for the farmer to pay for medical expenses in rice or in other ways either. Often farmers would fall behind in payment, and I would volunteer to act as a bill collector. Hunger was my driving force.

The tradition-bound farmers and their wives would never let anyone come to their houses and go home hungry, even the bill collector. It did not matter what meal I happened to come upon, after many miles on the country road, I was pretty sure that I would be begged to partake of their repast. Gladly and politely I would accept their offer and stuff myself on their humble but ample country food in their warm house. Sometimes I was even rewarded with rice to bring home.

It was in the first Wonju winter that I had the most embarrassing moment of my youth. One of our church elders was a prosperous rice merchant, who also acted as the authorized distributor of rationed rice for the government. One frigid snowy evening, he celebrated his birthday as usual by inviting the church dignitaries, the minister and the elders without their wives, to a feast, unheard of in wartime. At one time, it was rumored, that he had worked as a cook for an American missionary before the war.

The whole town heard about the fabulous dinner and the lucky invitees always looked forward to his annual party. For months, the rice merchant's family slaved over the dinner preparations. A pig was butchered for thinly-sliced cold white meat. Whole chickens were boiled for broth. Pheasants were trapped for their special flavor on the noodle dish. Beef was slaughtered for broiled beef, marinated in spices. To top them all, fancy cakes were made with dried dates, chestnuts, dried persimmons, and sweetened red beans. I never knew until then that there were a zillion other ways to make kimchi — with apples and pears, oysters and fish fillet, and mouth-burning hot or mild "water kimchi."

For weeks, I heard nothing but the mouth-watering account of the fabulous banquet ever since my father was included in the most favored list. In the afternoon of the dinner party, my father took a sponge bath, trimmed his nails, and had his hair cut by my stepmother. Since my father was night-blind, one of us had to take him to the party. I eagerly volunteered, out of a faint hope that the escort might be invited in, too.

When my father and I arrived at the rice merchant's gate that evening, I was told to come back for my father later. Something snapped within me. I decided to wait for my father just outside the gate, instead of going back home and returning for him. The walk of five long blocks four times in the snowy night was a daunting prospect to a starving girl. Other guests began to arrive shortly and saw me standing near the gate in the dark. One of them must have reported me to the host.

A girl was sent out to urge me to go home but I wouldn't budge. Finally, the mistress of the house came out to bring me into the house. Plainly, she was put out. Instead of taking me into their warm kitchen and offering me some food since I was not dressed for the party, she led me straight into the dining room with the dinner guests sitting around the magnificent table loaded with eye-popping dishes. I was mortified, but I could not back out. I searched for my father among the guests and caught fleetingly his beet-red face. I wanted to die.

I don't remember eating anything at the table. My deep shame took my appetite away and turned the ambrosia into dry dust in my mouth. I'll never forget the high price I had to pay for inviting myself where I was not wanted.

CHAPTER 25

My Government Work

Shortly after the 1945 New Year, I was hired as a Red Cross clerk by the Wonju County government. Actually it was the Japanese head of the Domestic Division, who was impressed by my academic record from middle school in Nagoya, Japan. During the Japanese colonial rule, the Japanese middle school education was considered an equivalent to the Korean high school diploma.

As I watched my father struggling to get his medical practice established while the family suffered from cold and hunger, I could not sit still. My family was skeptical, but one day I simply walked up to the county office and asked for a job. To my shock, at fifteen I found myself a government worker, possibly the youngest in Korea. I was one of three female clerks, all unmarried, among the male bastion of Wonju County government. Those days, the bureaucrats were regarded as local elites, educated beyond the elementary level.

The ancient county building seemed to hush all the noises from outside and muffle the inside with huge timber beams overhead and heavy board floors, polished smooth under countless feet. There were no office machines to disturb the calm except for the discreet click of abacuses. The only telephones were in the private offices of the division heads.

My Red Cross section had one other official who was my superior; he was in his thirties and married, but did very little supervising. My job was a simple one. For months, I was copying the names of the Red Cross members in Chinese calligraphy; hundreds of them. At times, I sent out official notices or memos to the local government of towns and villages in the county, and occasionally money in hard cash for special projects.

Our routine communication was hand-delivered in leather pouches by two messengers, a young man and an older, married man, on bicycles. We did not trust the haphazard postal service. Besides being our human carrier pigeons, these two men acted as jacks of all trades, repairing, janitoring, and running errands for a lesser wage than mine.

One time I forgot to sign the consignment sheets accompanying cash to local governments for a Red Cross project. To my dismay, only half of the targets received the money. Realizing that I goofed, the young messenger carried out my intent without my signature while the other pocketed the money, denying any knowledge of it. I noticed, though, the thieving man had a hard time looking me in the eye. The county treasurer, a chain-smoking, hardened man of experience, heard about the missing public funds and knew exactly what had happened. But he did not help me recover the money. I had to make up for the missing money out of my paycheck over a few months.

The old messenger must have been in dire poverty on his low government wage, and the temptation, rare in his lowly position, must have been too overwhelming to resist. It was a case of sacrificing justice for saving the man and his family from the disaster of losing the job.

The Domestic Division had other sections: treasury, education, and public health, and we all worked at our desks in one cavernous, open room in the old building, scribbling away with our fountain pens or clicking away on our abacuses doing computations. In the past, the caliograph-writing brush was used for all the government documents with black ink made in a black slate dish by rubbing an ink stick in water.

We did not yet have the modern office equipment like typewriters, telephone or teletypes, to disturb the solemn atmosphere or the government stupor. But we did have a hand-cranked mimeograph machine operated by two office girls.

These girls were about my age with elementary education. Every morning, they made barley tea using pan-roasted barley with husks

on for all of us. They arranged luncheons for the meetings and con-
ferences and ran a myriad of errands that the bureaucrats dreamed
up to keep them busy. Sometimes I saw resentment in their eyes
because of my higher status and bigger paycheck then theirs, even
though we were about the same age.

One of the office girls was exceptionally attractive with clear,
fair skin and comely features. Unfortunately, she became pregnant
by one of the university educated young bureaucrats who happened
to be a younger brother of the local prosecuting attorney in town.

In those days, all the male clerks took turns on night-watch-
ing the government building and stayed overnight in the janitor's
day quarters, an on-dul room and an adjoining kitchen. We all
noticed that the young man was much taken with the girl who, in
turn, was very flattered by the attention of a man from a prominent
family in Wonju. Now and then, I saw them whispering together
around the office and they must have gotten together somehow on
his night duty.

How the young man's family took their romance was another
matter. The woman had a baby girl after quitting her job when she
began to "show." And she became "damaged goods" thereafter,
abandoned by her boyfriend and denounced by his family. The
young man eventually married a suitable girl, chosen by his family,
and lived out his natural, respectable life as a government worker.
The girl just disappeared.

The county government had another division, Agriculture,
which was mostly concerned about enforcing wartime quotas on
farm products against rebellious farmers. The Agriculture Division
had its own smaller office abutting the Domestic Division on the
north side, but with fewer staff. We never saw any of the farm products brought into our compound. They must have been milled and
stored in warehouses or a grain mill on my street, between the
county compound and my house.

The Agriculture Division was headed by a jovial, bespectacled
Korean official in his forties who spoke impeccable Japanese and
had a high school or university degree from a Japanese school. All
other Korean bureaucrats were Korean school–educated with a
telltale Korean accent in their conversational Japanese and used

Japanese words incorrectly or imprecisely. No wonder that the Japanese colonial government placed a premium on the Japanese school degree and heavily discounted the Korean diploma.

A few years later, during the Allied military occupation after the Pacific war ended, I happened to see the former head of the Agriculture Division walking with a satchel on a busy Seoul street. To my surprise, he recognized me and told me, with a hint of boasting, that he was now working for the American occupation government.

In spite of the Korean populace's resentment toward former Korean officials of the Japanese rule — collaborators to their critics — the American authority had to fall back on the institutional memories and expertise these bureaucrats possessed, to carry out the immediate needs of governance. This explained how he managed to land on his feet, doing what he did best, being a bureaucratic cog in a new machine in Seoul, away from the previous "crime scene" in Wonju.

In wartime, it was not the nominal salaries which attracted educated, ambitious men or women to the government services. It was the unofficial, illegal fringe benefits of inside information, insider connection, and access to things not available and visible to the general population. Since I was on the bottom of the totem pole, I was not privy to all the dealings of government insiders which made their lives comfortable in the sea of poverty.

Occasionally, I had a taste of the shadowy world. One time, I was able to take home mochis with sweet red bean filling to my sick brother, Taikun. By the well-fed looks of my colleagues, they must have had all the things needed for a good life, including cigarettes, a luxury item, which they smoked all day, blanketing the entire office with an ever-present blue haze. No luxury consumer good was denied to the "essential" government workers, while the people were starving.

One day, the county treasurer told me in confidence that a local butcher shop had a fresh kill of cow for sale that day. By the time I got to the butcher shop after work, it was already mobbed by government workers from city hall, the police headquarters, and our county offices. So much for the secret tip. After a couple of hours of waiting in the chilly outdoors, I managed to buy a hunk of meat, about a pound, as I recall. My family had not seen beef since we came back to Korea. It was exhilarating to bring home such a precious food. I felt like a conquering warrior with a prize.

A few months after my government employment, a chance encounter saved my father from going to jail for black-market racketeering. One noon I came home for lunch, even though there was none waiting for me. My father had a guest in our main room, and I recognized him at once as one of the town policemen. When he left, I learned that my father was negotiating the sale of a man's woolen suit material which he brought from Japan, to buy food. I warned him of possible entrapment by the plainclothes policeman who posed as an ordinary citizen.

The next day, my father informed the policeman of his change of heart, but it was too late. He was arrested anyway on the charge of the attempted sale of contraband, and jailed at police headquarters. It took one week of Reverend Kim pulling strings through his judge friend and my stepmother's pleadings before my father was released, along with the suit material. It was a close call.

There were many tales of severe punishments including imprisonment and fines for economic crimes during the war. Often, the policemen arrested people on mere suspicion, and more likely pocketed confiscated goods and fines while the innocents rotted in prisons without charges having been filed against them.

The system of justice during the Japanese colonial rule operated on the principle of guilty until proven innocent, with the burden of proof squarely on the shoulders of the haplessly accused. Also it revealed a dark underbelly of corrupt police who supplemented their low salary with bribes and other illegal gains. Torture and forced confession by police was not uncommon, especially for the political suspects.

Also the Korean judicial system was modeled after the Japanese system. The judicial decisions were rendered by a judge or a panel of judges, not by a jury of one's peers as in the American system. Rarely was the trial an open public proceeding and most of the cases were disposed of before they reached the trial stage by bribery or inside deals.

The people really feared the police. Once they were in their clutches, their life, liberty, and property were in grave danger. It paid to know the right people, even bad and corrupt, at the strategic time to save oneself. Fortunately, my father was not subjected to any physical torture, but looked very haggard with one week's beard, and not having washed the whole time.

As soon as my father was released from jail, he obtained a live chicken and offered it to the judge as a token of his gratitude for his order to release him from prison. But shortly, through Reverend Kim, my father received a request from the judge that he would rather have the suit material for himself. My father, always painfully ethical, was appalled by the implication and flatly refused. Thereafter, he was known as incorruptible, and he was left alone by everyone.

CHAPTER 26

The Last Throes of World War II

For the townfolks in this inland provincial town, the fierce battles near the Japanese home islands might have been taking place on another planet. There was a local newspaper in town, but it was so skimpy in the number and size of the pages that the censored war news was rendered further incomplete. I suspect that the news was no more than straight copy out of a Seoul newspaper, delivered on the train, and became secondhand news by the time it reached us in Wonju.

My father kept up his subscription despite our financial straits. It was an expression of his unspoken concern for his children left behind in Japan proper and also gave him a peephole into what was happening outside Korea.

The publisher of our newspaper was one of our church elders. He lived in an impressive old Korean house, heavily timbered with tiled roof, on the northern slope, halfway from the third missionary house and the main road into town. Enclosed by a mud wall, the house stood forlorn without any houses or trees around it.

The publisher Park was interrogated, tortured, and imprisoned right after Pearl Harbor on suspicion that he was an American sympathizer due to his past associations with American missionaries. By the time we came into town, he was running his printing press. I always thought he looked a bit more like a Westerner than Korean. He was big boned, over six feet tall with graying hair, a prominent nose, and sunken eyes. He could have been easily mistaken for a Caucasian in his natty European suit and hat.

His wife was tall for a Korean woman and their daughter, in her twenties, was living at home after finishing at a prestigious girls' school in Seoul. Their daughter was in danger of becoming an old maid because there was no suitable man in sight for marriage in that backwater town. She had one younger brother who was away at the university in Seoul, though he came to church when he was home from school on his vacations, summer and winter. He was more delicate of feature than his sister, and definitely cultured in his mannerisms, a stark contrast to his boorish contemporaries in town.

I was naturally attracted to him because of my interests in all things Western. Under the Japanese domination, the Korean elite tended to be influenced against their will by what was trendy among the Japanese intelligentsia. Before virulent military nationalism in the 1930s and the Pacific war which tried to eradicate all the vestiges of Western influence from Japanese thinking and life, there was a wholesale infatuation with the Western civilization from the nineteenth century Meiji modernization. It was not surprising to see a similar fascination with the West, and what it stood for politically, among Korean intellectuals. The Korean intelligentsia's pre-war association with Christian missionaries further reinforced their pro–Western inclinations.

Without any words ever being exchanged between the publisher's son and me, I felt a kindred spirit in him. Despite my self-inflicted superiority, a defense I developed against ethnic taunting I had received from the Japanese kids, I began to see him as my equal, an honor I rarely bestowed on anyone outside my family. But I never had a chance to let him know how I felt about him.

Still, war news crept into our lives one way or another and the ripples of war seemed to touch even the remotest corners of the world like Korea in unexpected ways.

After the spectacular Normandy landings in June 1944, the Allied forces were advancing toward Germany while the Russians were pushing back the Nazi forces from their motherland and beyond. By January 1945, the Russians were fifty miles from Berlin, on the Oder River, and took the Eastern European and Balkan countries one by one. The Allies, meanwhile, had to contend with the last ditch counteroffensive by Hitler's forces in December 1944, and the agonies of the Battle of the Bulge before they could even enter Germany. Seeing the end of the European war in sight, in January 1945, the Big Three, Roosevelt, Churchill and Stalin, met in Yalta, Crimea, to decide what to do with the defeated Germany.

In April 1945, the race was on to see who would be the first to enter Berlin. The Russians won the race but also the ignominy of the beastly behavior in plunder, rape, and the wanton slaughter of civilians. The brutal behavior of the Russian soldiers seemed to sicken even the neutral Japanese government whose soldiers were also known for their own atrocities in China and the Pacific. Mussolini and his mistress were hanged by a Milanese mob, while Hitler and his bride of a few hours committed suicide in his Berlin bunker.

In declining health over the past few years, Franklin D. Roosevelt, who looked ashen during the arduous Yalta conference, finally succumbed to a cerebral hemorrhage in April while taking a curative treatment in Warm Springs, Georgia. After the deaths of Hitler and Mussolini, the war was over in Europe and VE day, May 8, 1945, turned into gigantic merry-making in Europe and America. But not on the Pacific battlefields.

After July 1944, the Americans set up bases on the Marianas Islands and were ready to bomb the Japanese home islands and Formosa in November. They soon found out that Iwo Jima, halfway between Guam and Tokyo, was minimizing the impact of the air raids with three bases and a radar station which detected oncoming air attacks and took defensive measures.

On February 19, 1945, the legendary Iwo Jima battle was waged on the small, rocky island. It lasted a month and caused 20,000 American casualties besides untold Japanese casualties. After Iwo Jima was taken, the American B-29s had a free hand in bombing Japanese targets from March 10, 1945, until the surrender of Japan on August 15.

The night firebombing of Tokyo on March 10 flattened downtown completely, and decimated the population by estimated deaths of about 100,000. From then on, all major cities, all military targets, and eventually even mid-sized towns became sitting ducks to be picked and attacked at will until the end of the war.

As the final push was under way, the American forces needed a staging base for the anticipated invasion of the Japanese home territory. Okinawa was their choice. It was only 370 miles from Japan. The attack on Okinawa commenced on Easter, April 1, 1945.

In a final ditch effort to stop the invading forces, Kamikazes were deployed with young pilots suicide-diving into the American warships. Kamikazes, this time, were powerless against the overwhelming firepower of the American forces. I remember the newsreels of the young pilots drinking the ceremonial sake with white-gloved hands, pledging eternal homage to the emperor and the country after the solemn Shinto worship. They knew that they were not coming back alive. To be sure, they had only enough fuel for one way.

On the Chinese mainland, the Japanese forces were in total retreat from the Communist forces under Mao Tse Tung in northern China, and from Chang Kai Shek's Kuomington forces elsewhere, reinforced by covert U.S. military assistance.

In April, shortly after the Tokyo bombing, Taiam came home with a degree in acupuncture from the Nagoya Acupuncture Institute. Still no letters from my sisters, however.

In May, when the long awaited spring was in full swing, Taikun came down with typhoid. Even a rare treat of mochis I brought him from my work didn't seem to perk him up. I knew then he was very ill.

It took only a week or so before Jinju and I succumbed to the typhoid epidemic that was sweeping through the town's communal wells, our only drinking water source, and the town river, the communal laundry place. The townfolks were already weakened by malnutrition from a food shortage that winter and thus had no resistance to the disease. My family caught it in different degrees of severity. My father and Taiam suffered least with only a couple of days of headache. My stepmother was down for a week, but bounced back quickly.

I was hit hard. Unlike my plump stepsister, a couple of weeks of fever and vomiting left me skin and bone, with hollow cheeks.

My clothes hung loose around my waist, and I looked like one of the concentration camp inmates just liberated in Europe. When the active symptoms of the disease finally stopped and my appetite was slowly returning, there wasn't enough food in the house to fatten me back, even to my normal, skinny self. The illness thinned out my hair so noticeably that my friends and our neighbors were visibly shocked by my gaunt look. Their well-meaning, ill-concealed reactions made me ashamed of my appearance. It took some weeks to muster up the courage to overcome my shyness and the strength to venture outside the house.

One day during my recuperation, a middle-aged Chinese woman came to see my father about her ailment. She had heard that my father practiced authentic Chinese acupuncture. Except for the Japanese people living in town, a foreigner was a rare sight in Wonju during the war years. The only thing I knew about her was that she lived near the railroad station about a mile out of town.

Koreans always felt a special kinship toward the Chinese, through historical and cultural ties and in the ongoing struggles against a common enemy in Japan. This feeling was intensified after the 1931 Japanese control of Manchuria and the subsequent all-out Sino-Japanese war on the Chinese mainland in 1937.

The first time she came to see my father, she had on a traditional Chinese dress in silk brocade, with a high-necked, sleeveless sheath with side slits. Her black hair was chignoned at the nape of her neck and her bound feet in the colorfully embroidered silk shoes seemed to pain her with every gingerly step she took.

We in Korea heard about how the Chinese girls' toes, except big ones, were bound with cloth before she reached her first birthday. The bound feet marked the respectability of her family and later prevented her from running away from her husband, who paid a great sum of money for his mate. The people, so we were told, who were exempted from this Chinese practice were men and peasant women who had to work in the fields. For women, big feet meant a lifetime of labor and no class. Maybe the Korean penchant for a woman's dainty feet could be traced to the Chinese root.

In the course of my father's examination, she had to untie her feet, which were virtual stumps with toes stuck to the soles. Even my father seemed to recoil at the man-made deformity. Seeing malformed and malfunctioning feet by aesthetic design reminded me of the Japanese art of bonsai which dwarfed a tree sapling into a pleasing art. Whenever I saw a hobbling old Chinese lady later in Seoul and San Francisco, I thought of a miniature pine tree with pine cones, hundreds of years old, still growing in a ceramic pot.

That summer, from our back vegetable garden, we saw our Japanese schoolteacher bidding a tearful goodbye to his weeping wife and their two little boys. He, in his thirties, had been belatedly drafted for military service on the Manchurian front. Our Japanese neighbors knew, deep down in their hearts, that they might never see each other again. The man was rushed to Manchuria to fight the ruthless Russians once again, and only God knew when and how his family was going to face the inevitable surrender of Japan, or the tragic end without him. The future offered nothing but the darkest of prospects.

In spite of the Japanese government's furious diplomatic efforts to keep the Russians from declaring war on Japan, she could see that the Russians could not be trusted to keep their 1941 neutrality agreement. She was too familiar with Russian treachery dating back to the czar's time.

During the Potsdam Conference in mid–July 1945, Stalin confided to Truman that he was amassing one million Soviet troops on the Manchuria-Siberia border. Japan was scraping the bottom of the barrel, rushing older and married men to a new battle front in Manchuria. It was too little, too late.

Having succeeded Roosevelt, Truman was anxious to pin down Stalin on his promise at Yalta to enter the Pacific war against Japan. Stalin promised anew to go to war against Japan three months after the German surrender in May, but did not give an exact date or other details.

During the conference, Truman also received a series of test results on the atomic bomb, and the final word that it could be deployed against Japan in a matter of days. Churchill already knew about the Manhattan Project from Roosevelt, but Stalin was supposed to be in the dark. When Stalin was told about the bomb without any elaboration, he was, strangely, not at all impressed or curious. Later, it was revealed that Stalin had known all about our atomic project. He was initially tipped off by a young staff scientist, Theodor Alvin Hall, a recently exposed American Communist spy. The information supplied by Hall was later confirmed and elaborated on by the naturalized British scientist, Klaus Fuch, a Soviet spy. Both men had worked on the Manhattan Project at Los Alamos, New Mexico.

The Soviet Union not only knew about the nuclear bomb project but also was working on its own in a race against America, Germany, and Japan.

After I returned to work at the county office in midsummer, I noticed the increased activities of Japanese soldiers in town. Before this time, they were discrete about their presence in Wonju. One day, I was asked to serve lunch and tea to the Japanese military officers' meeting at our local elementary school. It must have been on Sunday as there were no schoolchildren around. I was the only Korean present and, shortly after that meeting, I was summoned to my Japanese division head's house one evening.

The regional commanding officer who presided over the officers' confab wanted to adopt me for his daughter to look after his ailing wife left at home in Choonchung, our provincial capital. They had no children. When my father was told about the proposal, he was not at all amused by the preposterous suggestion, and took it as a personal insult.

The Japanese military and civilian officials must have been planning the evacuation of the Japanese nationals in the Wonju region and my Japanese superior at the county office probably recommended me to be at the meeting as a harmless Korean who would not spy on them. Or he might have mistaken me for a half–Japanese with a Japanese mother and was genuinely concerned about my safety when Japan surrendered. He remembered that my mother had died in Japan.

When the education department of the county announced the recruitment of students for the Normal School for future teachers to be trained at government expense in Choonchung, I jumped at the opportunity. I had always dreamed of being a teacher, just like my first grade Japanese teacher, Mrs. Shigeko Matsuii. My application was readily accepted, the only one from my county. I was to report to the school on August 15.

While I was waiting for my departure to Choonchung, our newspaper printed a small article on a "new kind of bomb" dropped by an American B-29 on Hiroshima a few days before. It was almost overlooked by everyone for the screaming headlines of the spectacular exploits of the Kamikazes against the American armada in the Pacific. As usual, there were no casualty numbers, or other details of the bombing. We had to wait until after the war to find out about the atomic bomb, a terribly destructive, revolutionary weapon devised by man.

After the German defeat in May, President Harry Truman was compelled to bring a swift end to the remaining war in the Pacific. The American forces had experienced high casualties from stiff Japanese resistance on Iwo Jim and Okinawa, and were staring into the daunting prospect of invading the Japanese home islands. The military estimate of invasion casualties for the Americans was one million. The time for complete subjugation was estimated at one year.

On the Japanese side, the military government was preparing for mass national resistance and suicide.

Even though concerned about the civilian casualties in Hiroshima, President Truman felt bound as commander in chief to decide what was best for *his* country. He thought perhaps this awesome bomb might persuade the Japanese military to surrender and save all the bloodshed. It was a gamble.

There was no conclusive evidence that the bomb itself changed the minds of the ultranationalistic military or the cabinet members about fighting to the bitter end, but it had a profound effect on Emperor Hirohito. The emperor had been ready, for about a year, to find an honorable way to stop the fighting, and seized the bomb as an opportunity to make his urgent case for ending the war.

Neither the Hiroshima bomb nor the nightly firebombing by the American B-29s might have made a decisive impact on the ultranationalistic leadership, but the Russian entry into the war against Japan on August 8 was another matter. The Japanese government knew that Japan would face worse under the Russians than any other conquering power.

Above everything else, Soviet Russia would not let Japan retain its emperor. By order of Lenin, the Communist Russians massacred their own Czar Nicholas II and his family on July 17, 1918. The preservation of the emperor and his rule became the only thing around which the military and the Japanese people could unite. So intense was the debate in the highest quarters of the Japanese government that they barely noticed the second nuclear bomb dropped on Nagasaki on August 9.

On August 10, Foreign Minister Tojo cabled the Allies that Japan would accept the Potsdam terms of "unconditional surrender" with one condition: the emperor and his rule must be retained. On August 11, the Allies, surprised and delighted at the quick reaction from the Japanese government, replied that they could not guarantee keeping the emperor, but promised that the Japanese people would be allowed to decide what form of government they wished to have.

The fate of their emperor was, thus, left in the hands of the Japanese people themselves. This satisfied the Japanese wish for the preservation of their emperor, and at the same time the democratic principles of the Allies, an honorable out for both sides.

On August 12, the Allies received a report that Russian troops had reached Korea on her northern border with Manchuria and Vladivostok.

Shortly after the acceptance of the Japanese peace, the thirty-eighth parallel was picked by the Allied command as the dividing line between North and South Korea. According to Joseph C. Goulden in *Korea, the Untold Story of the War*, the thirty-eighth parallel was adopted at the suggestion of Dean Rusk, then a young colonel on General George Marshall's staff, and Colonel C. H. Bonesteel III, as a barrier to stop the rushing Soviet troops trying to grab as much territory as possible, a replay of what had happened in eastern Europe and the Balkan region. The Russians weren't facing any credible resistance from the lightly armed Japanese units in Manchuria and Korea, and the Allied forces were not near enough to slow down the Soviet advance either.

The selection of the thirty-eighth parallel revealed that Rusk and Bonesteel were aware of the historical precedence. In 1896,

Russia and Japan signed a formal agreement to establish the spheres of influence in Korea at the thirty-eighth parallel, roughly halving the country at midriff, with Russia taking the north and Japan, the south.

It was quick thinking on the part of the American military which prevented the Russians with heavy armor divisions from taking over the entire Korean peninsula and invading the Japanese home island, Honshu, across Tsushima Strait before the United States and Great Britain. The Americans could not let the Russians have a strategic presence in the Pacific.

Also surprising was Stalin's ready agreement on the thirty-eighth parallel as the demarcation line to divide Korea into Russian occupation in the north and U.S. occupation in the south. When he was negotiating with the West about the post-war arrangements at Yalta and Potsdam, Stalin was concerned mostly about setting up a protective buffer zone over the Russian backside in Asia. To that end, he insisted on dominance over Manchuria by Russian control over Port Arthur, the Dairren harbor, and Manchurian railroads.

Taking Korea was an afterthought. He must have thought that half of Korea was better than getting into a fight with the United States at this juncture. After all, North Korea was an unexpected bonanza, and very profitable, especially after only one week's fighting.

After the Allies' response to the Japanese offer to surrender was received, the emperor insisted that Japan accept the Allies' conditions to end the war. He offered, hopefully, the possibility of rebuilding the vanquished country, if the people, the land and the imperial family survived, to rise like a phoenix from the ashes.

The emperor's resolve was unshakable even in the face of the last desperate coup by the superpatriot military fanatics, who breached the imperial residence to destroy the tape of the emperor's surrender address the night before the fateful date. At noon on August 15, 1945, for the first time the Japanese people heard their emperor's voice on the radio, announcing the end of the war.

CHAPTER 26

Peace at Last

August 15 dawned innocently enough like any other summer morning, cool and serene. I got on the north-bound train to Seoul in the morning, along with a sundry bunch of town and country folks and reached Eastgate railroad station in Seoul around noon to change trains going east to Choonchung, my destination.

I noticed agitated whispers at the station and quickly learned about Emperor Hirohito's radio broadcast announcing the end of war. Stung by the news, I was thrown into a quandary whether I should push on to Choonchung as though nothing had happened, or turn back home like a beaten dog. Something deep inside of me rose up against the unfair turn of world events messing up my future. Defiantly, I took the train to Choonchung.

The train was buzzing with excited chatter about the Japanese surrender and the emperor's voice on the radio. The implications were slowly sinking into the minds of the people. What happens now to Korea and how will our lives be affected by this momentous event? The shocking news put asunder the usual caution that people took in discussing political matters in public. I only wanted to go to school.

Choonchung was eerily quiet and the streets were empty that afternoon, not even a dog in sight, as though the whole town was holed up in its houses, trying to digest the big news. When the Normal School's tall, black iron gates stood forbiddingly mute and locked in front of me, I knew I had lost my gamble. There was no sign of people inside or outside the silent gates. I was forced to turn my back on my dream.

On my train ride back home I was dazed by the enormity of the day. I felt deepening despair over my dashed dream, while the passengers on the train were visibly excited. When I reached Eastgate railroad station for the second time that day there was complete chaos. People were getting on the trains without paying on the excuse that the Japanese yen was worthless. No ticket seller was in sight. So the last leg of my dismal train ride home late that night was free.

In a way, I was glad to be with my father and family on this historic day we had all waited for so long. My father was beside himself with joy, brimming with patriotic fervor unleashed after many years of suppression.

The next day, we noticed that our Japanese neighbor was letting one of her husband's students and his grandfather take out the furniture, household items, and even sacks of grain, leaving behind only an iron, potbelly stove. My father was asked if he would like to buy it from her. So my father acquired a stove for his medical office. We knew the student's family from our church and were ashamed of their vulture-like behavior, taking advantage of the vulnerable Japanese housewife with two small children. That night, our neighbor and her boys slipped away quietly, evacuated by the Japanese soldiers.

There were some rumors that the Koreans had taken revenge on Japanese civilians and government officials in other towns, but I didn't see anything like that happening in Wonju. Since I resigned from my county job to go to school, I never saw my Japanese boss again. He, too, must have left in the night with his family.

The first week of Korean liberation from the Japanese colonial rule was sheer pandemonium, throwing the whole country into anarchy. The Japanese currency became useless overnight and there was no new currency to take its place. The farmers' market sprang up spontaneously and all kinds of farm products, clothes, household goods, even luxury items we had forgotten existed, appeared openly on the market. So the time-honored practice of bartering became the medium of commerce once again to sustain life, until the new Korean won was printed.

One of my girlfriends had a big brother in the watch-repairing business and he prospered nicely in the spontaneous free market, however primitive, providing a comfortable life for his three-generation extended family.

Overnight, the Japanese language was banished from Korean life. Japanese was no longer spoken or used for writing anywhere. All the signs on shops and establishments were redone in Korean and all public announcements were made in the familiar everyday tongue. During the dark days of a forty-year foreign rule, the native language was kept alive and well somehow.

Since our church services in Japan and Korea were always conducted in Korean with Korean Bibles and hymnals, the transition was seamlessly smooth for my family. At the same time, the Chinese characters used in both Japanese and Korean retained the same meanings, so all we had to do was learn Korean pronunciations with slight variations of sound. There was a great advantage in growing up bilingual, as the political climate could be very fickle in this fast moving Third world.

As the Korean elite readily adjusted to a new reality of polity, the rest of the Korean people seemed to make the political sea-change effortlessly, too. After all, the Japanese language requirements were confined to institutions like schools, government offices, judicial courts, and publishing houses. The majority of the population and non-governmental workers were very much left to their own expedient devices, illiterate and very Korean.

They remained essentially un–Japanized in daily life throughout the Japanese rule and would go on with their unrepentant ways without missing a beat. Now the schoolchildren had to learn only the Korean alphabets, simplifying their schizophrenic world of bilingual requirement.

Korean flags sprang up everywhere, like eager spring flowers popping up after a long winter. A red rising sun was replaced by a Mongol symbol of Yin (red) and Yang (blue) in the center, with four clusters of black-bar symbols around it on a white field. The symbols reflected the Mongolian root of the Korean culture filtered through many centuries of Chinese contact.

A Seoul newspaper began to appear on a regular basis in Wonju, though it was still a couple of days old as before. Once again, it acted as a window on a nation-in-making and a world in post-war turmoil.

The people and events eagerly vied with each other in wiping out any reminders of the Japanese domination, a blight on the Korean history of over five thousand years. Suddenly, all Koreans seemed glad to be themselves, openly proud and quarrelsome about politics and all.

During the lull between August 15 and September 2, when the Japanese surrender was signed aboard the USS *Missouri* in Tokyo Bay, there was an eerie buoyancy of a political vacuum in Korea. There were rumors and speculations flying about regarding various political factions of Korean expatriates, with diverse political bends, returning home to claim their rightful places in a new Korean government. To the ordinary Koreans, their conflicting political views were all confusing and baffling after the Japanese dictates.

One day in the "suspended animation," I happened to see an old Japanese lady in her somber, dark kimono, walking slowly, with a parasol for shade from the late August sun and a bouquet of flowers in her hands. She was passing through the alley between my house and the Japanese inn, now vacant, on her way to visit her husband's grave. I wondered why she was still here.

She and her Japanese husband had a mochi shop in town for many years and, since her husband's death some years back, she had been running the business with their adopted Korean son.

She was once a geisha in Japan, so the local gossip said, until her husband purchased her to be his wife, and they had lived in Korea ever since. She must have been very beautiful once, in the classic Japanese way, with a slender nose and a cherry blossom bud for a mouth, in an oval face perched on a long, slim neck. She aged gracefully with her high cheekbones and well-defined eyebrows, but her wrinkles and transparent skin gave away her age and her strenuous life as the wife of a mochi maker.

She was at least in her seventies and had no relatives left in her hometown in Japan. She only wanted to stay with her husband and be buried beside him in Wonju. Though being befriended by a stranger, she was really glad to talk to someone in Japanese, now that the language was taboo among Koreans. She did not speak Korean.

She was still living in the Japanese-style, residential portion of her house, which had the mochi store facing the street, across from the south wall of the county office. From the street, nobody suspected that the interior was completely Japanese with tatami rooms, an indoor Japanese privy at the end of a corridor connecting the rooms, and also a typical Japanese kitchen. This house was only part of a compound, as her adopted Korean son and his young family lived in the Korean-style house with on-dul rooms in the enclosure.

Now and then, I would drop by her house through the back gate to her compound, as the mochi shop was now closed. I noticed her Korean son looking at me as if wondering why I was there. After the war, she was truly alone in a foreign country, waiting for death to unite her with her husband in the next world. From my visits, I sensed that her relationship with her Korean son had deteriorated since the end of war, to the point that it was no more than a commercial arrangement. She received very little emotional support from him.

One winter day, I came upon her lying ill with a terrible cold in her chilly, unheated tatami room, with no sign of anyone caring for her. I insisted, against feeble protest from the old lady, on cooking some soft rice for her poor appetite, making charcoal heat for her futon bedding, and staying nights with her until she was better.

A couple of years later, the lady's futon caught fire from the charcoal futon warmer one winter night and she died three days later.

On September 8, 1945, American occupation forces arrived in Seoul and the Wonju people knew that it was a matter of time before our share of American soldiers would be here with us. We waited for their arrival with a great deal of trepidation, still remembering the Japanese propaganda about the Americans.

For the majority of Koreans, this would be the first close encounter with the blue-eyed, blond-haired foreigners who smelled like wet sheep. We had already heard the horror stories of what Russian soldiers did in North Korea. Some of them sported arms covered with wristwatches snatched from the Koreans on the streets at gunpoint, and carried their long, black Russian bread in their dirty winter boots.

Sometime in September an American army unit rolled into our town, dusty from an eighty-mile drive from Seoul. It was duly welcomed by hastily assembled local government officials and townfolks with Korean and American flags, lining the town's main street. To my father, this was a historical moment for the town that he did not want to miss. But just in case the Japanese propaganda was even half correct, he told the girls and my stepmother to stay in our house behind locked gates. So I missed all the excitement of unprecedented history being made in Wonju. We all waited for our father's first-hand account of what he saw.

My father was amazed at the enormous sizes of the soldiers and the blueness of their eyes. A daring old Korean gent went up to check if a soldier would blink when he passed a hand over his "glass" eyes. My father's clinical observation took in the huge hands and feet, and noted their large heads which, to his thinking, explained the advanced technology and civilization of the West.

He was unprepared, however, when he saw a Negro soldier in the marketplace one day. He was aware of the Negroes in American society through his readings on the American Civil War and Abraham Lincoln, but this was the first time he had come face to face with a black man. He was fascinated by his black skin, the whiteness of his large eyes, his thick lips, kinky short hair, the contrasting paleness of his fingernails and the palms; he didn't miss a thing.

My father, a lifelong admirer of Western technology, was most impressed by the equipment the occupation force brought with them: trucks with huge tires, novel vehicles called jeeps going everywhere under any condition, ambulances with crosses, trucks pulling water tanks sloshing water inside, and even power generators. By contrast, the Japanese trucks looked tinny and flimsy, and toward the end of the war, there were very few around town.

To our alarm, one of the American units set up camp in the vacant Japanese inn right next to our house, across the alley, and installed a kitchen and mess hall in the back of the inn. The soldiers would line up in the alley to relay boxes of food and other supplies from a truck parked on our street. The alley was too narrow for the truck.

When the supply relay was in progress, the soldiers could easily look over the top of our cornstalk fence into our front courtyard and back vegetable garden, in essence taking in the whole inside view of our u-shaped house. This unexpected public viewing trapped us girls and my stepmother indoors until their chore was done, and it became a cat-and-mouse game for us all.

In the beginning, we were afraid to go to the communal well for water, just a block away, but gradually got used to the American presence and their occasional whistles. Whistles were the first American gesture the Wonju girls came to accept, though it was considered rather brassy until then.

Taiam somehow made a friend out of one soldier, a radio man, who came to see him now and then in his room at the end of a wing. My brother had a Western desk and a matching chair in his room, which came in handy for the American's long legs. They had to make do with an awkward seating arrangement, as my brother had to converse with his guest from the floor cushion.

His soldier friend often brought us gifts, candy bars and canned food. I am not sure how they managed to communicate with each other since Taiam's middle school English was not good enough for even rudimentary conversation and the most recent foreign language he had studied was German.

While his American friend was visiting, I was forbidden to go near his room, even though I was not afraid of him. When the soldier had to go home to America, he gave my brother a black desk telephone as a farewell gift, which sat silent and unused on his desk, because there was no telephone line to our house.

Shortly after the American soldiers moved in next door, my jittery paranoia caused a real scare. One evening, I was in the privy. The small window of the privy was right on the alley side, aligned with the fence. All of a sudden, I heard a whispered conversation in a foreign tongue among a few shadowy figures in the alley, peering over the fence into our front courtyard. I thought the war propaganda–fed nightmare was about to be enacted by the lawless soldiers.

I waited, deathly quiet, until I could hear no noise from the alley. I crept out of the privy, ran to the main room, crouched low in the dark and alerted my family about the imminent danger. My stepmother, Jinju, and I slipped out the back door of the room, ran around the house and scaled the scratchy cornstalk fence on the west side; it was amazing that the flimsy fence didn't just collapse under our combined weight. We then ran to a nearby church member's house. After a while, Taikun came to tell us that our great escape was all for naught.

When the American military settled in our town, an unanticipated cottage industry sprang up for the local housewives, doing the American soldiers' laundry for good pay. In those lean days, bars of soap or canned meat were prized things, fair compensation for labor.

My stepmother decided to take in laundry, and the family began to taste rich, greasy meat we had never had before. Those American meats tasted so gamy, as we had been, by necessity, vegetarian for some years. This was my introduction to the American Spam and lamb meat.

I still remember the pungent tobacco smell from the G.I. clothes, even after being subjected to the harsh Korean laundry treatment. They were boiled in lye water to kill lice and taken out to the river to be beaten with a wooden paddle on a smooth rock. They were dried on lines in the fresh air, even in the frigid winter. Then they were trampled under feet, wrapped in cloth and partly dry for easy ironing. Finally, they were ironed with a flat pan containing red hot charcoal. How beautifully the clothes turned out despite the primitive laundry method! We mistook the tobacco smell for the white man's odor and decided that the Americans were a very smelly bunch indeed.

In spite of our natural apprehension toward a foreign presence, the townfolks gradually accepted the American soldiers well and got along with them better than expected. The American soldiers were better disciplined and behaved than the propaganda or the tales of the Russian soldiers had prepared us to believe. The soldiers were particularly kind to children, and Taikun, then twelve years old, took readily to their easy, friendly ways. Candies helped. He wanted to learn English from them and started to pore over my old English textbook I brought from Nagoya.

I wished I too could talk freely to the American soldiers without being branded a tramp for life. I wanted to practice the elementary English I learned in the first year of my middle school in Nagoya before it was yanked off by the Japanese government as the enemy language.

As required of all the public institutions and businesses, my father had to put up a sign in English to let the Americans know what kind of trade he was in: Acupuncture Clinic.

In spite of the social taboo of fraternizing with foreign soldiers, I began to notice one particular soldier, younger than the rest of the Americans. He looked no older than I. I had just turned sixteen that fall. He had an open, boyish face with no sign of shaving yet.

One day he whistled at me over the fence, driving me straight into the house, mortified. But I was pleased that he noticed me, even in his crude American way. In those days, I was very self-conscious about my gawky appearance with sparse hair. Thereafter, I found myself looking for him surreptitiously, whenever I was doing outdoor chores, hoping to get a glimpse of him.

This one-sided interest didn't last long, though. As the golden autumn melted into frosty mornings and Old Man Winter was at the door, the American soldiers vacated the inn, taking him away forever and leaving piles of garbage behind. I wonder if that young soldier ever knew that he left behind a broken heart in Wonju in late 1945.

Even though our next-door Americans left for home, a detachment remained in town for the provisional military government. One of my girlfriends from church had an older sister who became an interpreter for an American officer who commanded the local detachment. My friend's family was the Korean expatriate from Shanghai, where they lived a sophisticated, cosmopolitan life for years. They were fluent in four languages: Korean, Chinese, Japanese, and English.

My friend's mother was always stylishly dressed in hand-knit sweaters, and her hair was braided from both temples, ending up on top of her head, or wound into balls over her temples, like earmuffs. She brought her two daughters to Wonju around the time the Pacific war was coming to an end. The family rented a house, part of an old farm compound owned by an elderly church couple who still farmed, with seasonal harvest hands, several acres of rice paddies and a plot of vegetable garden.

I never met my friend's father who lived in Seoul with his mistress and was employed in the American military occupation government. Probably his past connection to the Korean provisional government in exile in China and his multilingual skills became valuable assets to the Americans.

I saw my friend's sister ride to and from her American military government office downtown in a jeep driven by an American soldier. She seemed to have escaped the townfolks' censorious opinion for consorting with the American military. She was always smartly dressed in well-tailored Western clothes with a devil-may-care air of supreme self-confidence. Her brimming authority seemed to overcome her plain, plump look. After all, she was making an unheard-of salary by the Korean standard, especially for a woman. I envied her flawless English with impeccable enunciation of difficult sounds like "R," "L," and "th," a breathy diphthong.

As an interpreter she commanded any price she asked, according to the law of supply and demand. This period of a hastily cobbled military government was known, therefore, as the "interpreters' government." The American military heads had no choice but to rely on the educated Koreans who spoke fluent English as deputies or interpreters for governance.

In the fall, my father diagnosed my lingering malaise and failure to gain weight as incipient tuberculosis. He promptly started daily acupuncture, combined with suut treatment. A tiny mound of finely ground suut, a medicinal herb, was lit over each acupuncture hole to let the medicinal steam seep through into the strategic places of my body.

I could bear the needles by gritting my teeth but the burning suut on my skin was sheer torture. The needle holes all over my body became infected and I was covered with draining sores sticking to my clothing, uncomfortable day and night. I knew then what the lepers went through.

The first post-war Christmas was memorable for my frost-bitten toes. That year, the teenage boys and girls had the first-ever Christmas Eve party in the parish house with the mondu soup and rice. Mondu is a Korean version of Chinese wonton dumpling, with a filling of minced kimchi, tofu, and minced pork. This was the only party of the year for us and we girls bunched together on one side of the room, separated from the boys like the two halves of the Red Sea. For entertainment, we played musical chairs and the losers sang.

The Koreans were born singers just like the Irish, singing melodic and melancholy folk songs, along with popular Western ballads — the Irish "Danny Boy" and "Brahms's Lullaby" in Korean. Koreans weren't called "the Irish of the Orient" for nothing. Since the liberation day in August, the traditional folk songs had come out of the woodwork, and were sung openly and passionately.

Around midnight, we were sung out, bellies full, and fanned out by foot to the countryside for Christmas caroling at church members' farms. Usually these farmers would treat us to the steamy hot mondu or rice-cake soup and rice, even though we couldn't get there until the wee hours of the night.

That Christmas Eve was a bitterly cold night with sub-zero wind chill. The powdery snow particles in the night air made the whole countryside into an ethereal, sparkling crystal paradise enveloped in a diffused white light. The starlit heaven and the snow-covered earth met in a shimmering glitter. Stupidly I was woefully underdressed for the penetrating cold and miles of frozen country roads.

None of the farmers expected us that Christmas night and we came home, hungry and frozen, just before dawn.

CHAPTER 28
The Family Tragedy

We had a relatively calm year while Taiam was finishing up his last year of acupuncture training in Nagoya. When he returned to Korea in the spring of 1945, the old tension and antagonism between my stepmother and him returned in full force. My brother's anger was boundless when he learned that the only photograph we had of our beloved mother was gone.

War was declared then. Unforgiving self-righteousness afflicted both sides. On Taiam's part, his youthful sense of absolute justice was egregiously offended. On my stepmother's side, the Confucian code of one's filial duty to respect parents, no matter what, was violated by his anger.

At the time, Taiam was footloose, wondering about his future — medical practice with our father in Wonju or to strike out solo elsewhere. He, for a time, tried his hand at helping our father, but the examination room was not big enough for both of them and there were not enough patients to keep them busy.

It was early 1946, after the holiday season was over, Christmas through two New Year Days, one by the solar calendar and the other by the lunar, that Taiam, only nineteen years old, almost died.

One Sunday evening at the dinner table, Taiam had another terrible argument with our stepmother over some now-forgotten matter. After dinner, my father and I left for Sunday vespers at the church, leaving the rest of the family behind, still troubled by the unpleasant dinner scene. In the middle of the service, when I heard hurried, unapologetic footsteps, I instinctively knew something terrible had happened at home, and my most-feared nightmare became a reality.

Taikun, from the back of the church, was frantically gesturing to us, and my father and I hurried out of the church. I started to run toward home in the pitch dark winter night while pulling my night-blind father along. Between sobs, Taikun told us on the way that Taiam had shot himself with an American military revolver and was dying. He gave us a sketchy account of what had happened while we raced home.

Taiam tried to apologize to our stepmother for his bad behavior at the dinner table, but she coldly rejected his peace offer. Whereupon, Taiam went back to his room and a gunshot was heard, summoning my stepmother, Jinju and Taikun to his room. They found him bleeding uncontrollably from the gunshot wound under his chin.

When we reached his room, Taiam was all alone in a sea of blood. The bullet had entered the underside of his left chin, pulverized his left jaw and some teeth, and exited right below his left cheekbone. I saw right away an urgent need to stop his bleeding.

Unexpectedly my father reacted with rage at my brother's attempted suicide as a personal affront to him, his father. By his reckoning, my brother had no right to take his own life without his father's permission. He refused to do anything to save his son's life and stomped out of the room, shouting incoherently.

While Taikun was summoning us from the church, my stepmother and Jinju tried to stem the blood flow with some cloth but only managed to break further the already shattered lower jawbone. They were so frightened by the bloody wounds and their undeniable implication in the tragedy that they fled, leaving Taiam to die alone. If my brother was to live, it was up to me to save him.

In a flash, I remembered that there was a doctor living a couple of houses below the Methodist church on the slowly rising, winding road. I knew that seconds meant life or death. I fixed my eyes on the lights in the doctor's house and ran toward them on a straight line across the frozen, snow-covered rice paddies stretching out from our westside fence to the foot of the hill. I remember the dream-like, slow motion of jumping over low fences, climbing an alley between houses below the church, crossing the road, clambering up the hillside, and finally pounding on the doctor's wooden gates with my fists. While running, I had a distinct sensation that my feet were not touching the ground, just flying through the frosty night.

To my eternal relief, the young doctor quickly sensed the urgency out of my breathless babbling, grabbed his bag, and ran with me to the house, this time following the road.

The doctor examined the wounds and bound my brother's jaw and the left half of his face with cloth bandages to stop the bleeding. By then, the bleeding was slowing down on its own. The doctor gave him a shot of some kind, but Taiam was in agony with pain as the day was breaking.

I stayed with him in his room all night and could not sleep, so scared that my brother might die. I was inconsolable, realizing that, even if he survived, my handsome brother forever ruined his square-jawed good looks and his great future as an upstanding man of good character in the community. Koreans took suicide as a dishonorable character defect and something to be ashamed of both as a family and an individual.

As the day was breaking, I was totally drained physically and emotionally, but I had to see that the family had some breakfast. My stepmother and Jinju were nowhere to be seen around the house. Thus began the true endurance test for my stamina, emotional and physical. Alone, I had to care for my brother in great pain and to look after my grieving father and younger brother. I forgot all about my own health problem.

The doctor came several times to check on the wounds and change the dressings. A few days after the incident, the Wonju police sent a detective to investigate the shooting. Taikun had to show how he retrieved the gun from the trash thrown into the well in the inner courtyard of the Japanese inn after the Americans left late in December. He lowered our ladder into the covered well in the presence of the detective to prove his point. It was illegal for citizens to possess any firearms at that time. To our great relief, the police did not press charges against my younger brother or anybody else.

Also the police took Taiam's statement that it was an accident. Was he protecting my stepmother, or his reputation, or our family honor? I have my doubts, but then, nobody knows the truth, except Taiam who never talked about that night, ever.

As soon as my father got over the initial shock of his son's near-death and realized that he was going to live, he started his own fail-safe, Chinese herb treatment to boost his son's greatly depleted blood supply and his weakened immune system, to ward off infection and start the healing process.

As my father did not have his own Chinese herb pharmacy set up in Wonju as yet, he went to a local practitioner for the appropriate herbs. He also sought out a slaughterhouse to get fresh cow blood, and made my brother drink it, still warm.

Producing the Chinese herb drink three times a day was a twenty-four-hour enterprise of continual brewing, perfuming the room and the whole house with a sweet-herby fragrance. A dozen varieties of Chinese herbs — dried roots, leaves, barks, and berries measured precisely into proper proportions by a small hand-held scale, a small version of the one held by the blind American lady justice — were boiled together in an iron teapot with water. The reduced liquid with herbs was strained through cheesecloth to make about a cup of bitter, dark liquid, drunk while warm. Requiring constant attention, it was a precarious, nerve-wracking undertaking. In the beginning, many times herbs were scorched black on the bottom of the pot until I had the hang of it.

This was the first time my father faced the gunshot wound and realized that it was beyond his competence. For his son's sake, he forgot his usual contempt for modern medicine and sought out all the advice from any source. He was a humble man now. After one month of home care, my brother was transferred to the Provincial hospital on the southside of the town, on the doctor's advice.

Before I could accompany Taiam to the hospital, I had to fetch my stepmother and Jinju from their friend's house where they had taken refuge ever since that terrible night. They were reluctant to return but for their friend's urging. Feeding two extra mouths was a burden to anybody, even to the family from Shanghai, in an inflation-crazed economy. For my part, I was glad that my stepmother could lighten my load by taking care of my father and Taikun at home.

In 1946, the hospital in Wonju was a glorified country clinic with a few upstairs rooms for occasional hospital stays. One doctor and one nurse covered all the medical needs of the region. It had no surgical capability, no modern medical equipment to speak of except an X-ray machine which was so antiquated that the pictures were too hazy to reveal anything definitive. We hadn't yet heard about penicillin.

The wooden structure of the hospital with modern architectural pretension had a woebegone, neglected air about it. Our room on the second floor was just big enough to contain a steel double bed for the patient and a cot for me at the foot of the patient's bed. I was to cook all the meals right in the room on a charcoal burner, clean the room daily, and wash Taiam's bandages for reuse. There was no bathroom in the room and we used a wash basin for cleaning ourselves. We brushed our teeth with salt using our fingers. I brought water in a bucket from a downstairs faucet for cooking and cleaning.

How dusty the room was! The first time I tried to sweep the floor with a short broom, the cumulus cloud of dust was so choking that my mouth tasted of grainy sand, and my nose smelled the dryness of Sahara desert. The next day, I tried it with water sprinkled on the floor and, thereafter, gradually the wooden floorboards revealed their wood grain, worn smooth.

The young resident doctor visited my brother every day and examined his disintegrated left chin and missing lower teeth to check the healing. Even though we never explained how this injury occurred, the doctor seemed to know all about its circumstances. Gossip traveled fast.

He was most solicitous toward my brother and me, when he saw that only my father and Taikun visited us regularly, bringing food supply and charcoal. My stepmother and Jinju never came. Usually it was the mother who would come and fuss over the sick child in the hospital and my stepmother's absence explained everything.

I don't know how my father paid for all of the medical expenses. There was no room for an extra financial burden after he paid for the heavy house mortgage and living expenses. He might have sold, now legally, the wool suit and coat material he brought for himself and his sons from Japan. Later, my stepmother had to give up her prized Singer sewing machine.

Not only was our family fast impoverished by the tragedy, but there was a loss of face in the community, rubbing salt into the wound. I could see a heavy blanket of gloom descend on the entire family, sparing no one. My father' silent suffering, Taikun's helpless hurt, and even Jinju's scared look told of incalculable tolls exacted from the unwilling cast of the tragedy.

My stepmother was an enigma. She tried not to betray her emotions by avoiding eye contact with any of us, but there was no question that the event must have had an effect on her. But she remained taciturn and cold as ever. To my knowledge, she never expressed any regret about the part she played in my brother's near-death encounter.

After the daily examination by the doctor in the morning, there was not much happening except living an ordinary apartment life with the usual housekeeping chores. After the nightly visit from my father and Taikun, the evening was quiet without a radio or phonograph to break the silence. Just reading, and plenty of it. My brother and I would walk in the deserted upstairs corridor, back and forth in accompaniment to our echoing footsteps, so that Taiam could sleep well at night. For an additional assurance, I gave him nightly back rubs before going to sleep. Many a night, the pain, physical and emotional, kept my brother from sleeping soundly.

I had no trouble sleeping, but my night was often interrupted by my brother's nightmares and sleeplessness. In those dark hours, sleep for me was a welcome comfort and an escape from living hell.

After one week into our hospital stay, we had a new patient move into the next room. To our surprise and to my delight, he turned out to be the university student son of our local newspaper publisher. I never found out the nature of his ailment. He looked a tad pale, but otherwise his problem was not so obvious. There had been a rumor about his suicidal tendency, but I dismissed it as idle gossip. His family was a loving, good Christian family for all to see. They came to visit every day with hot meals and anything he needed. He did not have any family member stay with him in his room.

The very first night after he moved in, my brother and I heard the most dreamy, melodic music coming from his room. It was the "Moonlight Sonata" by Ludwig van Beethoven, on the piano. His family had brought his phonograph player and some of his records. Every night thereafter, when the whole building fell silent with no one but us three upstairs, we were indulged in after-dinner music until our bedtime. He played the "Pathétique" by Peter Tchaikovsky, the Beethovens, and my favorite, Chopin's "Nocturnes."

We already had a nodding acquaintance with each other through our families in the church. My brother visited our neighbor in his room, but I was too shy to even say hello. Besides, our social protocol forbade me to visit a young man's room, even a hospital room.

So the rest of our hospital stay turned out to be more pleasant than we had a right to expect. Sometimes, I wonder if he ever knew how much his beautiful music meant to me then. I never saw him again after my brother and I left for Seoul.

In late spring, the doctor recommended that Taiam consult the best dentistry available at Seoul Dental College, for his destroyed left chin and missing teeth. The gunshot wounds were mending nicely. So off we went to Seoul.

CHAPTER 29

Seoul

When the decision was made to take Taiam to Seoul, the spring was in full swing. The countryside had moved quietly from deep winter, through thawing March, into fragrant impressionistic pastel with fruit tree blossoms coloring pale greens everywhere.

Out of our train window, we could still see some yellow dandelions here and there in the fields and along the country roads, overlooked by wild-green pickers earlier in the spring. At Eastgate train station, Taiam and I felt ourselves slipping into a familiar urban scape as naturally as a bird taking to the blue sky after being cooped up in a cage. We were exhilarated by city clamor and vibrancy after a quiet life in the country.

In the spring of 1946, Seoul was a bustling, joyful city with the streetcars and people rushing every which way. The streets were clogged with American G.I.s on the sidewalks and the military jeeps and trucks spilling over with boisterous soldiers, whistling indiscriminately at all the girls in sight. Unexplainably, these whistles sent a piercing thrill through me as though they were meant only for me. It was not unpleasant at all.

I should have been well prepared for the natural American exuberance from the Hollywood movies I had seen after the American occupation forces came into Wonju in the fall. *San Francisco* with Clark Gable and *Chicago* with Tyrone Power were spectacular sunbursts after the predictable war propaganda movies. But it was entirely another matter to see it all around me on the streets — so exhilarating.

For the first time, I saw American white women in military uniforms which tried to negate the feminine identity, but failed. They looked stylish in straight skirts, revealing well publicized, long, slender American legs, and with jauntily perched overseas caps over short, light-colored hair. By the time we arrived in Seoul, the foreign soldiers, blond or black, became familiar, common sights in the city. I didn't see any sign of Russians on the streets, however, even though there was enough noise made on the front pages by the Russians, objecting to everything and anything proposed by the United States and the United Nations about the fate of Korea. It was as though the U.S. Army had taken over the whole city.

In political reality, a military occupation was precisely what was happening against the wishes of the American government and the Korean expatriates returning to Korea. The joint trusteeship of the United States and Russia — agreed upon by the Big Four foreign ministers in Moscow in December 1945 — was falling apart due to too many Russian "nyets." Russia had its own political agenda of taking the whole of Korea for Communist rule under Kim Il Sung.

Stalin's strategy was to keep South Korean politics in constant turmoil by any means possible, including subversive tactics, so that the United States would become thoroughly disgusted and leave Korea. Then, the North Korean Communists, with its well-disciplined army, would swoop down on the South and take over the entire peninsula, like catching a ripe plum falling into their waiting hands.

Meanwhile, the Korean political leaders in the South were fighting among themselves (there were over one hundred political factions) and couldn't even coalesce enough to form a manageable number of political parties. With the military threat from the Communist North and the political constraints from American domestic politics, which resulted in downsizing the wartime standing army of twelve million to one million by July 1947, the American military government found itself in a dilemma.

The American military was forced to govern the country with the help of Korean interpreters, earning the label of "interpreters' government." Major General John R. Hodge was a soldier who commanded the taking of Okinawa in April 1945, and lacked savvy diplomacy and political training. But as the head of the occupation government, he kept the South from sliding into anarchy and maintained a semblance of order in the post-war chaos.

It is often overlooked by historians that the Korean interpreters, during this critical time, played a significant part in keeping the American government interested in the fate of Korea. These interpreters were by and large educated by American missionaries before the Pacific war and were true believers in the democratic principles of government. By acting as interpreters, they were in a position to influence American thinking and policies toward Korea.

The children of the American missionaries, too, played a vital role in the post-war military government. The navy doctor George Zur Williams and army Major Clarence Weems, for an example, served on the headquarters staff as interpreters and advisors.

Being Christians, these interpreters were also staunch anti–Communists, thus drawing the definitive line of ideological and political difference between North and South Korea at the thirty-eighth parallel.

The Seoul Dental College was located in the bustling city center. The "modern" building was rather imposing but visibly shabby, like other public edifices around the town, due mostly to wartime neglect.

For a medical school, the unkempt interior was rather disconcerting. After an examination of my brother's injury by one of the professors, we were ushered into a large room next to the main entrance hallway on the first floor. We stayed almost the entire summer before an inconclusive verdict was rendered on his case.

The room was a classroom converted into a makeshift hospital room with a metal hospital bed for the patient and a wooden platform on the concrete floor for the accompanying attendant in charge of housekeeping. We used the same restroom on the main floor used by everyone: students, faculty, and the general public. For cooking, I drew water from the nearby laboratory faucet and, for laundry, the lab sink came in handy after the day's classes were over. I strung laundry lines in our cavernous room to dry the wash.

An electric hotplate provided the cooking heat source for a linear cooking process: steam the rice first, make some soup next, sauté vegetables or broil fish.

As soon as we had settled into our daily routine of the "hospital" living with Taiam's morning dental examination by the teachers and students alike, we took off for sightseeing. Around late May or early June, all the peonies, the ancient Chinese transplants, were in full bloom, perfuming the public parks and the inner courts of Kyong Puk Palace, now the national museum.

It was sad to see the Korean imperial palace and its grounds so drab and bleak in stark contrast to its Japanese counterpart in Kyoto with its exquisite garden and well-preserved ancient buildings. The Chinese-influenced Kyong Puk Palace buildings of heavy timber and tile roof were weather-beaten, bare of paint, and thickly caked with dust by centuries of use and latter-day neglect. Perhaps the sorry sight of our national museum was simply a reflection of our recent subjugated state, not fully recovered for nationhood yet.

When the Yi dynasty ended with the 1910 annexation of Korea by the Japanese, the five-year-old crown prince was taken to Tokyo to be reared by the Japanese imperial family. He eventually married a Japanese princess and had a son. Some time after the end of the Pacific war, the prince and his Japanese wife came to Korea for a visit, and I understood that they were generally well received by the Korean people. But there was little interest among the Korean people in the restoration of the monarchy. They had not forgotten nor forgiven the last king for his role as the Japanese puppet around the turn of the century.

My brother and I started to attend the Sunday services at Westgate Presbyterian Church, next to the Severence Hospital–Medical School run by the Seventh-Day Adventist mission, near the main Seoul railroad station. Taiam was getting stronger, able to walk quite a distance, with a bandage over his chin, more to hide his scar than for medical need. His exit wound, under his left cheekbone, was completely healed, leaving a hardly noticeable scar.

Shortly after we arrived, a new patient, an elderly widow, came to share our room with her daughter in attendance. Her daughter was a bit older than I. The room was divided by a wooden screen in the middle of the room and patient beds were placed on both sides. The room divider was no more than a pretense at privacy. All the conversations, the noises, and cooking smells freely traveled over the imaginary line of propriety.

Our co-tenants were Seoul natives and their extended families visited often with prepared food and groceries. From silk Korean clothes, brocade beddings, and pricey food materials, I surmised that the lady's son was a prosperous merchant of some sort.

Her accompanying daughter was a stunningly beautiful girl, not the traditional Korean beauty but the Western type with large eyes shaded by luscious lashes, a handsome nose and shapely lips. I noticed that, whenever she and I went shopping in the open-air market for our groceries or walked together to church on Sundays, the passersby did double-takes at her striking looks.

Soon, I noticed that one of the young professors at the dental school was smitten by her and began to show up at our room on the flimsiest of pretexts. At the same time, a recently graduated assistant, who lived in one of the garret rooms on the top floor (he could not go back to his home in North Korea after the thirty-eighth parallel was closed) also showed his interest in the same girl.

The classical drama of a triangle was unfolding right under our noses, even though Taiam and I did our best not to notice it. The young professor was a most unlikely suitor for this gorgeous creature. He was shorter than she, and stocky with a flat nose on a round face. But he was evidently brilliant and from a good family. By contrast, the assistant was a tall, nice looking young man, but poor under the circumstances.

There was not much contest as the playing field was decidedly skewed in favor of the professor, who dazzled the vain girl with his pedigree and timely gifts. One late evening, the poor assistant in sheer despair got himself roaringly drunk, and my brother had to help him up to his garret before anybody saw him in this disgraceful state. The next day, sober, the assistant whispered a heartfelt thanks to my brother and they became friends.

Taiam and I did not stay long enough that summer to see the outcome of the romantic entanglements, but a couple of years later I happened to see the girl at a sporting event one summer afternoon.

She was dressed to kill in a flowing Korean summer dress, shimmeringly sheer pastel, with a silk parasol to shade her ever more beautiful face from the scorching sun. A pair of binoculars hung from her neck.

I was delighted that she recognized me, then a student at the Methodist Mission School in Seoul. It turned out that the professor had won out in the end. They had been married happily for a year and had a baby girl. Just before he was to embark on an advanced study program in dentistry in America, he suddenly died.

Her family must have prevailed upon her to marry the professor, a great step up the social ladder from the trademan's class. In those days, the scholar outclassed all other professions. From her enticing appearance in a public place, unchaperoned, I did not detect any sadness or sign of mourning over her dead husband. Somehow, she reminded me of a tigress roaming in the bamboo forest for another prey.

The primary reason my brother went to the dental college was to find a way to reconstruct his destroyed left chin. Soon we discovered that Korean dentistry in 1946 did not have the required knowledge, nor the technology for plastic reconstruction. For the rest of my brother's life, he had to live with a half chin which gave a caved-in, asymmetrical look to his jawline. When the final verdict came after countless probings and consultations, the summer was almost gone.

I wished we could have remained longer, not necessarily at the dental school, but in Seoul, away from the glum home under the dark shadow of my stepmother. However, there was no other reason for us to stay in town. Besides, our stay was putting a financial burden on our father. About the time my brother and I were preparing to leave Seoul, unexpectedly our oldest sister Kiyon and her husband came to visit us.

Around the end of the Pacific war, the Kims came to Seoul from Fukuoka, Japan, with their two small sons and a toddler daughter, to escape the last inferno. They were barely spared from the final furies of the war, living in Fukuoka which was roughly the midpoint between Hiroshima and Nagasaki, the nuclear bomb targets on August 6 and 9, 1945.

They came to Korea with only the clothes on their backs, and somehow my brother-in-law, a mild-mannered man, managed to land a policeman's job, of all things. He was not mean or dishonest enough, however, to supplement his pay with bribery or extortion, as expected. They were living in a rented room with an adjoining kitchen, in a house where the landlord also lived, on the far north hillside overlooking the sprawling city below.

After leaving the hospital in late August, we visited the Kim family for a couple of days. It was a mistake. We were partaking some of their thin meal of boiled water with flour, soy sauce, and nothing else.

Kiyon, my father's one-time favorite daughter, was a prematurely old, worn-out woman in her twenties, who had lost both youth and spirit. Poverty and malnutrition seemed to make everyone, including the children, languid and lethargic. In the post-war chaos with high unemployment and inflation, I wondered how long my gentle brother-in-law could stand the brutal profession of being a policeman, climbing the winding dirt road up and down the steep hillside every day to get to work for a pittance.

Seeing Kiyon's miserable living in one room, crammed with her three children, we could not stay one second longer. Our house in Wonju was spacious, especially in the summer when the wooden verandahs brought summer living out to the fresh and cool outdoors. My brother and I came home at last.

CHAPTER 30

The Return of Duli

In the waning days of summer, Taiam and I came back to Wonju with mixed feelings and a certain amount of anxiety. We came home to an all-too-familiar, gloomy scene of our still-despairing father, cold stepmother, taciturn Jinju, and silently stoic Taikun.

However, Taiam and I came home changed from Seoul. We had seen possibilities for a new life of our own making, away from our sad home under the damning influence of our stepmother.

One day, I happened to remember a letter from Duli we received months ago but had forgotten all about in the aftermath of Taiam's injury. In defiance to my father's order not to communicate with her, I hastily wrote to Duli at the Masan address given on the envelope, hoping that she could still be reached there.

Rereading her letter, I found out that she had had a very rough life since she and her husband, along with her brother-in-law, were thrown out of our house by our enraged father, when they came home for a reconciliation in Nagoya in 1943. The humiliating rejection by her own family left Duli a non-person in the eyes of her husband and his family.

Shortly they too returned to her husband's birthplace in Kyonsan nam-do, the southernmost province, to escape the imminent air raids on heavily industrialized Osaka. Her husband for some reason didn't stay long in Korea, and returned alone to Japan, leaving Duli behind with his extended family. Innocent of the harsh world, and illiterate, Duli was at the mercy of her in-laws, who considered her nothing, abandoned by her own family and husband.

Somehow, she ended up working at a whiskey house in Masan. Her brother-in-law, the head of the family, borrowed money from the establishment, and my sister was to work off the debt as an indentured servant. She was an unworldly twenty-four year old, fair game for any predator, family or stranger. My letter finally reached her, begging her to come home, no questions asked. I did not mention our father's objection, nor our stepmother's cold indifference out of fear that Duli might hesitate to come home.

One day in September, Duli came home, our prodigal sister. If the truth were known, our father was glad that I disobeyed his edict and brought his daughter out of a den of iniquity, the whiskey house. This time he let her stay after an obligatory protest.

Duli came home chastened by the experiences and consequences, unforeseen by her naiveté, of her first act of independence. Somehow, she came through the unspeakable ordeals without any bitterness toward anybody — her husband, in-laws, or our unbending father. She was reluctant to talk about the mistreatments she had suffered and wanted to forget about them. After her arrival, we never received any inquiry from her husband or his family. They, too, wanted to forget her.

Duli had a calming, moderating effect on the too frequent, tense family scenes between our stepmother and us. But before long, our stepmother waged a campaign of elimination on Duli by complaining loudly about the food shortage, as though my sister had caused it. At the same time, she was blaming me for the extra mouth to feed. The mounting tension was too much for Duli who soon developed a bleeding ulcer.

Meanwhile, our stepmother was inquiring around for any prospect to marry off Duli while on her weekly visits to the church members' homes as the woman elder. So Duli became a ne'er-do-well farmer's wife after just a few months' stay with us. A woman church member had a recently widowed brother with three small daughters ranging in ages from twelve years to five years old. The marriage was arranged by my stepmother and his sister in town and there was no wedding ceremony of any kind.

Kiyon, by contrast, was given away in a Western church wedding with all the pomp and circumstance, though visibly pregnant, because she was marrying a man my father picked. This time my father pointedly stayed out of the whole affair, except for giving his nodding consent at the end.

Duli was a generous soul, even at her own expense. I knew that she never cared much for her new husband, a worn-out, uneducated, country jake, twenty years older than herself. He was such a departure from her first husband, who was educated, urbane, and handsome. I suspect that Duli took the marriage offer as a way out of the family friction her return caused, and at the same time to ease the family's food problem. Duli thought that she could bring some rice or even a chicken from the country instead of being a burden to her folks.

Thus, against her own desires, she became a farmer's wife and stepmother to the girls. But all of her good intentions and efforts toward the arranged life could not overcome the absence of her genuine love for her husband. Hers was a loveless marriage of expedience, born of hunger.

Now and then I visited her farm in a little hamlet, five miles north of Wonju. She worked as though she never knew any other life, getting up with a rooster and fast learning the myriad of farm chores folded into the unchanging demands of growing cycles. She mastered the fine arts of a farmer's wife, seen but not heard in tradition-bound, country life.

Duli tried to be a mother to her stepdaughters, but failed to bridge a gap between the girls and herself. From day one, her predecessor's ghost stood in her way, judging everything she did and said, and finding her lacking. It was a difficult life, emotionally and physically, for my sister who had forgotten what it was like to live on a farm since our family had emigrated to Japan in 1930 when she was only seven. But she gave it all she had in her steady and conscientious ways. Even though her poor farm did not produce big enough margins of farm products for giving, she always urged me to take food home after every visit. I loved Duli and felt her silent pain and suffering. But I was powerless to do anything about her predicament.

Duli's Herculean efforts and Job-like endurance came, however, to an abrupt end by an apocalyptic event of the Korean war on Sunday, June 25, 1950. The surprise invasion of the North Korean Communists unexpectedly liberated Duli from her self-imposed bondage.

Like the rest of the countrymen, she was driven out of her farm life and found herself dislodged from her second marriage by the brutal force of the war. When her domestic life was destroyed by raging battles, there was little emotional attachment to tie her to her marriage. She left her second husband with no regret amid the turmoil of war.

While trying to survive the ravages of war, she set out to find our family which was scattered all over the land by the hurricane wind of the war. When the war began, our father was away visiting our relatives in the south. Our stepmother and Taikun lugged our valuables to the church basement for safekeeping before being driven out of the town by the fighting. Taiam and I were away in Seoul, and only God knew what would happen to us.

CHAPTER 31

Carpenter Lee

We knew Mrs. Lee well through our church, where she attended our Sunday services regularly with her children. Mr. Lee was not a church-going man. In spite of his skills and steady employment as a carpenter, Mr. Lee had trouble keeping the wolves of poverty from his doorstep. His wife and children were always in various stages of raggedness and illness.

As the old saying that the cobbler's children go barefooted, Mr. Lee failed to shelter his own family under a decent roof. The Siberian chill seeped through the thin, uninsulated mud walls of their one-room shack and the thinly thatched roof did not keep away the freezing wind rushing down the hillside.

The hut sat right at the roadside, on the way to the Methodist church. In summer, the hut was completely engulfed by thick clouds of fine dust and was splashed generously with muck from the road traffic on the rainy days.

Earlier, Mrs. Lee came to consult my father about her latest ailment. She had suffered a mild stroke, which left one-half of her body paralyzed and shriveled a little from head to toe. With half of her face drooping, one arm dangling, and one foot shuffling, she was still trying to keep her little ones fed and cared for with no outside help whatsoever, except from her oldest boy, who had just started going to school.

One cold winter day, the seven-year-old boy came for help. While his father was away working on a carpentering job, his mother gave birth to their fourth child, and there was nobody to cook for the family, and nobody to keep their little home warm against the frigid winter.

I volunteered to help the family. Fortunately, the carpenter had enough firewood and food in the house for the family. It was a simple matter of cooking the usual big breakfast in the morning and the hearty supper in the evening, keeping the only room in the hut toasty warm at the same time. For lunch, the morning soup and rice were warmed over the charcoal heat in the hibachi, which was kept going all day in the room.

For the childbirth, I cooked the traditional seaweed soup for the nursing mother. In those days, the Koreans believed that the black, rubbery seaweed, rich in iron and iodine, was essential to the mother's milk production. It was a joy to see smiling little faces and a beaming mother, warmed through inside and out from the heated floor.

Conveniently, the house was just a stone's throw away from the communal well and there was a little stream running through the back of the house for diaper washing. It was an icy cold washing, but there was no other way. The diapers were fashioned out of old cotton clothes, cut into rectangles and worn soft; they were anything but white.

While I was taking care of their meals and washing, I noticed that Mr. Lee had some cotton yarn he had received from a farmer as his wage. Seeing the little children shivering in thin clothes, I asked Mrs. Lee if I could knit some longjohns for the two older boys and the little girl.

So, the following weeks were taken up for knitting sweaters, socks, and mittens which they had never had before — all in off-white, natural color and the cable design as the only decoration — while I told them fairy tales from Grimm brothers and other Western writers I remembered. Wide-eyed, the children and the nursing mother, all huddled together around the hibachi, were mesmerized by the wild stories from the West.

Mr. Lee was a large, silent man who spoke not one word to me the whole time I was at his place, out of shyness or propriety, I do not know. I was there at the crack of dawn for breakfast so that the oldest boy would be off in time for a long walk to school, and stayed until after the supper dishes were done. Most of the day, Mr. Lee was gone working. But it seemed that he studiously avoided being in the same room with me and even refused to eat with his family when I was present. He ate his supper after I had gone home for the night, and usually he left for work before I got there in the morning. Once I saw him come home drunk, to his wife's embarrassment.

CHAPTER 32

Running Away from Home

It was early spring of 1947 when the long-awaited, dazzling white light of the spring sun was still tinged with a touch of chill that Taiam and I ran away from home.

During the long winter of 1946-47, Taiam and I concocted a plan to go to Japan, pretending to be Japanese refugees, siblings escaping from the northern harbor town on the Sea of Japan, near where Manchuria, Russia, and Korea came together.

We chose the farthest northern Korean town we could find on the map, as an insurance that the South Korean police could not readily check our story, if they had any doubt. To the unsuspecting Koreans, we spoke like Japanese, even with a distinct Japanese accent in our Korean. We looked Japanese, except for Taiam's six feet height.

After our brief taste of freedom in Seoul, we knew that our salvation lay in getting away from our home, one way or another. Our unrepentant stepmother assured us that there was no hope of fulfilling our dreams if we stayed in Wonju.

I didn't want to be married off to a local clod, like Duli, couldn't see myself subservient to a mother-in-law, and pretended that there was no other life out there for me beyond the surrounding mountains. My brother knew too that he had no second chance with our stepmother.

We had also heard through the grapevine that Fukui, across the

Sea of Japan, where we had had a happy childhood under our mother's wings, was spared from war devastation unlike the cities on the Pacific coast. Subconsciously we might have been drawn to Japan through the memories of our Fukui home, hoping to recapture the lost paradise.

In 1947, there was no Korean government yet to grant a visa to emigrate anywhere, especially to Japan. The most expedient way was for us to assume Japanese identities. We still had our Japanese names, Matsuko Nagayama for me and Taikan Nagayama for my brother. We would let the Japanese government agency, stationed in Pusan, process us as Japanese nationals. Ever since the end of the war, there had been a stream of Japanese stragglers, military and civilian, trying to reach their homeland from Manchuria and North Korea after missing the initial mass evacuation.

We told our parents that we were going to Seoul to look for work and kept our plan secret in fear that they might try to stop us. Surprisingly, they did not object or ask questions.

My poor brother Taikun. My preoccupation with Taiam's injury and long recovery left him forgotten and out of the loop of our conspiracy. We did not tell him about our harebrained scheme either.

Something told us that what we were about to do was not legal or honest, but we did not know how risky and dangerous an enterprise we were about to undertake.

We traveled on the train from Wonju to Seoul as ordinary Korean passengers in Western clothes with a couple of bundles. As soon as we reached the Eastgate railroad station and melted into the anonymous street crowds in the bustling city, we shed our Korean identities and donned those of Japanese evacuees. While walking from the Eastgate to the main railroad station by the Westgate, our metamorphosis was accomplished simply by covering my head with a somber-colored scarf, which I had often seen done by the Japanese women in the field.

During our plotting days, we took a precaution to take out any hint of the Korean accent which might have crept into our seldom-used Japanese language since the liberation. It paid off. The casual encounters with the Koreans on the city sidewalks convinced us that we were taken as Japanese. The only fear was that we might run into some of the acquaintances from the dental hospital days: my brother's towering height, easily spotted from afar, might give us away.

Finally, we reached the main railroad station, undiscovered and thoroughly used to the new identities. But we were not out of the woods yet. We still had to face the Korean police or the train station officials if we were to get on the train to Pusan. When we approached a railroad official standing on the platform and explained in Japanese that we were trying to reach Pusan to return to Japan, he without hesitation took us personally onto the Pusan-bound train as though he had done this many times already.

The railroad man took time to settle us into our seats, explained our circumstances to the train conductor, and instructed that we be delivered to Pusan safely. The first big test of our masquerade was an unqualified success.

The fellow passengers on the beat-up wooden bench across from our seats were cordial, but left us pretty much alone. No doubt, they took in the conversation between the rail official and the conductor, but showed no hatred nor rancor against their former oppressor. To our relief, our fear of possible assault on the Japanese refugees from vengeful Koreans never materialized.

April is the prettiest time of the year in Korea, especially throughout the rice bowl of South Korea along the west coast and the southern region. We passed through a rich farmland of rice paddies, greening fields, and fruit orchards in full bloom. Spring comes to the Korean South a few weeks earlier than Seoul. On that train, the succulent Southern pears, crunchy apples, and the delicate white peaches were farthest from my mind, and I was a nervous wreck.

Taiam and I were gripped by the fear of discovery and by a growing apprehension of what was awaiting us at the end of the interminable train ride. We needed to catch our breath. Ever since leaving Wonju, we had been on tenterhooks, with no time for eating or resting. Thankfully, our free train ride from Seoul was rather uneventful, but we were not prepared for what happened in Pusan.

As directed by the Pusan station agent, we went straight to an old warehouse building on the pier in the harbor. The Japanese government had their representatives waiting for Japanese nationals straggling in from former colonies in Manchuria and Korea.

When I saw two middle-aged men and one young man warming their hands over the charcoal hibachi in the tatamied section of a spacious, open room, I was suddenly seized with terror. I remembered the same fear I felt before the entrance examiners for a girls' high school in Nagoya in 1942.

Fearfully, Taiam and I related our well-rehearsed story of our narrow escape from the Russians' rapid invasion of North Korea around the time of the Japanese surrender, through the mountains and the countryside, disguised as Koreans. Our uncontrollable stammering and Taiam's height must have tipped them off. The men exchanged suspicious glances and decided to talk to us separately.

They asked my brother about the wound on his chin — he still had a bandage over it — and were trying to engage in general conversation in Japanese to determine his true identity. Then, they turned to me to ask if I was truly his sister. I realized then their point of suspicion. They determined that Taiam was too tall for a Japanese and believed him to be Korean. They suspected that I was his Japanese wife who was trying to smuggle her Korean husband into Japan by pretending to be his sister.

I must have looked Japanese enough, but under the hard-edged questioning, I was completely unnerved and a Korean accent crept back into my responses, thus blowing my cover. Our charade was exposed unmercifully by their sharp eyes and discerning ears.

I don't know why they let us leave without calling the Korean police to punish us for a number of illegal acts we had already committed: false identification, an illegal emigration to Japan, and misleading the Korean railroad. These Japanese officials saw through us as naive kids running away from home and Japan didn't need dumb kids like us to take care of in post-war hard times in the devastated country.

When we left the building late in the afternoon, we felt as if we had escaped, by a hair, from the jaws of a real disaster. We went straight to the railroad station for the next train home, fearful that the Japanese might still report us to the police.

This time, as ordinary Korean passengers, we paid our fares.

Surprisingly, the railroad station employees did not recognize us as the Japanese kids who had asked for directions to the Japanese Evacuation office just a couple of hours before.

Our journey home was depressing and we hardly said a word the whole time on the train. To our family, we must have looked like stray dogs coming home late at night. We never told our parents about our misadventure, and they didn't ask any questions either. We eventually confided in Taikun.

CHAPTER 33

Miss Laird

As spring blossomed into a full growing season, one Sunday our minister announced that the American Mission–owned land between three missionary houses and the main town road was now available to the church members for vegetable growing. The slope had been fallow since the stored sweet potatoes for war fuel were gone. Along with other church families, my family claimed a patch of land big enough to till several rows of potatoes across the slope.

Early summer mornings, still dewy and cool, I carried a ceramic "honey pot" on my head, filled with human manure collected from our latrine, several long blocks from my house. Each of the young potato shoots was fertilized with a wooden dipper. My constant hunger drove me to the demeaning labor which was frowned on for a girl of my class. A small voice in my head told me that honest work was nothing to be ashamed of. Yet, I chose early morning to avoid the townsfolk seeing me this way.

That spring, we planted annual cutting flowers: cockscombs, balsam flowers, and zinnias, in the front courtyard flower bed. In the back garden, we set out corn, green onions, red-leaf lettuce, Chinese cabbage, Daikon, all from seeds. Even the long-stemmed succulent Korean watercress was started in a little ditch next to the well.

After being vacant for a time, the former Japanese teacher's house had a new tenant, a Korean government bureaucrat. He was a married but childless North Korean refugee. We already had several such families in our church with distinct North Korean dialects, arriving in Wonju with nothing but what they could carry on their backs. They were fleeing from the persecution of Christians by the Communist government. These refugees were all Presbyterians but joined our Methodist church, the only Protestant church in the entire region.

That summer, 1947, we heard rumors that the American missionaries were finally coming back to Wonju to reclaim their houses and resume their mission. Shortly after the Japanese military vacated their brick buildings on August 15, 1945, the American military had to repair and restore the plumbing, the wiring, and the wells before their officers and men could occupy them.

After initial delays in the post-war economic chaos, the lack of housing, no postal or banking services set up as yet, and no dependable American groceries and gasoline for automobiles available, American missionaries of all denominations began to slowly filter back into South Korea.

Miss Esther J. Laird, affectionately called Miss Ram by the Wonju people, was one of the second wave of returnees allowed in by General Hodge in 1947. General Hodge not only had to look after the military personnel, but also all American civilians acting as advisors to the Korean leaders who were setting up a new democratic government. The general saw to it that the American missionaries, too, had their necessities taken care of by extending the privileges of the military mail service (APO), and the Post Exchange for groceries and gasoline.

One summer day, one of my girlfriends breathlessly told me that Miss Ram was back in her house. My friend had known her since her kindergarten days, until Miss Ram was forced to leave Korea following Pearl Harbor. I begged my friend to introduce me to her so that I might meet the legendary lady from Ohio, a nurse-turned-missionary, for her wonder work with orphans and abandoned babies.

I already had caught glimpses of her around the town and on my street, driving a magnificent new automobile unlike any I had ever seen in Japan before the war — a large boxy station wagon with woodies — through the bumpy, mud-packed, crooked streets and the milling crowd in the open market. Her driving skill was sorely tested by the primitive road conditions of post-war Korea.

One afternoon, my friend and I went up to her house and knocked on the front door, uninvited and unannounced. A Korean housekeeper, a widow with a school-aged daughter who had worked for Miss Ram before the war, let us in. Nothing could have prepared me for the grand, exotic furnishings of the Western house with well-proportioned, high-ceilinged rooms, and the smell of the house. Intermingled with the smell of the freshly waxed hardwood floor, there was the rich, buttery smell of freshly baked bread. It reminded me of a European bakery displaying pastries in Nagoya before the war.

While I was taking in the fascinating American furniture in the drawing room and the adjoining dining room, a smiling American woman appeared. A petite lady with sparkling blue eyes and short graying blonde hair greeted my friend familiarly in Korean. And I was formally introduced. Little did I know then that this encounter would have a profound impact on my life.

It wasn't just Miss Laird's exquisite gentleness which intrigued me most. It was her genuine politeness toward us teenage girls without the dismissive ways so common in Korean adults toward minors. Unlike the brusque American ladies in the movies, Miss Laird was gracious and welcoming as though we were important guests.

No doubt she was interrupted by us in her busy work to put her house in order after the military occupation for some years, and to set up a new nursery in town for orphaned babies. But she never showed any hint of impatience or irritability. Even her sing-song accent in her good working Korean was charming. I liked her.

Whenever I had time on my hands that summer, I would bring cut flowers to Miss Laird's house since she did not have a chance to plant any flowers herself that summer. This was how our lifelong friendship was forged.

As the summer flowers were fading away, Miss Laird asked me if I could help her in her nursery. I was thrilled. The idea that I would be working with her was an honor even though she had to teach me everything about infant care: how to measure baby formula, warm up the bottles, and hold babies properly. Miss Laird made up the formula with powdered milk, donated by the Ohio Methodist churches, and boiled water from the well. All of this was so new and exotically American. In those days, the only milk the Korean babies depended on was their mother's milk.

So quickly, Miss Laird found a dozen babies, mostly girls, abandoned at their mothers' deaths or illnesses. Their fathers were very reluctant to keep them. She must have known that her rescue operation was slowing down the silent infanticide practiced on girl babies by the boy-crazy Koreans.

Miss Laird had the building owned by the American Methodist Mission, near the city hall in the town center, repaired and cleaned up after its wartime neglect. A major part of it was used for the nursery and infant clinic while a smaller portion was made into a meeting-library room with still bare bookcases against one wall.

There was a small Korean house, one on-dul room and a kitchen, attached to the building for the resident nurse and her family, so that there would be someone on hand for the babies at night. The nurse was a recent arrival from the North with a child but no husband.

There was also a charwoman who kept the wood-burning, iron pot-belly stove going day and night in the nursery all winter. She boiled the water from the well in the kitchen, and kept the place clean with the help of her handyman husband.

As soon as the building was made livable, Miss Laird had twenty wooden cribs, on waist-high legs, constructed by the local carpenters to her specifications. The nursery was an airy, light room with glass windows on three sides, decorated with crisp cotton curtains. She had the cribs well padded and had procured baby clothes, blankets, cloth diapers, and plastic toys from the church ladies in Ohio. Even in the dead of winter, the room was kept toasty warm for the staff's hands and the sleeping babies.

Considering the precarious line of supply for anything those days, it was a near miracle that she managed to keep that many babies fed, bathed, and clothed better than two-parent babies in Korea.

I do remember one particularly sick baby whose mother had died from tuberculosis. She cried incessantly, stirring up the rest of the babies, night and day. To give some rest to the resident nurse and the rest of the babies, Miss Laird took the baby to her house for her personal care at night and her housekeeper's during the day until the baby was stronger and gaining weight. We weighed the babies right after their daily baths and fresh clothes in the morning to see how well they were doing under our care.

I stayed on helping Miss Laird even after the summer turned into autumn and my girlfriends went back to the new girls' high school, opened after the war in Wonju. Now we had separate high schools for boys and girls besides the old agriculture school. A whiff of equality for girls at last.

I don't know exactly when Miss Laird approached me about going to school that fall. Her suggestion hit me like a bolt of lightning out of the blue and my answer was unequivocal.

CHAPTER 34

Methodist Mission School

In spite of appearance, my family could not afford to send me to the Methodist mission school Miss Laird recommended. No problem, she said. She would pay for my tuition and room if my father would pay for my board — one mal, a Korean bushel, of rice per month.

In the postwar turmoil, rice and other precious food commodities acted as currency for commerce for their intrinsic value. I knew even one mal of rice per month was a difficult expense for my father to bear, but I was determined that this minor glitch was not going to quash my last chance for more education. As expected, my stepmother was dead against it, but in the end my bull-headed will won out.

Once again I headed to Seoul, this time for the second semester at the Methodist mission school for women in February 1948. With the postwar fuel shortage, there was a two-month (December and January) hiatus between the first and second semesters so colleges could save on fuel during the coldest winter months.

It was a bone-rattling ride in the unheated train, which, after much delay due to a coal shortage, finally arrived at the Eastgate railroad station near midnight.

Streets were completely deserted, frigid, and pitch dark. There was no taxi or streetcar in sight to take me to my destination. With my suitcase and a bedroll, it was humanly impossible to walk from the eastside to the northside of the city where the school was located. For some reason, the dark, deserted streets did not frighten me.

The only place I knew how to get to with any certainty that night was Seoul Dental College in the town center, roughly a halfway point. So I headed toward that little glimmer of hope, dragging my burdens and stopping to rest as often as I had to in the empty black streets. The streets were deathly quiet except for my footsteps and no policemen in sight, Korean or American, in that deep winter night.

It was in the wee hours of the night that finally I pounded on the front door of the dental college with my fist to arouse somebody from sleep. After an interminable wait, the sleepy-eyed dental assistant friend peered out and let me in, surprised to see me.

He quickly sized up the situation and persuaded the janitor and his wife to let me stay with them in their cramped attic room with a slanting ceiling. He avoided a delicate situation of having a young girl stay in his bachelor quarters, even in an emergency. On my part, I was so exhausted that I would gladly have risked even my reputation.

Never have I had such a warm, peaceful sleep, before or since, in this hastily made-up bed with soiled thick bedding in a stranger's home. In the morning, well rested, I resumed my walk with my burdens to the school in the northside.

Awestruck at the imposing Western stone structure of the mission school, I forgot all about the aching, torturous climb up the unpaved driveway winding up the hillside from the busy city street. The school was perched on a level shelf among trees and bushes, midway up the hill, looking over the bustling, low-lying city sprawl disappearing into a hazy horizon. The school stood as the "shining city on the hill" for my hope and salvation.

The east end of the three-storied structure with a separate entrance was reserved for the American single-woman missionaries' residence. The rest of the building, with its main entrance, was used as a boarding school for the female students and Korean women teachers for now. Before the Pacific war, it used to be the coeducational Methodist seminary.

The main floor had a chapel which doubled as an auditorium,

the school administration office, and classrooms. The second floor had a library where students studied, and the Korean teachers' bedrooms. The third floor was the students' dormitory. In the basement, the kitchen and dining room were at the west end, and the bathroom and toilet for students were at the other end. The cook's family lived in two rooms in between.

Our cook's family was a young, North Korean refugee couple with two small children, a toddler and an infant. An old mother helped out in the kitchen and baby-sat her grandchildren.

The students were a motley crew of young women, mostly recruited by missionaries from town and country. The missionaries had a history of educating the best and brightest Korea could offer, for future leadership in the church and the nation, ever since they had been allowed into the country late in the nineteenth century. These girls came from all walks of life and the Methodist-controlled regions in Korea, even from the North. There was a rosy, high-cheeked peasant girl, a young widow, a crippled spinster from my town, and some Seoul girls with city attitudes.

The mission school or Bible school for women was run under the instructional head of Miss Katherine Cooper and the generalship of Mrs. Anna B. Chaffin, a widow.

Miss Cooper was prevented from returning to her former mission, north of the thirty-eighth parallel, and was waiting for the resolution of the conflicting views between the United States and the Soviet Union on the fate of Korea.

Mrs. Chaffin was a widowed, long-time missionary with an ample bosom and generous nature, with a practical nose for creature comforts. Her tremors from Parkinson's disease did not slow her down one bit in doing anything she wanted.

Both of these ladies were in their sixties and from the American South. Age and birthplace were the only common things they shared. They were, otherwise, exact opposites in physical appearance, personality, and quality of spirituality.

Miss Cooper was the embodiment of pure Christian spiritualism, a self-imposed ascetic. Never married, tall and willowy, she had blue eyes, clear pale skin, and no makeup to mar her soft appearance from her white hair to her toes.

Decades before the Pacific war, she had come to Korea in her early twenties, right after college, for missionary work in a seaport town on the Sea of Japan, north of the thirty-eighth parallel. She too, like all other foreigners, had to endure rude curiosities and natural xenophobia prevalent in feudal Korea.

Many a time, she had to suffer uncouth Koreans pass their hands over her pale blue eyes and touch her lily white skin in her early days of Christian evangelism. Her towering height might have been intimidating to the natives but her gentle, lilting Korean, accompanied by her angelic smile, must have been irresistibly disarming. In her flowing Korean dresses, her preference over Western dresses, she looked like a heavenly creature.

Mrs. Chaffin, on the other hand, was an earthy person for a missionary, her spirituality well concealed by her jovial, outgoing nature, and enjoying all the pleasures of living well, with no apology. We saw her everywhere in her silk brocade Korean robe warding off the chill from her generous size, fussing over the precarious supply of coal to heat the whole building with steam heat. Miraculously, she managed to revive the heating system after the wartime non-use.

In her high-pitched Korean with extra emphasis from an involuntary shaking of her head, she used to scold us for turning on the heat in our bedrooms for the cold nights. By her managerial calculation, the heat rising from the lower floors during the day should have warmed up our bedrooms sufficiently enough to be comfortable by the ten o'clock curfew in the evening, even in the coldest winter days.

In postwar shortages and inflations, Mrs. Chaffin used all her charms and wits to obtain all the necessities of a good table for the students and missionaries living with her in the east end. She was ever vigilant that there be electricity and hot water for the building, more precious commodities than gold in those days.

Miss Cooper and Mrs. Chaffin were a classic study in contrast, but sisters under the skin in running the boarding school for the mission. Miss Cooper took full charge of the spiritual needs and Mrs. Chaffin, the mortal side. They were the perfect team.

Mrs. Che-Hong — the wife of the Reverend Hong who was away

in America, doing an advanced study in church ministry — was our housemother in charge of housekeeping, meals, and living arrangements for the students and Korean teachers. According to tradition, she kept her maiden name even after her marriage, but we called her "Sunsen [teacher]-nim," nim being a gender-neutral honorific suffix.

She, her husband, and her aging mother fled North Korea as the Russians and Korean Communists swept through their town after the end of the war. With the help of their American missionary connection, they resettled in Seoul, with an American scholarship for her husband and a job for her at our school in his absence.

She and her mother, an older version of Mrs. Che-Hong, lived in an oversized closet next to the school library on the second floor and took meals with us. Mrs. Che-Hong was a delicate, small-boned woman with a refined, chiseled look, in her thirties, childless. Her wire-rimmed glasses made her look like a delicate bird. Her dainty appearance, however, belied her keen intellect and iron will. Nothing escaped her sharp eyes, whether it be dust on the windowsills or guilty excuses for being late from Sunday outings.

Mrs. Che-Hong oversaw the menus, the purchases of groceries for two dozen students and the Korean staff, and figured out how to incorporate donated American canned food into Korean cooking. American powdered milk and canned meat were cleverly Koreanized in cooking to supplement our calcium and protein-deficient diet.

For a long time, we had a hot rice gruel made of powdered milk, rice and water boiled together, served up with ever-present kimchi, for breakfast. She had our own kimchis made in giant stone jars in the fall, using our cook and their aged mothers, just like any other Korean household.

Her mother, in her seventies, was an unobtrusive, helping hand in the kitchen, and a gentle grandmotherly presence to homesick students. She negotiated the broad stairs from her second floor bedroom to the basement kitchen many times a day, gingerly clinging to the banisters. She was never in anyone's way and carefully avoided being crushed by students rushing to classes and meals, summoned by the handbell.

Miss Esther Park, a second generation Korean born in America, came to Korea to resuscitate the YWCA after the war. She was a quintessential American in every way except for her Korean face. Her Korean was practically nonexistent, poorest of all the American missionaries living with us. English was her native tongue. Her stylish dresses and jaunty hats on her slim, tallish frame cut a rather fashionable silhouette among the conservatively dressed missionaries.

While the missionaries had to rely mostly on the military jeeps to get around, Miss Park had a large black Buick sedan, which she drove around with such a flair. Even though she had a room on the Korean side of the second floor, she took all her meals with the American ladies and used the bathroom in the American end. Her Americanized stomach could not tolerate the hot, spicy Korean fare.

The east end was a little America with an American kitchen and Korean cook who knew how to roast and make pies in the wood-burning iron stove. The bathrooms were all equipped with hot and cold tap water. The bulky Western furnishings in the drawing room, dining room and individual bedrooms completed their Americana way of life. Its own entrance marked the separateness of their personal life from that of the Koreans.

Before the Pacific war, Mrs. Che worked with Miss Cooper in a North Korean seaport town. Now as a refugee, she was living with her daughter, an Ewha college student, on the second floor, and took meals with us. Being a student at the prestigious, first women's college, Miss Che took pains to let us know that she was better than we even though she had to share the basement bathroom and toilet for bathing and laundry with us.

For a time, we had a former Ewha college instructor for public health living with us while waiting for paperwork to be processed for her advanced study in America. It wasn't her rosy health with blooming cheeks and scrubbed look but her pathological obsession with all the invisible germs which made an unforgettable impression on me.

To fill her time, she gave us lectures on health matters, but her mortal fear of those pesky, insidious germs on doorknobs and commonly used furniture warned us of imminent dangers we were in from unsuspected sources. She always carried a clean handkerchief ready to wipe the doorknobs, to cover the eraser for the blackboard, and to dust off chairs before sitting on them. She never accepted money from anybody, except on a tissue.

Her apparent good health, however, did not improve her sour disposition. Red-faced from hard scrubbing or zeal, she was wont to rant and rave about our not washing our hands often enough and turned herself into a nag in no time. After a while, we simply didn't hear her.

For our own good, luckily we did not escape totally from her crusade about good hygiene. All the students and staff including the cook's family had to take American manufactured pills to kill intestinal parasites which were contracted through raw or undercooked fresh vegetables grown with human waste, the only fertilizer used by Korean farmers. With kimchi being part of every meal and the fresh lettuce-wrapped rice marking the coming of summer for Koreans, the parasites were an unavoidable price to pay for our way of life.

We forewent one meal, usually the Sunday breakfast. When the intestinal worms were hungry with their mouths wide open for food, they got bellyfuls of poison instead. The procedure was quite effective, but had to be repeated at least once a year. In Korea, the intestinal parasites were a national problem affecting rich or poor, city or country, indiscriminately.

The academic work was not that taxing, intellectually speaking, but simply time consuming. There were classes for Old and New Testaments, Korean grammar, English, hygiene, and music lessons in organ playing.

There was a great deal of memorizing passages of the Bible so that one could quote any appropriate verse and chapter to fit any particular situation or lesson offered. No critical thinking was required or encouraged, and the orthodox Christian dogmas were accepted as the absolute truths. There was no mathematics, no science, no physical education.

The school life was a lark for me, away from gnawing hunger, Taiam's tragedy, and above all my stepmother. Our strictly regulated day started with early morning cleaning chores before breakfast. Classes began promptly at eight o'clock in the morning and ended at three o'clock in the afternoon, with a one-hour lunch break at twelve, Tuesday through Saturday. There was no school on Monday. After supper, the daily vespers brought students and teachers together once again in the chapel. There was barely enough time for all the assignments to be done in the library before ten o'clock curfew. On rotation, students did the dining room duties of serving and dishwashing.

There were no radios or record players allowed to lighten up the regimented life. Also there was an unspoken ban on any cosmetics on our faces.

Dating was not forbidden, but frowned on. One Sunday afternoon, one of my classmates, a widow in her twenties, was spotted by Miss Cooper walking up the hillside with a man. The young man happened to be a student at the nearby Methodist seminary, recently opened in temporary quarters.

That evening, she was called in by our housemother, Mrs. Che-Hong, for questioning. It turned out that both came from the same country church, and, to the young woman's misfortune, the seminary student was already married. Their meeting might have been completely innocent and purely social, but Miss Cooper did not tolerate even an appearance of impropriety. I saw the young widow in tears, packing her things the next morning. She had been summarily expelled from the school.

We had several girls attending the Methodist seminary, living with us on the third floor. Even though they were students at the coeducational institution, they did not have any male students calling on them for dates. We had no lounge to receive them. The Korean society itself did not know how to deal with the revolutionary idea of unchaperoned dating between sexes, the latest import from America with the American occupation forces and Hollywood movies. It was waging a valiant holding action against the waves of the new morality, an alien idea in the postwar turbulence, but it was a losing battle.

I could not quite understand other girls complaining bitterly about our bad food. To me, the food was plentiful and nourishing, served predictably like clockwork, far better than anything I had had at home since my family returned from Japan.

I was finally happy and excelled in my studies. I was in my own element.

Meanwhile, South Korea was having the first ever democratic election under the supervision of the United Nations for the national assembly on May 10, 1948. After agonizing over what to do with Korea since the end of the Pacific war, the United States decided to shed its responsibility for Korea under the constrains of downsized military forces and the low strategic priority assigned to Korea by the Pentagon in 1947. At the same time, the United States was not about to offer South Korea on a silver platter to the Russians either. Since the Soviet Union refused to participate in the United Nations–sponsored elections in Korea, the United States went ahead with its own plan for the South.

The independence-hungry Koreans registered to vote in record numbers, eighty percent out of the eligible voters. Ninety percent of the registered voted for the historical election. Syngman Rhee was elected from Seoul by ninety percent of assembly district votes, and subsequently elected by the newly constituted national assembly to be the first president of the government of South Korea in July 1948.

The Communists did everything to sabotage the elections by killing about one hundred people around the polling places. They failed to disrupt the voting or dampen the people's patriotic fervor.

I was ineligible to vote in Seoul, but the excitement was palpable in my school; the Korean teachers, older students, and even our cook all went to vote.

Our summer vacation started in July, passed through the height of summer in August, and took in some of September, in deference to the demands of the rural economy — the rice harvest time. I hated to leave school even for a vacation, but I made up my mind to survive three months somehow.

Miss Laird put me to work at the nursery right away. Then, I noticed that, in my absence, she had spruced up the library of the mission building and stocked up the bookcases with some books donated by Ohio churches. She even had a young missionary teaching English and American folk songs to the vacationing high school students.

The new missionary was in her early twenties, fresh out of

college, the most graceful and statuesque Western woman I had ever seen. She was at least six feet tall, but well proportioned with an exquisitely sculpted face and proud carriage.

Her English class was coeducational, but the boys and girls were, like water and oil, separated by the invisible force of social taboo. With no makeup on her face, not even lipstick on her well-defined thin mouth, and her hair loose on her shoulders, she gave the timid students the feel of informality and easy access to the English language and herself. Perhaps her young age made us more comfortable and her inability to speak Korean as yet gave us the sense of equality, in handicap.

Our young missionary also had a good voice and introduced us to the old American favorites — "You Are My Sunshine," "Old McDonald Had a Farm," a round of "Row, Row, Row Your Boat." Soon our library became an American singing fest.

Among the books on the shelves, I came across *Uncle Tom's Cabin* by Harriet Beecher Stowe. Even though I did not know some of the words and had difficulty in comprehending some of the American scenes in cultural and historical terms, the story itself was gripping. So emotionally wrenching that even today I could see the hair-raising escape of a slave, jumping from one ice floe to the next, floating on the frigid Ohio River, for the freedom in Ohio from the slave state of Kentucky.

As the summer moved on, I began to notice definite changes in our English teacher's appearance. She came to the library with her hair curled, wearing lipstick. Her long bare legs were shaved clean, and even her toes were painted red in her sandals. She began to teach us in her pretty summer dresses, revealing her slender neck and white arms.

Then one day, I saw her walking downtown with an American soldier who was as tall as she, holding hands. The mystery was solved.

After the late 1945 withdrawal of the American occupation force from Wonju, there remained a small unit in town for the interim military government. Somehow Sergeant Wood must have come across my beautiful teacher in that little Korean town, and fallen in love under exotic and improbable circumstances.

I didn't stay in Wonju beyond summer vacation to find out what happened to the romance, but in 1952, my teacher came to see me, a patient at the National Jewish Hospital in Denver, Colorado, as Mrs. Wood. That was the last time I saw her on her way to or from Tacoma, Washington, where she made a home with Sergeant Wood.

That summer, Mrs. Charles Stokes became my conversational English tutor. Dr. Charles Stokes was an old Korean hand, reared by missionary parents in Korea, and more fluent in the Korean language than I. He was also a musician, playing hymns and classical pieces equally well, either on piano or organ. His young wife, Irene, was rather new at missionarying and struggled with Korean as I did with English.

One hour a week with Mrs. Stokes was more than a foreign language lesson in her beautifully appointed living room with chintz covered furnishings. It was a time for me to soak up the elusive thing called the American ambiance through my pores.

She was from Kentucky, soft and genteel in her speaking and mannerisms, which had the effect of rounding off all the sharp, guttural sounds of Korean words and expressions. From the leisurely small talks with her that summer, I had a distinct feeling that she was homesick for her home and sisters back in America, while trying to fill her life with a child of her own.

By that summer, we had another young couple, Mr. and Mrs. M. O. Burkholder, who occupied the middle missionary house, which was more elegantly furnished than the other two. I smelled private money of their own. I am not quite sure what particular mission work they were engaged in, but one incident in our church brings back to me the feel and flavor of the time in which we were living that summer.

One Sunday, our congregation was treated to a rare recital of a duet with an organ and a violin. Dr. Stokes played the portable organ and a Korean assistant to Mr. Burkholder, the violin. They played "Barcarole" from Jacques Offenbach's "Gaieté Parisienne," enrapturing the whole congregation on that beautiful morning.

The violinist had recently come from Seoul with his attractive young wife and their infant to work with Mr. Burkholder. The assistant turned out to be quite a handsome man with his urbane ways and curly luscious hair, more befitting an artist than a church worker.

As the recital was over and the people were leaving the church, there was a loud outburst of angry voices exchanged between the violinist's wife and the wife of our church elder. From the self-righteous accusation by the older woman and the tearful response of the young woman, I managed to understand the cause of the unseemly disturbance marring an otherwise beautiful summer Sunday.

It was revealed that the violinist left his first wife, who happened to be the niece of our church elder, to marry the current wife. As far as the elder's family was concerned, the new wife was nothing but a homewrecker or worse. It was odd that the same elder who took advantage of our Japanese neighbor's wife in the aftermath of the Japanese surrender would pass judgment on someone else's ethical lapses.

For me, even the unpleasant ending could not diminish the delicious sensation of being bathed in the dreamy melodies of Offenbach. For some years after that morning, I did not know who the composer was, nor what opus the music came from, but I always carried with me the melodic strains of "Barcarole."

The return of our missionaries signaled the onset of the postwar American generosity in CARE packages reaching the far corners of Korea, like Wonju with its ragged people.

Our townsfolk were liberally showered with used clothes of all conceivable varieties and second-hand shoes in good condition. Our church congregation had the first pick of everything because the missionaries used our church as the main distribution conduit. Soon a dispute arose, indignantly advanced by my father, that the best things were taken by the church leaders including the minister himself.

For the first time, I saw a bra. Up to that time I did not know that I was supposed to tame my growing breasts from bouncing around so freely beneath my summer dress. Ironically in the country where public nakedness was viewed as a cardinal offense, a woman's exposed breasts escaped societal condemnation. Nursing babies — anywhere and anytime, in the field, on the market street, or on the train — was regarded as natural as eating. A woman's breasts, stripped of any lascivious connotation, were simply baby food on the hoof.

It was like bringing back the 1930s prewar world to see a woman's high heels. I hadn't seen any since my stepmother wore hers to church in Japan before World War II, before the Japanese government ban on all things American. I tried on a pair of high heels with my summer dress and was pleased to see the slimming effect they had on my plump legs. In Japan, clunky girls' legs were called daikon legs from sitting on legs all the time. It took some practice to walk around on tiptoes, in heels and with confidence.

After years of drab, wartime clothes, the American clothes were like sunbursts of exuberant colors, imaginative designs, and infinite styles. We knew then that the war had ended.

The peddlers in the open market sported suit jackets or heavy overcoats, men's or women's indiscriminately, to ward off the Korean winter cold. Even the farmers were seen tilling their land in Western hand-me-downs, and the housewives did their laundry at the river in men's tweed jackets.

Just before returning to school in the fall, Mrs. Stokes surprised me with a school wardrobe: skirts with matching jackets, versatile blouses, underclothes and even nylon stockings, the essence of Western fashion, daring to be chic. A pair of beautifully made penny loafers completed my Cinderella outfit.

In the fall of 1948, I returned to the mission school for the second year. The austere, gray stone building of the school was like an old friend waiting for me with welcoming arms wide open.

But no sooner had I settled into the academic routine than the whole school was afloat with rumors that our days in that building were numbered. Our mission school for women was to be moved to another location, a couple of miles farther north, into a more residential area for the next semester, February 1949.

Already Miss Cooper had picked out a fairly spacious Korean house. Seven on-dul rooms of good size, a large kitchen and a gated courtyard were to accommodate two dozen boarding students, the resident housemother, Mrs. Che, with her Ewha College daughter, and the new cook with her family.

The stone building was to revert back to the Methodist seminary, whose curriculum included two years of the preparatory school. It was announced that the entrance examination for the preparatory and the seminary would be given in April of 1949.

There was no question that I wanted to try for the prep school and eventually go on to the seminary as I was about to graduate from the mission school in the spring. Since the seminary took only four-year high school graduates, the prep school was to even out the spotty educational backgrounds of some of the aspirants like me with only a middle school education. I felt lucky to be taken as a candidate for prep school before the rigorous demands of seminary.

There was no time to waste, preparing for the exams on world history reaching back into the Babylonian and Assyrian civilizations in Mesopotamia, English, Korean history, and even current events. While I was carrying my full course works at the mission school, reading for exams began in earnest. Passing the entrance exams became my consuming obsession from then on.

During the fall semester, one Sunday Taiam came to see me at school unexpectedly. He had come to Seoul after I had left for school, looking for work in the city. My breakaway for independence must have given him hope and courage, pushing him out of Wonju. On his own, he found a practicing acupuncturist who was willing to take him on as his assistant in the sprawling suburban area across the Han River, which skirts around the south edge of Seoul. From him, I also learned that Taikun was enrolled at the Wonju high school for boys.

In the fall semester, I had Mrs. William E. Shaw as our English teacher. Dr. Shaw and his wife were old-timers as missionaries, having spent their entire adult lives in Korea since before World War II. They were fluent in Korean, and knew the culture and its people like the natives.

Dr. Shaw and his wife were a well-matched couple, both being tall, big-boned, and well-muscled without being fat. To ordinary Koreans on the street, they were a formidable presence, even scary, if it had not been for Dr. Shaw's utterly charming, warm smile and loud, hearty way of talking in our native tongue. Mrs. Shaw was a little restrained and even austere. Her infrequent smiles were meant to meet the minimum requirement of the occasion. Nevertheless, they were a perfect couple in their dedication to their calling.

Mrs. Shaw wanted to teach us English by phonetics. Most of my classmates had not been exposed to the English language as I had, in grammar, vocabulary or enunciations. They had to learn English cold turkey. She asked the whole class to sound out the sentences she wrote on the blackboard and expected us, after a few repetitions, to understand the meanings and replicate the sounds correctly. Without the basic foundation of grammar, vocabulary, and associated sounds, the class was completely at sea. Except me.

Reluctantly I ended up answering all the questions put to the class and unwittingly became proof that the new theory on language did not work with the class. We all could see her increasingly frustrated and irritated at the blank looks of my classmates.

Mrs. Shaw would hiss, with great emphasis on the "L," "Listen," thinking that if the girls were hearing all the sounds articulated clearly, they might catch on. After all, human infants learned to talk by repeated sounds, didn't they? Her experiment was a valiant effort on her part but a dismal failure. We never went beyond "This is an apple" stage before the semester was over, mercifully for both teacher and students.

Dr. Shaw and his wife later gave the ultimate sacrifice to the Korean cause in their son's tragic death during the Korean War. Their son, William Hamilton Shaw, was studying at Drew Seminary, but shortly after the North Korean invasion on June 25, 1950, he was assigned to the staff of General Douglas MacArthur, commander of the Allied forces, and later as his interpreter for the Inchon landing. He was killed just outside of Seoul.

I was so engrossed in my studies and preparation for the entrance exams that I remember only two things happening that semester.

One unusually cold night, just before the Christmas recess, several of us decided to break the ten o'clock curfew. We stealthily sneaked down from our third floor bedrooms, tiptoeing past the housemother's bedroom next to the second floor landing, to the still warm kitchen in the basement, to study for our final exams by candlelight.

Our kitchen had a huge Korean oven, waist-high and made of mud encased in cement, against an outer wall. It was big enough to hold three, two-feet-in-diameter, black iron kettles in a row with three separate wood-burning holes under these kettles. To take the cooking steam and smell out of the building, there was a giant tin vent hood hanging over the kettles. After the full day of cooking, the oven was kept warm long after the six o'clock supper, and the kitchen was the warmest spot during the cold winter night.

One of my co-conspirators was a big-boned, rosy-cheeked country girl who decided to crawl under the vent hood into the warmest space between two kettles and study cross-legged with her book on her legs, like a Buddha. The rest of us sat on the edge of the warm oven, legs dangling, and started to read quietly by the candlelight. Warmed by the oven and thrilled by our daring act, we felt as deliciously wicked as blood sisters.

Suddenly, somebody heard the swinging dining room door squeak, and we all stopped to listen for footsteps but didn't hear a thing. As we relaxed, the door to the kitchen burst open and our housemother was standing in the doorway in her nightgown and slippers with a flashlight.

In an instant, pandemonium broke loose. Books and papers flew, and flailing arms and legs struggled to get off the oven. The peasant girl sitting on the top of the oven got up, hitting her head against the vent with a big bong, one foot stepping on one of the kettles and letting fly the iron lid, which crash-landed on the concrete floor with ear-splitting clamor.

Mrs. Che-Hong was as stunned as we by the noisy stand the girl made. She was absolutely transfixed with one foot in the kettle, scarlet-faced, her petrified eyes bulging out of her skull, and her gaping mouth letting out a silent scream. It seemed an eternity before our housemother collected herself and found her voice to march us back to our cold bedrooms. She did not scold us as we expected but with a fleeting glance, I saw her smother a chuckle in her attempted stern look.

Another thing I remember was the Christmas play we students put on just before we went home for the winter vacation. The play was about the conversion of a self-indulgent, spoiled daughter of the Roman commander who ruled over Jerusalem after the execution of Jesus. To her father's horror, her chance contact with the outlawed followers of Jesus led to her conversion to Christianity.

I suspect that one reason Miss Cooper chose me to play the commander's daughter was that I could memorize her long dialogues without much trouble. Furthermore, her sharp, perceptive mind might have detected a worldly inclination in me to play the role convincingly.

For the first time in my life, I wore a long Western evening gown, borrowed from one of the young missionaries, with a revealing, low neckline. It made me feel glamorous, like a Hollywood star.

While still in school, I caught a cold which was aggravated by the heavy burden of schoolwork, reading for the entrance exams, school finals, and the Christmas play. During the Christmas vacation, I got worse at home. My head was woolly, my throat was aflame, my ears were stopped up, and my tongue could taste nothing. I had full-blown pneumonia. I had trouble breathing and felt so spent that I just wanted to lie down and sleep all the time.

But I did not want to admit to myself, nor to my family that I was very sick, afraid that I might be prevented from studying for the exams and, worse, going back to school. My fierce determination, however, kept my glazed eyes glued to the series of European crusades to take back Jerusalem from the infidels during the Middle Ages. Somewhere in my enfeebled mind, there was a voice saying that passing the exams was the key to my future.

I should have turned down the pleas from the wife of my girlfriend's brother, the watch merchant, for help in the kitchen. During the Korean New Year holiday season, her maid went home to celebrate with her own family in the country. The young wife with a high school education, a snob, didn't want to take up the slack and enlisted me instead to cook for her family. My girlfriend was away at nursing school at Severance Hospital–Medical School in Seoul.

There was no talk of any wages, but an understanding that I would eat with them. To the starving and cold, the offer was too good to be turned down. I had to will myself to get up at the crack of the cold winter dawn to cook the typical Korean breakfast of freshly steamed rice, hot soup, and some side dishes. I forced myself to eat as much as I could without tasting anything. They took care of their light lunch, but I prepared their more elaborate dinner. I had no lunch at home. The food-for-cooking job lasted until I went away to school in February.

I hated it the minute I laid eyes on the new school house, an old tile-roofed, typical Korean residential structure with a wooden gate. It just didn't look like a school should look. I didn't like the living arrangements of sleeping on the on-dul floor on our own pallets and turning the room into a classroom in the morning by putting away our sleeping gear in the closets. I missed the Western, narrow bed in the seminary building. I thought everything was so uninstitutional and improper for a school setting and the serious purpose of learning.

I didn't like our housemother, Mrs. Che, whose unusually high, rosy cheekbones looked like stuffed lumps, making her more a comical than an authority figure. Her stuck-up daughter, an Ewha student, did not help easing the gulf we felt between them and us, even though we had to live in cramped space under the same roof.

The new cook wasn't as good as the cook we left behind in the old building, but I stuffed myself at each meal, determined to get rid of my lingering cold. Slowly, my taste buds were returning and my ears were opening up some, but I felt weak and exhausted all the time. I kept my physical condition all to myself, and kept up my late night studying for exams, come hell or high water.

In April 1949, I returned to the old seminary building for two days of entrance examinations. The exams were on the histories of the world and Korea, English, and Composition. I remember only a few questions now: on the European crusades to the Holy Land during the medieval age and on the Berlin blockade. I wasn't sure which Berlin blockade, the one in the final days of World War II or the 1948-49 Russian blockade. Later I found out that the examiner had the current blockade in mind. By not reading the current newspapers I missed the question by writing about the earlier World War II blockade.

For Korean composition, the school asked why I wanted to enter the seminary. Citing the miraculous conversion of St. Paul to

Christianity on his way to Damascus, I, too, wanted to serve God, as revealed by Jesus and his Gospels. All I could muster, however, was one page of my heart-felt determination to serve and couldn't risk writing anymore. I didn't have much confidence in articulating my thoughts in Korean then and I was trying to mask my inadequacy with sincerity.

It worked. I passed the inquisitions and was all set to return to *my* school, except for the last hurdle — a complete physical exam, including lung X-rays.

The X-rays taken at the Severence Hospital–Medical School revealed what I feared most, suspiciously cloudy spots on my lungs. My walking pneumonia had done its damage and left unmistakable marks. Dr. Hyungki J. Lew, the president of the Methodist Seminary, called me into his office to assure me of admission to the prep school in the fall on one condition: that my lungs should be rested and cured during the intervening summer. I was home free.

CHAPTER 35

Summer of 1949

When my medical verdict came down, I was swiftly removed from the school without much ado. I did not bother to ask about my graduation from the mission school in June, a moot point.

I was instructed to meet with my sponsor, Miss Laird, who happened to be in town, staying at the Grey House. The Grey House was used as housing for single-women Methodist missionaries, and doubled as hotel accommodations for the ladies who worked outside Seoul but had to come into town for supplies and meetings. The red-brick house was near the historical church, Chung Dong Methodist Church, which was right behind the old Kyong Puk Palace.

Chung Dong Methodist Church was the first Methodist church in Korea, built by the Reverend Henry G. Appenzeller in 1898. It was a Western red-brick building and became the model for the Methodist churches in Korea. Over the years, it had become a hotbed of breeding Korean leaders for national politics as well as the church.

My school friend's grandfather, the Reverend Phong Hyun Choi, was the first pastor in 1902, and her father was an officer in the court of the last Yi dynasty king. An old photograph shows him as a young man, unsmiling and serious, in his royal court costume with a sword at his side.

The American Methodist mission, like other Christian denominations, recruited the best and brightest from the yangban classes for leadership training. It was no accident that the first president of the Republic of South Korea, Syngman Rhee, was from this class.

On that bright spring day, coming home with Miss Laird in her Ford Woodie station wagon was an outing I will never forget. An impromptu picnic, American style, was exactly what I needed to wipe out the long, hard months of studies and fighting illness. The Grey House cook packed us a picnic basket of sandwiches, hard-boiled eggs, pickles, vegetable sticks, and cookies. I had never before had American celery, whose stalks were rather stringy, compared to the Korean variety grown in water.

Years later, when I was reading *The Wind in the Willows* to my young sons and came to the joyous spring picnic Ratty and Moley had after the dusty spring cleaning, I could not help hearing the echoes of my own first American picnic.

From her frequent trips to Seoul, Miss Laird found a shortcut to the eighty-mile trip between Wonju and Seoul through rather precarious backcountry roads. Since the countryside was still thawing out under the warm spring sun after the hard winter, the roads were muddy in places and, for the most part, too narrow for a car and oxen-driven wagon to pass each other.

Eventually we had to cross the Han River at some point. It originates from southeast headwaters deep in the central mountain range and empties into Inchon harbor, rushing past the southern edge of Seoul on its way to the Yellow Sea. Away from the populated urban area, the river did not have any bridges to speak of. The local people had to improvise their own crossings by rigging rafts with wood beams and heavy ropes for the local traffic, sturdy enough to transport carts, beasts, and people. Our Woodie and local farmers crossed the river on a raft at the point where the water was too deep for fording.

At another place on our route, Miss Laird placed two heavy planks over a small stream to reach the next country road. It was an amazing sight to see her maneuver her big car precisely on the planks onto the solid ground, with me standing in front, signaling with my hands. She always carried these planks in her car as an instant bridge. As we approached home, she told me that she had a plan for my medical condition.

While I was in school, Miss Laird was busy building the first sanitarium for tuberculosis in Wonju region, among the pines in the southwest hillside of the town. Initially, she had six modest wooden cabins, three for patients, one for the kitchen, one for the medical office, and the last one for the outdoor privy, separated a little ways from the rest.

I was one of her first patients. The patient cabin had two windows looking out into the wooded hillsides. It had an unpolished wooden floor, and uninsulated board walls to let in the pine-scented forest air unimpeded. A bunk bed was built against one wall, and a bedside table and chair were provided for meals on the tray. Plenty of bedding was piled on the bed to ward off the chilly night air.

This was a rest I needed badly, a retreat from everything and everybody. Surprisingly, my parents were amenable to Miss Laird's suggestion to care for me at her sanitarium. Despite my father's misgivings about the efficacy of the Western rest-cure for tuberculosis, he was willing to try anything for his ailing daughter.

I thrived on being sequestered in my little cabin with the Bible and light reading brought by my visiting family. I was fed on nutritious meals of high protein: milk, meats, and vitamins. Sleeping all night undisturbed under the warm blankets with pine-scented night air seeping through the cracks in the boards, taking a daily nap in the afternoon, and just being idle were sheer luxury beyond my wildest expectation. No question, this treatment was a mere play, compared to my father's acupuncture remedy I endured right after the war.

While I was preoccupied with my school and health problem, my father had a once-in-a-lifetime adventure of his own — an audience with the president of South Korea, Mr. Syngman Rhee. After corresponding with the president earlier in the spring and with his form reply in hand, my father hopped on the train to Seoul and showed up at the presidential residence without any appointment.

His guileless audacity won over the president's aides against their better judgment and he was given a fifteen-minute audience. It was an emotional encounter he would recount again and again for the rest of his life.

He took a box of the best quality ginseng he could find in the market as a gift to the president. Mr. Rhee needed vigor and good health to carry out the heavy responsibilities of a newborn country after 40 years' subjugation. "Forty years" because my father always traced the loss of the Korean nationhood to 1905 Russo-Japanese war mediation by President Theodore Roosevelt, not to the 1910 annexation. Teddy Roosevelt, fearing the ravenous Japanese imperial expansion in the Pacific, particularly in the Philippine islands, attempted to mollify Japan by permitting her to take Korea as her war prize.

Along with the U.S. government, my father was very concerned about an aged president then in his seventies. Besides, there were obvious effects on his health from the prison torture he had suffered at the hands of the puppet government of the Yi dynasty under the thumbs of the Japanese for his Korean independence movement around the turn of the century. Ever since, whenever Mr. Rhee was emotionally distressed, he was known to blow on his fingertips unconsciously. One of the tortures he underwent was to have his fingernails pulled off, one by one. At one time, he was sentenced to life imprisonment, but was released by the 1904 amnesty.

In spite of my father's confessed ignorance of Syngman Rhee's underground agitation while being questioned by the Japanese secret police during the Pacific war, my father was well aware of the patriot's long struggle for Korean independence from foreign dominance since his 1912 self-exile. He could not return home from America where he was visiting, being warned of the Japanese warrant for his arrest.

I could easily imagine that my father couldn't have said much to Mr. Rhee once he was in his presence. His joy of seeing the president would have dissolved his composure into free-flowing tears.

Every day Miss Laird visited the sanitarium to take our temperatures and check on our progress. I had two fellow patients, a middle-aged man and a housewife in her thirties, but we stayed in our own cabins and were discouraged from socializing as a medical precaution. I could feel strength returning to my body in June and July. Finally, Miss Laird thought I could go home, provided that I continued resting for the remainder of the summer.

Knowing that I could not get the kind of peace of mind I needed at home, I asked to be sent to my cousin Youngii's family in Pohang.

He was then married with two small children. My illness seemed to give me an unmitigated gall to assert myself, and my family simply acquiesced to whatever I demanded, no matter how impossible it might have been.

On the train to Pohang, I felt I was finally going home to my true roots after five years as an exile in a foreign province. This was the first holiday in five years for me to spend the whole month with my cousin's family, to see my dear aunt, and to go to the beach.

From the train, I could see all the dry rice paddies green with maturing rice stalks, bowed slightly with budding grains swaying in the August sun. This was the time the farmers and townsfolk enjoyed the cornucopia of the summer garden: cucumbers, eggplants, zucchinis, new potatoes, watermelons, and yellow, smooth-skinned Asian melons. I smelled the pungent sun-ripening yellow melons from the train.

For the farmers and their families, August was a nature-forced slack between the feverish planting and rice harvesting, relishing the fruits of the earth, cooled off by the cold watermelon chilled in a basket kept in the deep well, and indulging in a languid pace of summer days.

Youngii's family was living in the former Japanese teacher's house in the residential part of Pohang, just a couple of blocks away from the elementary school where he had advanced to teach the sixth grade.

It was a modest, one-story house with only two rooms: one ondul room and a small tatamied room which was cornered by the main room and the kitchen. The kitchen was typically Japanese with a wooden platform and a wood-burning oven on the concrete floor. There was a small, enclosed backyard, just big enough to have a water pump and clothesline criss-crossing overhead.

The family had a scullery maid in her teens to do most of the housework while baby-sitting. The girl was perpetual motion from morning till night. She was a wedding gift from Youngii's father-in-law, the wealthy owner of a fishing fleet, who saw that a schoolteacher's salary didn't go too far toward maintaining his daughter's accustomed life of leisure and her unsoiled white hands. The house was another wedding present from her family.

Youngii's wife was not a beauty by any stretch of the imagination, but she was a good catch for any young man, particularly for a man with a humble beginning like my cousin. He was the most sought-after heartthrob in town, but he used his head, not heart, to pick his future wife. Thus, he assured himself and his offspring improved social standing and financial stability.

She was a typical rich man's daughter, unaccustomed to any kind of work and with unblemished white skin. She still had a languid air of wealth, in spite of being the wife of a poorly paid schoolteacher. Her high school education was no more than a social requirement for good marriage and her intellectual pretension was given up altogether at her wedding.

In time, as expected, she produced a son and a daughter, and my cousin was all set to live the preordained but contented life of the middle class professional. Their four-year-old boy was a spitting image of his father with a comely yet serious look, and their one-year-old daughter resembled her mother in her plump, self-satisfied way.

I shared the small tatamied room with the maid for sleeping until one day Youngii's unmarried younger brother, also a schoolteacher in the rural school, came to visit. The maid and I then moved to the big room for sleeping, joining Youngii's family. Shortly my cousin's mother came to see me from the country where she still farmed with the help of her rich farmer lover.

Nights became hot and sticky for all seven of us, three generations sleeping on the oil-papered floor, packed like proverbial sardines, decently covered for propriety in the sweltering August heat. We had to endure the sleepless nights followed by debilitating, scorching days of a heat wave, with no electric fans to ease sweating.

At one point, Youngii's wife couldn't stand it any longer, and went home to her parents with her children and husband for a few days, leaving the rest of us to fend for ourselves.

I felt guilty, causing such discomfort for my cousin. After a couple of weeks, I could sense that I was fast becoming the well-known smelly fish, especially to the poor overworked maid, but I had to stay until my train ticket was sent from home.

To Youngii and my aunt, I must have changed greatly for the worse in the past five years. I was a young girl of marriageable age and to their dismay I had become a Christian zealot, reading the Bible every day and offering a silent prayer before every meal, while the family politely waited, not knowing what else they could do. My relatives on both sides remained adamantly Buddhist, particularly after hearing the horror stories that my siblings and I had to suffer under my Christian stepmother.

They could not see any good coming from the foreign religion when it could not even keep peace in the family. After all, my handsome brother almost died and I had to leave home aided by the helping hands of foreigners. They feared for my future and what would become of us, the orphaned kids. My visit did not reassure them and they saw only dark clouds on our horizon.

Perhaps my relatives' anxiety over my future in the postwar world was further heightened by the tragic death of my first cousin on my father's side, the farm boy in Uchong-myon, my birthplace. My cousin Che was caught up in the Communist campaign of subversion to take South Korea after being stopped at the thirty-eighth parallel by the Americans. After the war, the North Koreans sent out saboteurs, assassins, spies, and recruiters to indoctrinate the young and the malcontents of the South. My farm cousin Che was a perfect target for the Communist indoctrination. Back in the summer of 1944, I saw the brooding rage against his family's hardship and poverty after his father's untimely death.

In no time he became the leader of the local communist cell, attacking rural police stations, killing local government officials, and sabotaging the electrical or telephone lines whenever possible. They made general havoc out of an otherwise tranquil countryside.

The police retaliated by hunting down the elusive and well-armed Communist guerrilla fighters. One day, the police cornered my revolutionary cousin and his men in their farmhouse hiding place, and they set the thatched roof on fire to smoke them out. When my cousin rushed out of the burning house, seeing the police lined up waiting for him, he turned on his heels and jumped right back into the inferno. He would rather die in a fire than by horrible torture at the hands of the police.

Shortly after the tragic death of my cousin, his widowed mother and his uncle had to move away from our family place in Uchong-myon to new farms they had purchased deep in the interior region about thirty miles out of Wonju. They had to sell off their farmland, the houses my father and his brothers built, along with beasts, wagons, and farm implements. Only the bare essentials they carried on their backs and heads to new homes, hundreds of miles away, away from the family disgrace. They could not stand being ostracized by the village where their children had been born and their loved ones were buried.

To my chagrin, I didn't get to the beach as much as I had wanted to do, out of my hesitancy to impose on my host and because of the unflinching heat waves we were having. But just days before my departure for home, I finally had my swim in the sea.

One afternoon, Youngii, his little boy, and I stuffed our swimming gear into a straw bag and walked a few miles in the dusty, sizzling August heat, to the beach. For the occasion, I put on a flowery cotton dress with short sleeves.

This was the first time I had Youngii all to myself since my arrival. I had dreamed often of this moment and wanted to pour my heart out to him, detailing all my trials and tribulations since leaving Pohang.

Nothing remotely resembling what I long wished for happened. Maddeningly, I fell silent and remained speechless the whole time. Was it my deep desire not to spoil the precious moment with my beloved cousin, or the scorching heat? We trudged on all the way in total silence with his little boy trotting along beside us, uncomplaining.

The beach was completely deserted in the burning sun. We had the sand and the aqua-blue sea all to ourselves, while the townspeople waited for the dark to come out for a swim. For the first time in five years, I put on my big sister's jersey swimsuit of 1930s vintage, which fit snugly even with all the tucks out, and I plunged into the summer sun–warmed, pristine waters of the sea.

Countless times how I swam in my dreams with desperate abandon in those bleak years of Wonju. My soul soared with each stroke and an utter sense of freedom and peace washed over me, floating on my back in the clear blue sea fused seamlessly into the cloudless sky far on the horizon. I played with his little boy in the lapping waves of sparkling water, picking up shells and satin-smooth stones to take home for his mother. Fully clothed, Youngii watched us, hugging his pulled-up knees with clasped hands.

Even in the privacy of sea and sand, Youngii and I did not talk about anything of note to remember. He might have known that it was more than just shyness that made me avoid looking at him, or suddenly dumb with downcast eyes in his presence. He might have sensed that I loved him beyond cousinly love, though platonically, but he never did or said anything to breach the Korean taboo on unholy sentiments among first cousins. I loved him more for his restraint and the proper distance he kept between us.

In the end, my cousin had to lend me money to go home, as my family didn't send me the train fare.

After a whole summer of doing nothing, I was ready for a new page in my life.

CHAPTER 36

The Prep School

In 1949, the Methodist Seminary returned to the gray stone building where I had started my religious education a year earlier. When I entered the preparatory school in September, the school atmosphere was unmistakably changed by a better credential faculty and students. The school took on a more formal and serious academic air.

Dr. Hyungki Lew, an American-educated minister with a Ph.D. and an author/publisher of Korean-English dictionaries, became the president. He assembled impressive lecturers, mostly men, with divinity degrees, some with Ph.D.s, and a couple of women instructors for music lessons and health classes for female students.

Mrs. Che-Hong stayed on as the housemother to female students housed on the third floor. Her aged mother was still a welcome presence softening the institutional life. We had the same cook and her family, looking and clothed much better, still living in the basement rooms next to the dining hall. Her two little ones grew in leaps and bounds, literally right under our noses.

Under Mrs. Chapin's tireless hustle and procuring skills, we began to have better food and more of it. Miss Cooper was running my old mission school elsewhere, but often joined us at our vespers in the chapel.

The student body turned co-ed with a sprinkling of female students in each class. Living accommodations were completely segregated though. The male students lived in a separate dormitory about a block away, and had to return for lunch, while the female students lived, ate, and went to classes without leaving the building for the whole week. For girls, it was a self-contained cloistered life.

The female students were better schooled than I was; all had girls' high school diplomas. Passing the prep entrance exam equalized my spotty educational background to count me in among the freshman class. Only a handful of girls entered the prep school. The rest of female students were in the seminary.

The male student body was a mixed lot. Young ministers coming back to school for advanced diplomas, and recent high school graduates who were trying the seminary after failing more prestigious universities.

We were all so serious about our studies that we didn't even notice that we had no social life to speak of, sanctioned or not by the school. By and large, we were a docile bunch in comparison to politically active university students who indulged in the ritualistic, well-publicized street fights and protests. In those days, student agitation was the annual rite of spring in Korea.

I was kept busy from early morning until late at night, attending classes, keeping up with daily assignments, and following faithfully, for my fragile health, Miss Laird's instructions to take a daily afternoon nap, squeezed in between lunch and afternoon classes, and to snack on California sun-dried raisins, rich in iron.

The subjects we covered in classes were more challenging and interesting than the mission school's. Mrs. Shaw's phonetic English was replaced by the English translation of Guy de Maupassant's short stories. The English version of "The Necklace" was dissected by the class, word by word and sentence by sentence. Also we read the stories of W. Somerset Maugham, who became my favorite author. I was particularly touched by his sensitive portrayal of human frailty, nuances of human feelings, and subtleties of human relations. It wasn't the exotic setting he sometimes used for his stories which appealed to me, but it was the easy, unassuming way he wrote about the universal emotions and understandings transcending racial and cultural boundaries.

We learned English grammar by the parts of speech and sentence structure on the elaborate diagrams.

Following past policy and practice, the seminary returned to being the cradle of future church leaders and the brain trust for Christianity in Korea. It was not just content with producing new crops of ministers; it also sought to be a scholarly reservoir for the vitality of Christian faith. The missionaries acted as the link between the Korean scholars and the American universities later on. Hence, a great emphasis was put on the proficiency of English language as well as a good grasp of Western civilization.

Wasn't Christianity born out of the loin of the old Hebrew religion in Palestine? So the history of ancient civilizations was taught, starting with the Babylonian civilization in the fertile Mesopotamian Valley sandwiched between the Euphrates and Tigris rivers. After the rise and fall of Babylon, we moved on to the Egyptian civilization rising out of the rich muck of the Nile River. With Alexander the Great conquering Persia, eventually the Greek and Roman empires ran over decaying old worlds, spanning over hundreds of years, straddling the time of Jesus.

Besides the advanced studies of the Old and New Testaments taught in historical contexts, we started to read them in English, killing two birds with one lesson.

The hygiene lesson and organ lessons were easy enough, but there were no math or science classes to tax our brains or confuse religious dogmas.

At the seminary, I seldom heard any student complain about the food anymore. Every meal became a feast for me. Fresh meat replaced the canned meat, and the local, trucked-in vegetables, fish and fruits became everyday fare. So proud was Mrs. Che-Hong of her bountiful table that she invited all the faculty members to join us at lunch.

Our school bursar even had his supper with us every weekday before boarding a commuter train for home, outside the city. I often wondered how he managed to be at school early in the morning, while going home so late.

We never failed to celebrate birthdays for students and teachers with traditional birthday food, red-bean rice and sticky sweet rice cakes. Also the hangab (the 60th birthday) celebrations accorded to any church or school dignitary lightened our institutional life from time to time. Life became a bowl of rice, heaped high and steaming.

Speaking of a bowl of rice, in those days of pervasive hunger and poverty in Korea, it represented the very symbol of ultimate well-being. Above anything else, it signified wealth and unquestioned success in life. Only the very lucky few could afford polished white rice at every meal, while the mass struggled to stretch scarce rice by adding barley, beans, and sliced potatoes in the summer.

As a rule, even farmers ran out of rice by planting time in June and didn't see it again until the new crop was harvested in the fall. Summer was the time the country and townsfolk alike made do with less desirable grains: millet, wheat, barley, and beans, generously mixed and delectably lightened up by new potatoes and corn on the cob. Shorn of all the nutrients by fine milling, white rice, nevertheless, was more than a mere commodity. It was a potent symbol which separated haves from have-nots.

On Sundays, students were encouraged to attend any church service of their choice in the city, since most of us were out of town. I eagerly sought after the most exotic Christian services available in Seoul.

First, I tried Catholic mass on one Sunday before I turned to the Eastern Orthodox service, Greek or Russian I am not sure. What struck me most about the Roman and Eastern churches was the strong similarity between these Christian ceremonies and the Buddhist rituals — the glittery gold and silver cassocks the priests wore, the statuettes of saints lining the walls, and perpetual incense burning, shrouding religious rites in a pungent haze.

Unfortunately for these old churches, I was simply repelled by their unmistakable resemblance to the Buddhist temple. While I was growing up near a Buddhist temple street in Fukui, I was terrified of the cassock-clad priests with shaved heads. The priests' shaved heads always reminded me of dead Japanese with shaved heads, sitting like Buddhas with prayer beads draped over their praying hands in a barrel and cremated after the funeral rite.

The 1949 Christmas break brought me back home, which had changed noticeably in my absence. The Stokeses finally had a daughter, Carol, adopted from an American couple. The baby girl was blonde and blue-eyed like Dr. Stokes, and she became the core center of the Stokes' home. I even felt a tinge of jealousy as Mrs. Stokes forgot everything else, including me, for her baby. Mrs. Stokes became alive and joyous, and adoption seemed to be catching among the missionary community. Mr. and Mrs. Burkholder had also adopted a baby, an American boy.

My stepsister, Jinju, was gone, married off to a watch merchant in a seaport town on the Sea of Japan, arranged by her mother and a matchmaker. I knew that her husband could not have been Jinju's choice as she had been very much in love with a soldier in the ROK army the summer before.

In order to pay the bills, my father rented out a spare wing with two on-dul rooms and a kitchen to an ROK officer and his pregnant wife from Seoul in the winter of 1948-49. In spite of their low salary, the officer and his wife seemed to have everything they desired for a good life. They had fresh meat including live pheasant, vegetables and fruits, dried persimmon and dates for cake-making, and all the rice they could possibly consume. Fish and other exotic sea creatures like octopus and sea cucumbers were trucked in fresh by military vehicles from the coast.

To my father's dismay, they even had arranged a drinking party, now and then, for fellow officers, in which they got boisterously drunk, sang loudly, and smoked up the place. My father's ban on alcohol and tobacco was simply ignored.

There was an aide, a sergeant, attached to our tenant officers, who came frequently to our house to bring groceries and messages. When I was home from school the Christmas before, I noticed a remarkable change in my placid stepsister whenever the sergeant came around to our house on an errand. Jinju's round white face would turn crimson red, but her furtive glances in his direction were answered, in due time, by his obvious interest with bold stares.

Soon they were exchanging notes, surreptitiously. They could not have done much else as my parents' opposition was instant and final. The sergeant, a non–Christian from North Korea, was simply out of the question as her husband. Sometime in the summer of 1949, the sergeant was transferred back to Seoul with his officer, to my stepmother's relief, but her trouble was not yet over. One day, without telling anybody, Jinju took a train to Seoul to visit her soldier boyfriend, scaring her mother to death.

That fall, she married a young man of Christian faith, whom she met only once in the presence of both sets of parents, as arranged by the matchmaker. My stepmother won. No doubt, she reminded Jinju of what had become of my two sisters for their willful misconduct. My stepsister must have done the right thing as the last time I heard, her life was overflowing with five sons, born in quick succession, and with a prosperous tradesman for her husband.

There were two unforgettable events after I returned to school for the second semester in February 1950.

The first one was the moving memorial service for Dr. Alice Appenzeller, born on the day her missionary parents, the Reverend Henry G. Appenzeller and his wife, arrived in Korea in February 1885; she was the first president of Ewha College. The service was conducted in Chung Dong Methodist Church, the first Methodist church built by her father back in 1898.

Even though the presidency of Ewha was handed over to Dr. Helen Kim, the first graduate of the college, Dr. Alice Appenzeller, was a familiar sight at the seminary. She still taught at Ewha and lived in the east end of our building with Mrs. Chapin and Miss Cooper.

Toweringly tall, she exuded authority and authenticity. Unmarried, she devoted her entire life to educating the future Korean women leaders for church and society. Ewha and Appenzeller were synonymous to Korean women in the know.

Originally, Ewha College was started by Mrs. W. B. Scranton, the wife of a physician from Cleveland, as a girls school, Ewha Hak-Dang, or Learning Institute, with the queen's permission in 1885. Possibly it owed its existence to the post–American Civil War suffragette movement which prompted Mrs. Scranton to insist on the same educational opportunity for girls when the Reverend Appenzeller built the first brick school building for boys.

The most moving part of the Appenzeller memorial service, I still remember so vividly, was the singing by a young missionary, born in Korea to long-time American missionaries, the Reverend and Mrs. Jensen; she was married to a missionary and had two small children.

She sang a movement, popularized as "Going Home," from

Antonín Dvořák's "Symphony from the New World." Ever since, whenever I hear this Dvořák's music, I see the flaming red-haired young mother with her green eyes fixed upward, sending Miss Appenzeller's soul off to heaven on her clear, beautiful rendition of "Going Home" in that cavernous church.

The second memorable event was an American evangelist coming to town for a huge evangelical tent meeting. Up to that time, fiery preaching was done only by Korean preachers. The American missionaries, by and large, stuck to more sedate, dignified sermons.

Not this young American preacher — a tall, blond, Nordic man preaching with such passion and fire that the instantaneous Korean translation did not diminish nor slow the spellbinding impact on the audience, believers and nonbelievers alike.

Above all, the first year of prep school gave me the self-confidence I needed to go on with my future plans. My future became more clear, on the track to seminary and eventually to America.

The world I fashioned out of the American movies and the Western literature was calling me. The ultimate goal I envisioned for myself was to go to America, the land of opportunity, and be part of the free country where I could be whatever I wanted to be.

I never gave any thought, however, to what plan Miss Laird might have had for me. But the world had another plan, just around the corner, for me and Korea.

CHAPTER 37

The Korean War

June 25, 1950, dawned like any other early summer morning with a cool promise for a warm, pleasant Sabbath day. However, the invasion of South Korea by North Korean Communists across the thirty-eighth parallel that morning was anything but ordinary; it was remembered like no other.

After the usual Sunday breakfast, I was on my way to the Eastgate Methodist Church near Eastgate railroad station, on foot.

Strangely, for the usually quiet Sunday morning streets, I saw Korean military jeeps with megaphones, criss-crossing the streets, shouting something I could not understand. The church service was conducted as usual and not until I returned to my dormitory room around noon did I learn of the North Korean aggression. That explained the frantic Korean MPs shouting orders for the soldiers on the streets to report back to their bases.

There were questions raised later about the invasion, whether it was planned or was just another instance of frequent border skirmishes that were getting out of hand. But seeing the MPs trying to corral the furloughed soldiers and get them back to their units convinced me that the South Korean military was really surprised by the attack. On June 24, Korean military commanders had been authorized to give fifteen-day furloughs to soldiers from farming communities for rice planting during the coming rainy season.

As later discovered, the American intelligence was compromised by a beautiful North Korean spy who seduced an intelligence officer in the American command.

216

International espionage was even implicated through three Soviet moles in the British government: H.A.R. "Kim" Philby, Guy Burgess, and Donald Maclean. Around the time of the outbreak, Philby and Burgess worked at the British Embassy in Washington, and Maclean at the American desk in the British Foreign Office in London. They picked up the American government's reluctance to get involved in another war in Asia and the American military's intention to withdraw all the American forces from South Korea by June 1950. The timing of the attack was too convenient to rule out an intelligence leak.

By then, only a skeletal force of American advisors, numbering just a few thousand, remained to shore up the fledgling South Korean armed forces. Certainly the attack was Russia's direct challenge to the American postwar containment policy in Asia, after Russian postwar expansionism was thwarted by Harry Truman in Turkey and Greece in 1947, ushering in the Truman Doctrine.

The Sunday vesper gathered the girls, the resident missionaries, and other residents in the building for an anxious prayer and mutual comfort. We felt a serious threat this time, different from other Communist border incidents in the past.

The next day, Monday, was our usual no-school day as some of the seminary students had their regular church services to conduct and needed Monday to rest and study. All day, we tried to get the latest news on the fighting, but without newspapers or a radio there was no way of knowing how things were shaping up on the fighting front. Mrs. Che-Hong tried to relay secondhand information from the missionaries in the east end, but everything we heard only increased our fear and deepened our anxiety.

Around midday, we heard several airplanes buzzing over the city, but could not tell if they were ours or North Koreans. I tried to study in the library, willing the menacing dark cloud to go away from us all, but my pretended normalcy could not dispel my gnawing anxiety.

The Monday vesper turned out to be a gloomy omen for us all. The American citizens were preparing to evacuate, and none of the missionaries came down to the chapel that evening. Unknowingly, we parted without farewells.

The first thing grim-faced Dr. Lew did on Tuesday morning was to announce the immediate school closing to anxious students and faculty assembled, and he bade us a safe journey home. I knew it was war.

Quickly I said goodbyes to our housemother Mrs. Che-Hong and other teachers; all of us were worried and afraid. We never saw each other again. By grapevine later, I learned that Mrs. Che-Hong and her mother managed to leave Seoul before the North Koreans entered the city the next day.

For the moment, we had no idea if there was any kind of transportation available, public or private, or how long we would have to be away from the city. With no hard information or direction from anyone, each one of us was on her own. I knew that I could not possibly carry a leather suitcase, the bedding, and all the books I had accumulated in my room.

I tossed into two large scarves some undergarments, summer and winter clothes — just in case this thing lasted beyond the summer — my Bibles and a hymnal for spiritual comfort, and Dr. Lewis' English-Korean dictionary, a token for my dream.

I had very little cash left after paying for my room and board the previous week. Cloistered in the self-contained life of the seminary on a wooded hillside, we were effectively cut off from the mainstream life of the bustling city down below. On a moment's notice, we girls were literally thrown out on the streets that morning.

I decided to join two of my five roommates who had homes relatively close to Seoul. I could never make it to Wonju, eighty miles away, on foot, and with no money. My roommate Kim's mother was the director of a retirement home for the Methodist Bible women in a hilly, country place just across the Han River, south of Seoul. Lee's family lived in a little town, the first train stop on the major railroad line going south from Seoul on the west coast.

We decided to reach Kim's mother first, thinking that the fighting might be over in a few days. We were still hopeful.

When three of us hit the city streets at the bottom of our hillside driveway, the whole town seemed agitated to a fevered pitch with people scurrying around mindlessly. The streetcars weren't running, so we started walking toward the major bridge crossing the Han River, following the streetcar track Kim remembered taking to go to her mother's place.

As we walked toward the river, we noticed that more and more people were joining us out of side streets and alleys with bundles and children. Even cars with horns blaring and handdrawn carts, piled high with household goods and kids, began to muscle into the ever-ballooning, fleeing mobs. It was as though a giant magnet was drawing all the humanity and wheels in town toward one spot: the bridge, leading away from the town, toward the south. The panicky people all around us told us all we needed to know about how things were going in fighting.

Finally, around three o'clock in the afternoon, we reached the bridge, but the soldiers would not let us cross it. Somebody in the crowd told us that the Korean army was readying the bridge to be blown up to slow down the North Korean tanks and heavy armored cars. The Han River at that point was very deep and wide; the only alternative crossing was by boat.

The people with means immediately rushed down the riverbank to engage whatever boats were available at any price. The rest of us, stunned and stymied by the unexpected barrier, were milling about, helpless and fearful, while being pushed by ever growing mobs from behind.

The panic was palpable. Soon angry men and frantic mothers started yelling desperately at the soldiers to let us cross the bridge before blowing it up. We must have waited at least one hour before the military relented. We all sprinted across the bridge as though the North Koreans were right behind us, breathing down our necks.

By the time we reached Kim's mother, deep in the hilly, wooded country near the Han River bank, the day was finally fading away. We were far from the maddening crowd, serene and quiet, as though there was nothing wrong with the world.

Famished and tired, three of us gladly joined Kim's mother and her charges, a half dozen retired Bible women, for supper. Little was said but we all knew what everyone was thinking — what was going to happen to us all.

Some time past midnight, we were rudely awakened by a loud explosion from the direction of the bridge, shattering the forest tranquillity and our uneasy sleep. For days to come, we heard tragic stories of desperate people trying to cross the bridge, now broken in half, and the people, carts, and automobiles driving into the black river below.

The next day dawned with an ominous foreboding hanging thick in the morning haze-shrouded woods. Anxiously, we watched the early morning trickle of bedraggled people turning into a steady flow of humanity trudging along the hilly footpaths all day and eventually, in the fading twilight, the straggling Korean soldiers passed by, wordless and dejected.

That night ever louder artillery fires forced us on our next move. Lee and I decided to go south to her house, about twenty miles away, the first thing in the morning. Kim was determined to stay with her mother and the old ladies to face whatever came their way. The ladies were too old to walk.

This was a foretaste of a familiar scenario repeated again and again that summer. First, we would reach a relatively peaceful haven, far from the fighting we thought, and in a matter of a few days, we would be dislodged again by the approaching drumbeat of artillery thunder and a rushing human exodus. We were on the run, chased by the sounds of the guns.

After a sleepless night and in near panic, Lee and I quickly repacked our bundles for a long trek on the open road to elusive safety. My two bundles had to be reduced to one. I knew that from the previous walk through the city streets that together they were too much for a long haul. Into one scarf, I squeezed one bra, one blouse, one flower cotton skirt that I couldn't bear to part with, a wool blazer with a matching skirt, and one sweater, just in case this infernal fighting lasted longer than the summer.

My New Testament and the Korean-English dictionary survived the cut. Since then, once in a while I wondered what happened to my Old Testament with my notations on the margins, my wellworn hymnal, and a heavy winter coat left behind. Later the coat was sorely missed in the chilly winter days.

After breakfast, Lee and I joined the herds of people passing by the house and became war refugees ourselves, nameless and rootless. I put on the good penny loafers Mrs. Stokes had given me. We had then no idea that they would be in for rough hiking through uncharted mountainous terrrains and muddy country roads.

Lee and I, like the other fleeing people all around us, spoke very little as we trudged along the rough pathless forests in endless stretches of hills. It took all morning and almost all afternoon that day to reach level land at the southern end of the trail.

When we reached Lee's house, we collapsed in exhaustion. We had not had anything to eat or drink since breakfast. Lee's father was waiting for her. Her mother was dead, and her brother was away. I wondered then what was happening to Taiam working with an acupuncturist on the south side of Seoul, across the Han River, but there was no time for a search in the roiling chaos. Survival was the first and foremost on everyone's mind.

It took us only one or two days to see that the war was catching up with us. Lee's father kindly let me stay with them as long as I wanted. They packed what they could carry and needed most, some rice and clothes, and we went to the train station.

The trains came up north with fresh replacement soldiers and war supplies, and returned south with fleeing refugees. The station was mobbed with frenzied people loaded down with earthly possessions, babies, and children, trying to get on the train as though it was the last lifeboat in a shipwreck. We three pushed and squeezed onto the train, already packed beyond its capacity. We were virtually standing sardines packed tight with no room to wiggle or breathe in the humid June heat.

It was a slow, torturous train ride to Taejon, the mid-point between Seoul and Taegu. The ride was punctuated by my occasional faintings and the hazy semi-consciousness of suffocating heat, sweaty bodies and crying babies. Even though I fainted on and off, I was perfectly safe, well supported by bodies pressing all around me. Traveling light for myself, I felt for mothers with tired children and hungry babies, struggling to keep the families together in a cataclysmic time of war.

Why stop at Taejon? It was a human nature, hoping against hopes. No one dared to even think that the war was going to last the week, the summer, the year, let alone three long years. People didn't want to stray too far from home.

Taejon had a large Methodist church opened to all refugees from Seoul and elsewhere. As the church benches were all taken by earlier comers, we secured one corner of the wooden floor for our moveable home. The families were setting up makeshift housekeeping by washing rice and clothes at the water pump next to the minister's house, and building fires for cooking inside the circles of stones wherever they found any bare ground within the church compound.

The following day, I was delighted to see Mrs. Lew, our seminary president's wife, doing some washing at the water pump. The Lews were staying with the minister. Mrs. Lew was a second-generation American-Korean from Los Angeles before her marriage and very American in her ways. The Lews had one daughter and one son, both in their teens. Their daughter had been ill with tuberculosis recently.

The next time I saw Mrs. Lew, she was terribly agitated about spilled rice all over the concrete base of the water pump. I wondered why she was so upset about a few grains of rice when we were on the run for our lives. Perhaps in spite of herself, she remembered the Buddhists' teaching that each grain of rice contained three Buddhas, the Buddhist equivalent of "Waste not, want not."

It took no more than a few days of tranquil interlude before the familiar jitters sweeping through the refugees and the townsfolk alike, shutting down the shops and emptying the open market. I saw jeeps and trucks piled high with soldiers and civilians, leaving town. Soon we began to hear the rhythmic thud of artillery in the distance. It was time to go. The next destination, Taegu.

Taegu was the stronghold of Presbyterianism with only Presbyterian churches in town. This time we were lucky to have the church benches to sleep on. In raging war, the Christian churches, regardless of denomination, acted as beacons for fleeing Christians seeking shelter and safety. That was how I happened to see one of my prep school classmates.

Pak was one of the older, married students, with small children and a church in the country. He was trying to fill in his incomplete academic credentials with the help of a missionary. Initially, I was glad to see a familiar face in the sea of strangers, but to my surprise he was alone, without his family.

The next time I came upon him, he suggested that he and I go off to Japan together to escape the war. The idea was unexpected and, at the same time, so preposterous that I, though an innocent abroad, felt terribly offended. I was angry at his arrogant presumptions of me, but to spare his feelings, I declined as politely as I could. I never saw him again.

I remembered from dinner conversations at home that our Presbyterian ministers, the Reverend Pak (no relation to my school friend) and the Reverend Kim from the Korean churches in Japan, were now back in Taegu with their own churches. My father's first cousin Pek also settled in Tongsan, a crossroads village across from the Naktong River, about five miles out of Taegu.

As it was becoming burdensome to Lee's father to feed me with their diminishing rice, even once a day, I decided to strike out on my own. First, I visited the Reverend Pak, much aged since I last saw him in Nagoya in 1944. I learned that his gentle wife was dead and his Kyoto University–educated son, now a Presbyterian minister, had been trapped in Pyongyang, the North Korean capital, at the end of the Pacific war. One of his unmarried daughters was keeping house for him.

Seeing them in unmistakable hardship, I decided to try Cousin Pek.

CHAPTER 38

Tongsan

In spite of the distant rumbles, seemingly ordinary, local traffic on the road to Tongsan gave no hint of war in the bright July morning sun. I stood out among the country folks in Western clothes, carrying a bundle. As yet there were no refugees clogging the country roads around Taegu.

At that early stage of the war, it looked as though all of the war refugees were collected in the city of Taegu and dispersed farther south by rail, leaving the roads branching out of the city in their natural state of dusty, languid tranquillity. I almost believed that I was just visiting my second cousin in the country in ordinary peace time.

Cousin Pek was a born capitalist and a war profiteer with a nose for profit anytime and anywhere. Before he and his family barely escaped the American B-29 saturation bombing on Nagoya in the spring of 1945, he amassed a tidy fortune out of the Pacific war by supplying manufactured springs of all kinds to the Japanese government. Like us — the Ches — he came back to Korea with his liquidated assets from his factory in cash and personal properties intact. He settled his family in a crossroads village surrounded by rich farmland, orchards, and the Naktong River, west of Taegu.

When the Japanese people had to leave hurriedly in the middle of the night, following the emperor's radio announcement of the Japanese surrender on August 15, 1945, Cousin Pek swiftly bought up their farms, orchards, houses, stores, and even the Japanese teahouse on the Naktong River bank, for a song. Through his expertise in Japanese business ways and fluent business Japanese, he became, overnight, the richest man with considerable property holdings in that little village.

That was how I found him, his wife and their two high school daughters. They were living on a self-contained Japanese farm compound, facing the major road parallel to the Naktong River. Curiously, it had a storefront facing the road which, under the previous Japanese ownership, sold candies, sweet mochis, and farm produce from the vegetable garden and orchard in the back of the enclosure.

The storefront had a second story, tatamied room, but the main kitchen and on-dul rooms in the compound were typical Korean arrangements. There were the grain storage and the animal stalls at the far end of the compound, away from the living quarters.

Smack in the middle of everything, was a freestanding Japanese house, complete with tatamied rooms, a typical Japanese kitchen, a round hot tub, and an indoor lavatory. When the Japanese farmer owned the place, he and his family lived in the Japanese structure and the Korean farmhands occupied the on-dul rooms with the Korean kitchen for their own cooking. The Japanese farmer and the Korean helpers maintained their separate lives in the symbiotic embrace of the compound.

When I arrived unexpectedly at their door, Cousin Pek and his family were cordial enough, but not overwhelmed with joy either. I was bad news, a warning that the war was coming. Cousin Pek had had my brother Taiam living with him in Nagoya for a year, but he hardly knew me. He let me share the second floor tatamied room over the storefront with his daughters.

Soon I discovered that there were other war evacuees living at their place. The Japanese house was taken over by the entire Korean Air Force: about a dozen young pilots. I saw some soldiers coming and going with groceries: they were cooking their own meals. The pilots seemed to have plenty of meats and other precious food, even in the war emergency, by the looks of the surplus food gracing our tables.

Not only was Cousin Pek accommodating the Korean Air Force, but also American Air Force officers in the teahouse on the riverbank. Some of his orchards and rice paddies were expropriated for airstrips for American war planes. Once again, out of the jaws of war, Cousin Pek was making money, hand over fist, almost against his will.

My high school cousins and I tried to stay away from the young Korean pilots by playing hide and seek in the crowded compound but it was not easy. Whenever any one of the pilots happened to be in the common threshing ground within the enclosure, we made ourselves scarce. It did not mean that we girls were not curious, or did not have any interest in meeting them. The girls' mother made sure that it did not happen under her eagle eyes.

I remember one pilot in particular—the youngest one in the bunch, barely out of his teens, I thought. Whenever I had to go to the outdoor lavatory, just outside the back gate of the compound, facing a large kitchen garden and an orchard, he seemed to materialize out of nowhere, as if he was waiting for me. One time, he followed me out of the back gate, but I had nowhere to go but hide in the outhouse. When I finally came out, he tried to make awkward conversation. I was too embarrassed to say anything.

The whole month of July was spent waiting for the outcome of fighting, either going away or being overrun by it. All of us—the Peks, the pilots, and I—were simply suspended together in the Tongsan farmhouse, thrown together by the war. Those days, time hung heavy on our hands.

I wondered what happened to my family members, scattered to the winds by the war. Did my big brother get out of Seoul before the North Koreans came in? Did my sister Kiyon and her policeman husband escape with their three children? The rumors were rampant that Christian ministers and government officials including policemen were summarily executed by the Communists in Seoul. Was Wonju overrun by the enemy? If so, where were my parents and Taikun? What about Duli and her farm family? Jinju, just married on the east coast? Cousin Youngii in Pohang?

In the precarious time of the approaching battlefront, suddenly the most tedious, ordinary chores of living became precious privileges to be clung to as the last lifeline to normalcy. I learned to appreciate the predictability and stability that washing dishes and putting laundry on the lines implied. Daily routine became the silent chant to ward off the dark cloud of impending doom we all felt in our bones.

News, through the usual sources, such as newspapers and radios, was practically nonexistent and each one of us was on his own to make sense out of whatever one heard from other people, or saw stirring around him. In the latter part of July, I sensed an increasing nervousness among the Korean pilots, until one day they left without warning. Already, Cousin Pek was hearing the worsening news of the fighting. One day he told us that we would have to leave to a safer place.

So I decided to throw my lot with the Reverend Kim's family in Taegu since rumor had it that, because of the Communist hit list, the American mission was doing everything possible to evacuate ministers' families first. I hurried back to the city in search of the Reverend Kim whom I had not seen since my family left Fukui ten years ago.

I felt like a salmon swimming upstream this time, with the people pouring out of the city, loaded down by bundles and children, on carts and mostly on foot. I was gripped by fear that the Kims might have gone already.

CHAPTER 39

Taegu Churches Evacuated

Without a map or the Reverend Kim's address, it was really like a needle in a haystack to find his house among the similar dwellings on the serpentine streets with no names, and alleys to nowhere. By asking every passerby and with a little luck, I finally came to the Kims' door and found them home, preparing to leave momentarily.

In the past ten years, much had happened to the reverend who was widowed with two school children and remarried to a former Korean Bible woman who had borne him a daughter the year before.

I thought I might be a bother to the Kims, but surprisingly Mrs. Kim welcomed me. I found out why. Since her maid insisted on returning to her own family, she needed a replacement for her maid. With her three children and an aging mother, she needed someone young with strong arms and legs to carry things and care for the children, besides cooking and washing for the whole family.

Little did she know that I hardly qualified for the heavy lifting because of my weak lungs. In the turmoil of securing the house and getting to the military personnel trucks provided by the American mission, I did not bother to correct her false assumption. Was my fear that if they had known about my condition they might not have taken me, which kept me from speaking up? The Reverend Kim stayed behind to help evacuate other church members.

A convoy of a few trucks started on a hot, dusty ride under the blazing August sun. Only the drivers knew where we were going, though later I found out. We headed southeast toward the coast on the Sea of Japan, not too far to the north of Pusan. There we could be picked up by American Navy rescue ships, if need be.

Our trucks kicked up cumulous clouds of choking dust from the bone-dry, sunbaked dirt roads, covering everything in their wake with a fine dusting. I felt we were intruding, with bad tidings, into the still innocent, tranquil world of rural Korea. I felt sorry for the blissfully ignorant country folks, untouched as yet by raging war. By this time of the summer, farmers had finished harvesting wheat, barley, and millet, while the milky buds of rice grains were maturing under the searing midsummer sun.

We were all silent with our own thoughts, bounced around roughly by pock-marked country roads in the stifling, canvas-covered cab of the truck. Even infants and children were hardly complaining, perhaps sensing the urgency of the situation and, at the same time, thrilled by the new experience of riding in a truck.

Finally, the evacuees, veritable dustballs, were unceremoniously dumped at the side of the road in the late afternoon, greeted by a blast of roasting heat from the baked earth and the glaring sun from above. I looked around for shade, but there was none in sight, nothing but acres of yellowing green rice fields, bellowing in every direction. If we were to sleep under some sort of roof that night, we would have to do some walking.

We began to walk, with bundles on our heads and babies on our backs, toward the barely visible village far on the horizon. In a single file, along the narrow dike between the rice paddies, we trudged. It was a slow march of women, children, and old people, weighted down with loads and sodden in sweat, snaking through rice fields toward the promised oasis of shade in the village ahead. Even the summer songs of cicadas added mournfully to our misery.

All I could think of was a cool drink of water from a deep well under the thick shadow of a big tree. Otherwise, my mind was totally blank, but my legs seemed to take on their own life of motion, completely severed from the rest of my body.

When we reached the village, the Kims and I were escorted to a farmer's house while the rest of our group was directed to the school building for shelter. Rank had its privileges, even in the life of war refugees.

Despite Mrs. Kim calling me "Teacher Che," in deference to my being a seminary student, she expected full service in exchange for bringing me along to safety. I felt obliged. As soon as we got settled in a spare room, I was told to prepare a hot supper for the family. By the time I washed up cooking utensils late that night under the summer stardust, I was so numb from exhaustion that I could slip into oblivion, gladly.

At the first crowing of roosters the next morning, Grandma nudged me awake for breakfast cooking. I had barely drifted into sleep in the pre-dawn coolness after trying to sleep in the small, airless room crammed with six warm bodies and chewed up by ravenous mosquitoes.

For many months after that morning, I could not shake off an utter exhaustion I felt in my body and soul. All I wanted was sleep and this unmistakable familiarity frightened me. I just couldn't get enough rest with a one-year-old baby and two active kids around me day and night, and all the cooking and washing by myself.

One unbelievably peaceful Sunday morning, already sultry and sodden, abetted by the insistent singing of cicadas, Mrs. Kim with a parasol and I walked some distance from our village to get to a church service. Just around the bend on a deserted country road, we suddenly came upon a detachment of the American soldiers resting in the shade against the hilly side of the road. We surprised each other. The Americans, I am sure, didn't expect, in this war-torn, god-forsaken countryside to see two city women in American short-sleeved cotton dresses, with a parasol, as if they were out for fresh air on a Sunday stroll. Still remembering the Japanese propaganda, I was a bit afraid.

The only thing sharply etched into my memory was that I was completely unnerved by their stares, and I felt like melting into the ground. Amazingly, Mrs. Kim was acting so nonchalantly, as though this was nothing but a daily occurrence to her. We passed without a word.

Then, one day without any warning, a Red Cross ambulance

from Pusan arrived in the village to give all the refugees inoculations against communicable diseases. I eagerly asked two young Korean nurses for any news on the fighting, the American missionaries, or any mutual acquaintances we might have.

I learned that Dr. Lew and his family were in Pusan. The South Korean government was set up in the Pusan perimeter, a precarious foothold on the verge of being swept into the sea any moment. Dr. Lew was working with the United States Information Services as an interpreter in the American Embassy building. Doctors Charles Stokes, William Shaw, and Charles Sauer were evacuating Christians out of harm's way.

Hearing all these familiar names, on impulse I decided to go back to Pusan that afternoon with the nurses, to be with people I knew for whatever fate awaited us there. My momentary sting of guilt for abandoning the Kim family in a lurch was quickly quashed by my stronger desire for self interest.

I explained my wish to Mrs. Kim, who was most reluctant to let me go. I made the most plausible, face-saving excuse I could think of by saying that I wanted to find my family in Pusan. How could she object to my selfish reason camouflaged in filial duty, exacted even in extraordinary times?

The ride to Pusan with the Red Cross nurses, even in the stifling and uncomfortable ambulance, was the most liberating and joyous moment I had experienced since leaving Seoul two months ago.

Pusan stood for the refugees as the end of the line, a relief in itself, even though we might all die as a nation, momentarily.

CHAPTER 40

Pusan

When we reached downtown Pusan later in the afternoon, I saw at once that the city had been changed by the war. Before the Korean War, Pusan was an unhurried but important port with all the activities, commercial and transportation, centered around the wharves. It was linking the Japanese islands to the Asian continent by the wide-track Korean rail line threading the whole length of the peninsula.

Now the place was bursting its seams, spilling into its surrounding countryside, with the hurly-burly of Seoul, brought by the South Korean government on the run, and the refugees fleeing the fighting. The town was roiling with humanity, men in uniforms and ragtag refugees everywhere. It frightened me. There was no need to hear how the war was going.

I wasted no time in looking up Dr. Lew at the United States Information Service. Dr. Lew, elegantly attired in a Western suit, came out to meet me in the entrance hallway of the American Embassy building. I was surprised, and somewhat comforted, as a sign of confidence, by how easily I could come into the building without being challenged. Dr. Lew quickly filled me in on the latest news he had of the faculty members and the whereabouts of the church leaders. Some of them, he heard, had been executed, or disappeared without a trace. His family was living in a rented house. Seeing that I was alone without resources, he tried to land me some kind of job.

Eventually, Dr. Lew persuaded a group of Methodist ministers from the Seoul-Inchon area to take me in as kitchen help at their hotel, as they had left their families behind when they were evacuated. In those extraordinary times, the hotel guests had to cook their own meals in the hotel kitchen.

So I came to share a small, second-story tatamied room of the former Japanese inn with the recently-wed wife of a young minister, who refused to leave her behind when ordered to evacuate Seoul. Those ministers who chose to stay with their families and flocks gave up their lives when the Communists took over the city.

As I settled into helping the young wife prepare meals and shop for groceries, the sizzling summer heat was giving way to cool September nights for easy sleep. Mercifully, sleeping on the Japanese straw mat, even without any bedding, was much easier on my weary bones than on the church bench where I had spent some nights after my arrival in Pusan.

After a few days, I noticed that one of the ministers had brought an American-made, manual typewriter, complete with the typing manual. Leaving his loved ones behind to unknown dangers, this minister lugged around the cumbersome writing machine while fleeing for his life. But this incomprehensible act turned out to be a bonanza for me.

Between chores, with the minister's permission, I taught myself how to type with the manual showing which fingers to put on what letter keys and writing symbols; it was a bit reminiscent of organ lessons. It was easy to learn and, with practice my speed and confidence accelerated, even though I was in an awkward sitting position for typing, scrunched over the typewriter on the tatami floor.

On September 15, 1950, the American marines landed at Inchon in a lightning strike at the heart of the North Korean force. The news was electrifying to all the refugees, particularly the ministers who were on pins and needles, agonizing over the fate of their families. Within days of the American counteroffensive, the ministers were packing up, typewriter and all, to rush home in search of their families. Once again, I was out on my own.

Spreading like a wildfire, the news of the Inchon landing instantly turned the fearful atmosphere into euphoria and relief for the Pusan perimeter with its teeming population. With restored trust in the U.S. commitment to South Korea, the South Korean government and its skeptical people began to smile with a great sigh of relief that all was well.

The picture of General Douglas MacArthur coming off the warship *Mount McKinley* into the Inchon harbor, surrounded by his military officers, was more reassuring than his words of U.S. support at Syngman Rhee's presidential inauguration in the summer of 1948. An action spoke louder than a thousand words.

The show of American resolve to keep Korea from falling into the hands of the Soviet Union stiffened the spine of the Korean people and boosted the sagging morale of the ROK. America, with its mighty military power, saved a fledgling democracy from its premature death.

Everyone was going north to his home, on the heels of the victorious news of the U.N. forces. But I decided to stay on to look for a job in Pusan. For one thing, I was too exhausted from refugeeing the whole summer. At the time, I had no idea that it was the smartest thing I or anybody else could have done in those fluid, uncertain times.

Nobody foresaw the harrowing, seesawing battles waged after the relatively easy recovery of Seoul by the Allied forces in September and the sudden appearance of the Chinese soldiers across the frozen Yalu River from Manchuria in November 1950.

CHAPTER 41

Working for Uncle Sam

Since the hotel room was paid up to the end of September by the ministers, I had ten days to look for a job and a new place to live.

Armed with my newly-acquired typing skill and my English, such as it was, I had no trouble finding a job with a U.S. Army ordnance company across the harbor from the main wharf. The ordnance company was set up on a peninsula, wrapping around the north side of Pusan harbor, with its vast capacity for receiving and warehousing war materiels brought in by ships from Japan and elsewhere. I commuted by U.S. army ferryboat, along with other Korean personnel living in town.

Those days, the American military facilities seemed to have an insatiable need for Korean manpower with or without English language skills. With the command of English, one received the top salary allowed by the U.S. government pay scale for Korean nationals.

In my case, it was more pity than anything else that moved the interviewing sergeant to hire me as a typist in his section. By late September, my sun-bleached summer dressed looked too thin for the approaching autumn and my penny loafers I had on my feet day and night for the whole summer had detached soles and were gaping wide like an alligator's mouth. The wire to hold the shoes together did not keep water or oozing mud from sockless feet when it rained, nor did it quell the humiliation I felt about my appearance. I was a sunburned scarecrow, gaunt from long marches over rough terrain and muddy roads, and from the precarious existence of a war refugee for the past months.

I was a terrible typist at first. I kept making mistakes from nervousness and inexperience on the requisition forms with all kinds of numbers: date, serial numbers, and quantities of items with strange names not found in the dictionary. The eraser was not allowed on forms. Frankly, I was lucky if I produced one page without any mistakes in one hour. The U.S. government lost money on me, but she kept me alive.

While working for the ordnance company, I started to attend the Sunday church services held at the base for American soldiers and Korean workers, conducted by Chaplain Lunden. One day the chaplain introduced me to a Korean choir director who helped me find a place to live.

When asked about a rental room available, the choir director remembered his old music school classmate who lived about a mile away from my workplace. His friend taught music, before the war, at Pusan Technical School just outside the city, on the road to the American Airbase K-9, which had been installed on the tip of the peninsula since the outbreak of hostilities.

The chaplain also acted as a vital communication link to the world outside Korea and to the Methodist missionaries working in town. I had tried to leave a trail of my whereabouts every time I made a move from place to place in case someone like Miss Esther Laird was trying to locate me. Chaplain Lunden's APO address was at my disposal. My new address was left with the American Embassy in Pusan. The missionaries in Pusan had been notified about my current doings. All helped me to be spotted even from across the Pacific Ocean. It worked. Miss Laird, now settled in Oxford, Ohio, contacted me and we began our correspondence early in 1951.

In early October of 1950, I moved in with the music teacher's family, and for the first time since leaving Seoul, I had my own room, a small tatamied room. It was a luxury. The room was a former maid's room with only a closet and a window looking out on the vegetable garden.

The house was of typical Japanese construction, except for two on-dul rooms to ward off the far-reaching chills of the Siberian wind. Before World War II, it was originally built for the Japanese teacher at Pusan Technical School a half mile away. It was set back from the road, surrounded by a fairly large kitchen garden and fruit trees marking off the back property line. It was further secluded from the neighboring Korean houses by a creek running across the front yard. The creek bank path from the road led to the front door of the house.

My landlord had three children, the youngest still at his mother's breast, and a rather intense, thin wife with high cheekbones. It was obvious that the family had been going through a rough time financially, ever since the technical school was taken over by the U.S. Fifth Air Force for police and intelligence operations, thereby stopping the teacher's paychecks.

Without knowing one word of English, the music teacher found himself working as a day laborer for the new American employer at a fraction of his teacher's pay and a heavy dose of humiliation.

I commuted on foot to my ordnance job for most of October and November. With approaching winter and shorter daylight, I began to worry about my safety. My commute took in the deserted, barren mile of a side road from the well-guarded ordnance company gate to the t-intersection with the well-trafficked road to Airbase K-9. In the deepening autumn, I had to walk in the dark both ways, and an incident with an M.P. forced me to change the job.

The side road to the ordnance company from the airbase road was patrolled by an M.P. jeep. One evening an M.P. offered me a ride to my house. Initially, I was grateful for his kind offer, but when he began to give me gifts of candy and other things, rather insistently, in subsequent evenings, I became alarmed and worried about his unspoken, expected returns from me. I had nothing to give and was not keen on forming a relationship with a soldier. Socializing with American soldiers was viewed, even in the middle of war-induced social disorders, with disapprobation and, worse, I could be suspected of prostitution. The girls of my class were weary of the stigma such a relationship would be sure to bring on their reputations and families.

One evening, I simply declined the ride. He turned ugly at my refusal and tried to block my way with his jeep. Seeing that I wouldn't change my mind, he finally gave up and drove off in a cloud of dust. That prompted me to apply for a secretary-and-interpreter's job that opened up at the Fifth Air Force A.P. office in the former Pusan Technical School, closer to my house, on a safer road, and for much better pay. My landlord had told me about the job opening.

By then, the winter was setting in in earnest and war news from the north about the Chinese-reinforced, counteroffensive had ominous implications for South Korea, Allied forces, and the 1950 Christmas season. When the fighting was going well, pushing back the North Koreans beyond the thirty-eighth parallel in September and October, the American politicians and military brass were promising the American soldiers they would be "home for Christmas."

In December, the American and ROK forces were forced to withdraw from the Yalu River separating Korea from Manchuria because of the surprise entry into the war of the Chinese forces. The Chinese–North Koreans recaptured Seoul in January 1951, and the Communists didn't get pushed back north of the thirty-eighth parallel until the end of February, with the Eighth Army now under the command of General Matthew Ridgway.

December and January were the darkest days of the war for the South Koreans who had anxiously rushed back to their homes after the Inchon landing, only to find themselves running once again for their lives, this time in the dead of winter.

By pure dumb luck, I was sitting pretty and comfortable in Pusan with a room of my own and a job, far from the fighting. I was spared from retracing all the torturous steps of the previous summer.

Captain Robert E. Whitely, an Air Force Reserve pilot who was called into active duty when the war broke out, interviewed me for the job and promptly gave me the nickname Mary to simplify my exotic name, Pongsun. So I temporarily became Mary, as a wartime convenience.

Captain Whitely was close to forty, with weathered wrinkles on his neck and around his blue eyes in a lean, handsome face. He installed his Air Force police operation in the main school building office, next to the main entrance, but set me up with a typewriter and a couple of desks in a small, concrete-floored toolshed in the back, separated from the school building.

What I really appreciated, more than the top salary my typing and English skills garnered, was food as a fringe benefit. I was given a pass to eat three meals a day at the officer's mess set up in one of the school rooms at one end of the main building. Since I worked seven days a week, I was assured daily square meals for the first time in months.

After starving in peace and war for some years, the fresh oranges were manna from heaven, which I had not seen since before World War II in Japan. The varieties of meat blandly prepared in grease were a little hard on my vegetarian stomach, but gratefully devoured. The familiar carrots and potatoes, boiled to death with no trace of any spice, were reassuring, though tasteless to my hot spice–hardened Korean tastebuds.

And that pungent, black hot liquid called coffee, drunk in gallons day and night by the soldiers, was a sensational new experience to tea drinkers. However, I could not take to the coffee; it was too bitter and strong, even diluted with milk and sugar. I stuck to milk and delicious orange juice I had never had before. Other Korean personnel were fed, too, in a separate mess hall for enlisted men. My landlord brought home bread and meat left over from it in the evening to feed his family.

My typing duties were rather light and easy. I had plenty of time to retype the letters without any erasures for Captain Whitely to sign. Hunting down my boss for his signature was another matter. He was not always in his sparsely furnished office in the main building.

In addition to his responsibility for the Air Force police, the captain was also flying a World War II vintage airplane out of K-9 Airbase. I found him now and then in his living quarters, sleeping after long flying duties.

Captain Whitely, instead of sharing the second floor quarters for the officers in the main building, set up his own private quarters in another tool shed with a houseboy, a war orphan living in a partitioned space next to his master's bedroom. The captain turned the shed into a cozy place with a heater for warmth and hot water for his bath while the houseboy kept the life of the captain a little easier.

The first time I went, hesitantly, to his quarters, he proudly showed me the pictures of his infant twins and lovely wife, a college portrait, prominently displayed on a makeshift wooden crate serving as a table. His houseboy was a faithful gatekeeper, jealously guarding his master's sleep and privacy, and he did not hesitate one bit to turn me down for an audience.

Captain Whitely, despite his liberal attitudes, was very protective of me, naive, unworldly, and hung up on Methodism. He was an Episcopalian with relaxed views on the sins of the flesh. He teased me about my Calvinist views on drinking, smoking, and anything fun, but he trusted me unhesitatingly.

One time he asked me to talk to an eleven-year-old schoolboy who had been arrested for suspected espionage and temporarily locked in an empty school room for interrogation. He was caught sneaking into an American military installation in the Pusan area. I found him on the bare wooden floor in an airless, overheated room, covered with crawling lice from head to toe.

The boy was rather taken aback when he saw me, an ordinary Korean girl coming into his room. But he was very wary. I talked to him like a big sister and I didn't hear anything remotely suspicious of a politically motivated act of sabotage. Probably, he was one of the war urchins, roaming all over the war-devastated land, trying to survive by stealing anything, anywhere. This time, he went to the wrong place. I told my boss what I thought and never heard what became of this boy.

One downcast day in the early spring of 1951, still with frost on the ground, Captain Whitely took me to a Christian Sunday service conducted at the Chinese/North Korean prisoner of war camp, set against low-lying hills in the countryside outside Pusan. These prisoners of war were taken mostly during the U.N. forces' recapture of Seoul, and while straightening up the battle line along the thirty-eighth parallel in February 1951.

The first impression I had of the camp was a monochromatic

landscape in drab beige with its infinite shades and manifestations. Against the backdrop of the barren brown hills, the tents and high barbed-wire fences, the khaki-uniformed prisoners and South Korean guards alike, all seemed to spring from the ankle-deep mud oozing up from the earth.

When our jeep passed through the guarded gate into the compound, all the prisoners nearby stared at me with intense interest as though they had never seen a female before. No hostility, just curiosity. I spotted young faces here and there among puffy older faces. Most of the prisoners were in tatters. The padded Chinese uniforms were grimy black, and their feet were shod in once-military-issued shoes, stuffed with straw and newspapers, held together by strings and wires.

The service was conducted in Korean by a Korean preacher on a platform, all standing, the captors and the prisoners alike, in the chilly open air. The only parts of the service the Chinese prisoners could have understood, I was sure, were the hymns we sang and the prayers offered with our heads bowed.

As we were leaving the camp, I noticed one young boy looking at me intently, reminding me of Taikun. Perhaps he was remembering his home and his own sister, somewhere in the North or in China.

On April 11, 1951, General Douglas MacArthur was sacked by President Harry Truman, shocking everyone, especially the Koreans. For some months, since the Chinese intervention in the Korean fighting, General MacArthur had ongoing disputes with the American geopolitical positions taken by the Truman administration and the Pentagon. General MacArthur wanted to pursue the enemy into Manchuria, but President Truman did not want to expand the "police action," as he called it, into a major war on the Chinese mainland, thus inviting Soviet intervention and a possible nuclear Third World War.

To the Koreans, General MacArthur was a savior for their homeland and his dismissal meant a grave sea-change in American foreign policy toward Korea. The Koreans were deathly afraid that the United States would pull out entirely from Korea, leaving her to the Communist takeover.

Yet, Korea had no choice but to go along with American strategic dictates for their very existence. Once again, she was thrust into
the all-too-familiar role of "shrimp crushed in the battles of whales,"
a fate of all Third World countries in the Cold War period.

For all the death and destruction, Korea was to remain
unchanged from before the war, divided at the thirty-eighth parallel. There was nothing to show for all the suffering and sacrifice the
combatants gave and the innocent Korean people endured. Syngman Rhee's dream of a unified Korea never materialized before his
death in 1965. The unification still remains a dream.

While the Korean War stalemate was setting in along the thirty-
eighth parallel in the spring of 1951, the Fifth Air Force headquarters was moved north to Taegu, taking Captain Whitely with it. I
decided to stay on since the paperwork for my study in America had
been initiated in Pusan.

Miss Esther Laird obtained a full scholarship for me at Miami
University in Oxford, Ohio, despite the loss of my academic records
in the war. With all the turmoil and uncertainty around me, the
only real hope I had for myself was to have a brand new start in
America, leaving behind all the personal and political troubles in
Korea. Going to America became my sole focus.

The Pusan Technical School building was handed over to the
U.S. Army Replacement Company. It processed the American soldiers going home after their tour of duty. I had a new boss, Lieutenant Louis E. Namarich, in charge of all the Korean personnel
working there.

The U.S. Army, under Lieutenant Namarich, was all business,
strictly by the book. Gone was the informal, relaxed atmosphere in
personal and office conduct allowed under Captain Whitely.

Lieutenant Namarich was a devoted married officer, writing a
daily letter to his wife. He had moved up from the enlisted ranks
during World War II, and I could see why. He was an impeccable
example of an officer, always shaved clean, and spotlessly dressed,
with shoes shined. He had Captain Whitely's little haven in the tool
shed dismantled and joined his fellow officers in the upstairs quarters in the main building.

As much as I admired the lieutenant's exemplary behavior, I

somehow liked Captain Whitely better. The captain was so human while the lieutenant was a page out of the military code book.

By the time the Army took over the school building, my secretarial skills were much improved and I still commanded a top salary for indigenous personnel working for the U.S. government, except for a Korean interpreter assigned to U.S. Army Intelligence. He had been an oily street tough from Seoul before the war.

One night, this Korean intelligence man decided to raid my rooming house, hearing, probably from me, that a few girls were sharing my room. A few months earlier, two Ewha College girls came looking for a place to live as they had started to work as waitresses in the dining room of the Swedish MASH — Mobile Army Surgical Hospital — set up nearby. I offered to share my room with them.

I hardly saw them. They would come home late in the evening and get up early in the morning to serve breakfast seven days a week. Meanwhile, one of their college professors came to visit them when the raid took place.

At the insinuation of this Korean G-2, the American M.P. suspected that we were running a brothel with so many young girls living together. While the war was raging in the front lines, there was another war waged against venereal diseases by the military, brought by mushrooming whorehouses around the military installations.

After midnight, we were rudely awakened by loud voices coming from our landlord's room. The girls and I realized that the American M.P. with the Korean interpreter in tow was demanding to search throughout the house. Suddenly, the Ewha girls got panicky, remembering the silk parachute they had recently brought home from work for its silk cloth. In their groggy, confused state, they thought that the police had come to arrest them for taking the parachute. Given the wartime scarcity, the Koreans treasured silk, used in imaginative ways to keep themselves warm in the cold winter.

One of the girls wanted to throw the evidence into the toilet hole in the lavatory next to our room, while the other girl wanted to hide it in the closet. Actually, there was barely enough time to stuff it under some clothes in the closet. Seconds later, the M.P. and the interpreter burst into our room, flashing their lights into our blinking eyes. Finding only a frightened woman and three girls in their beds, they left without any apology.

During the late spring, when the warm sun greened everything it touched and a soft breeze scattered cherry blossoms all over the countryside, the Company commander gave me a document to be translated. The paper was the deposition of a Korean girl accusing an American sergeant of rape. I was acquainted with the accused, as he frequented our office. He was a supervisor of Korean laborers setting up the mess hall, sleeping tents, and toilet facilities for the herds of homebound American soldiers.

The sergeant was a red-haired, lanky, career army man, from Texas, I think. I didn't particularly like the crude, leering look about him and was not surprised at the allegation. He adamantly insisted that she was a prostitute and that he took her for a picnic on a boat in the bay.

While I was translating the accuser's deposition into English, I came to the rape scene. For some reason, I got it into my head that the word "rape" was too crude a term for a lady to use, even in a legal document. So I euphemized rape into "violation of virginity," to soften the harshness of the word.

When my translation was submitted, I watched closely at how the commanding officer took my liberty with the translation. In the middle of the reading, I could see that he was about to explode with laughter, and abruptly he left the room without words. I didn't hear anymore about the case.

My personnel office had a master sergeant, a crusty old army man, about to be retired after this tour of duty. The battles he had fought were clearly etched into the wrinkles of his craggy face. His low husky voice belied his piercing blue eyes, and his large rough-knuckled hands had seen unspeakable human suffering and tragedy in the wars of which he had been a part. He was soft-spoken but in firm control of all the Korean laborers he oversaw for the company.

One morning, I was shocked to see this giant of a man with bruised lips, a patch over his eye, and his stripes stripped off his sleeves, only their dark shadows remaining. He had been busted for a drunken brawl the previous night, just days before his discharge.

CHAPTER 42

The Last Days in Korea

While the paperwork for my passport and visa were being laboriously processed in Pusan by the respective governments in the spring and summer of 1951, I was increasingly afraid that my family would show up at my door. This close to my dream, I didn't want anything or anyone to stop me from going to America.

Had my parents found me in Pusan, I would have felt obliged to support them with my earnings and stay in Korea. In a way, I was once again running away from home and my duty.

That summer, my landlord, unhappy in his humiliating manual work at the American military installation, came home one evening, roaringly drunk and in a foul mood. He started smashing things with his bare fists in front of his wailing wife and crying children, and finally ended up cutting his little finger against the broken glass front of a china closet. The wound was deep enough to sever the tendon. The gushing blood sobered him up somewhat, but the damage was done. With his stiff, crooked little finger, he wouldn't be able to play the piano, possibly ending his music teaching career.

Just days before I sailed to America on the *Sea Serpent*, a portly, mild-mannered supply sergeant lost his life due to someone's carelessness. While he was loading turned-in rifles onto a truck, one of the rifles, supposedly emptied of all ammunition, still had a bullet left in the magazine and shot him in the stomach. He died instantly, leaving his many children fatherless in America.

Of all things, it is a few bars of the melody from "Frenesy" that triggers, even today, the memories of my days in U.S. government service with the full force of the sight, sound, and greasy smell of the place. The country-western music played by the Armed Forces Radio Network every day was broadcast from loudspeakers mounted under the eaves of the school building. With "Frenesy" as the intro theme, "Tennessee Waltz," "My Sentimental Journey," "Goodnight, Irene," and "Cold, Cold Heart" by Hank Williams flooded the whole compound with mournful, inescapable airs.

I don't know how the G.I.s liked the music, but the Korean laborers couldn't help feeling sad and homesick, without understanding one word of the lyrics. This was my first exposure to the other American music I had not known existed until then.

After all these years, I still do not know the details of how I was able to obtain such a highly coveted passport to emigrate to the United States during the wartime chaos. But there was no doubt that it took a miracle to satisfy all the bureaucratic red tape, American and Korean, without any official documentation of my very existence. It was, I am sure, the trust the respective governments must have placed in Miss Laird, and other missionaries, who took their precious time to vouch for me.

In the end, the post–World War II geopolitics and the Korean War conspired to shorten my wait to go to America by several years.

To this day, however, I live with a mistake the American Embassy clerk made in the spelling and pronunciation of my surname. My family name should have been spelled *Che* in English, the way it sounds in Korean, instead of *Choi*. For some unknown reason, the American embassy, and later the consulate clerk, insisted on pronouncing my last name by the Cantonese version of the Chinese pronunciation, *Choi*. The Mandarin version, *Chui*, would have been closer to the Korean way.

My birthday is also suspect. In all of my documents, my birthdate is listed as October 4, 1929, the year of the snake, by the lunar calendar of the East. But I never looked it up on the 1929 Western calendar.

Finally, my passport application required that my lungs be X-rayed to insure that I was free from the tuberculosis that was rampant in Korea around that time. There was only one X-ray machine at the provincial hospital for the entire Pusan area.

It was so old that when my lungs were X-rayed, to my untrained eyes, there was hardly anything to see, just foggy, blurred images on blank celluloid. To make things worse, I dropped the X-ray pictures in a muddy puddle in the rain on the way home. I had no idea then that I was seeding future trouble for myself later in San Francisco.

Chapter 43

Goodbye, Korea

My departure was auspiciously timed for my deliverance. August 15 was also a day to remember for the Korean liberation from Japan at the conclusion of World War II.

For months, I had been giving my entire paycheck to the landlord to ease his financial strait and, in the final days, I gave his long-suffering wife my accumulated clothing. I was emptying my pockets. After all, the streets of America were paved in gold and in its rivers milk and honey flowed. For the voyage, in the open-air market I bought a small, used leather suitcase and a Japanese lacquered tea tray as a gift for Miss Laird. With one suitcase in hand, I was ready to face the brave new world in America.

Early in the morning, Dr. Stokes came to take me to the American freighter *Sea Serpent*, docked at the Pusan wharf. After unloading war materiel, the freighter was going back to San Francisco by a northern route, hugging the west coast of Honshu, slipping through the Hokkaido strait, then east to the northwest coast of the United States and finally south to the San Francisco Bay.

The ship had a handful of other Korean passengers, but I remember only a college girl who was joining her sister in Kentucky, and a middle-aged minister. The early morning fog and the gray-green water in the harbor might have reflected the sad farewells of my fellow passengers. But nothing could dampen the soaring joy of liberation I felt — liberation from the miseries of my wounded family and the cold and hunger in the land of Morning Calm. I had no regrets, even at not seeing my family before my departure.

As the dark Pusan coastline, punctuated by jutting rocks, gradually melted into the lead-gray ocean mist, I prayed for my missing family and for Korea in her throes for survival. Goodbye, my love Youngii.

And I faced east toward the promised land of America, like a sunflower turning to the sun.

Index